T0330184

Strategy Making in a Crisis

To those who make imagination a way of life.

Strategy Making in a Crisis

From Analysis to Imagination

Michael Gibbert

Associate Professor, Bocconi University, Italy

Edward Elgar

Cheltenham, UK • Northampton, MA, USA

Published by
Edward Elgar Publishing Limited
The Lypiatts
15 Lansdown Road
Cheltenham
Glos GL50 2JA
UK

Edward Elgar Publishing, Inc.
William Pratt House
9 Dewey Court
Northampton
Massachusetts 01060
USA

A catalogue record for this book is available from the British Library

Library of Congress Control Number: 2009938397

Mixed Sources
Product group from well-managed
forests and other controlled sources
www.fsc.org Cert no. SA-COC-1565
© 1996 Forest Stewardship Council
FSC

ISBN 978 1 84844 240 5

Typeset by Cambrian Typesetters, Camberley, Surrey
Printed and bound by MPG Books Group, UK

Contents

Acknowledgments

Many thanks to all the imaginative ElectroCorp managers who participated in this study; to Francesca Golfetto, for encouraging me to write this book; and to Louise Bostock, Martin Hilb, Martin Hoegl, Mette Praest-Knudsen, as well as Marius Leibold, for trenchant comments.

1. Introduction

Strategy-making mirrors the economic environment. When overall economic conditions are favorable, resources are readily available, sales forecasts are met, customers remain loyal, shareholders are calm and strategy making[1] is about stating the obvious: a foreseeable future, making decisions about which we know the outcome in advance (e.g. Rumelt, Schendel and Teece, 1991, 1994). However, in a crisis, the business landscape is neither stable nor predictable, resources are scarce rather than abundant, customers disappear, and shareholders revolt, all of which can make prediction and control very difficult (e.g. Gibbert, Hoegl and Valikangas, 2007; Hoegl, Gibbert and Mazursky, 2008; Farjoun, 2008; Moldoveanu, 2009; Gavetti, Levinthal and Rivkin, 2005).

What lever to use for strategy making in a crisis? I believe that we can learn some important lessons for coping with the present (and eventual future) crises by taking an in-depth look into how successful strategies have been crafted in past times of crisis. In the early 2000s, I undertook an in-depth field study (Gibbert, Ruigrok and Wicki, 2008; Yin, 1994; Eisenhardt, 1989) inside a major diversified firm in the electronics and electrical engineering industry, here called ElectroCorp. What I found is that the problem, and the solution, is one of imagination. If there is not only one foreseeable future but several (or none), a company without imagination might either not be able to see the light at the end of the tunnel or, worse, mistake it for an oncoming train.

What do we know from previous literature? For decades, both scholars and managers have raised serious concerns about the extent to which existing approaches to strategy-making can help the firm in envisaging, conceiving, and realizing more imaginative strategies (Moldovenau, 2009; Pehrsson, 2006; Weick, 1989; Szulanski and Amin, 2001; Hamel, 1996; Porter, 1991; Chakravarthy, 1997). So it does not seem surprising that the most recent research increasingly calls for greater attention to imagination in the crafting of strategy (Szulanski and Amin, 2001: 537; Hamel, 2000: 3; von Krogh, Ichijo and Nonaka, 2000: 166–8; Roos and Victor, 1999: 348). As Porter argued, 'the most successful firms are notable in employing imagination to define a new position or find new value in whatever starting position they have' (Porter, 1994: 441–2, cited in Szulanski and Doz, 1995: 17). Never has this been more relevant than under the current economic conditions.

1

BACKGROUND

A number of prominent thinkers and practitioners in business have recently observed that the processes by which firms envisage, conceive, and realize strategies in general and in times of crisis in particular are not well-documented (e.g. Müller-Stewens and Lechner, 2001; Mintzberg and Waters, 1985; Hamel and Prahalad, 1994a; Lovas and Goshal, 2000). Two main streams of thought concerning the making of strategies stand out in the literature, namely strategy content research and strategy process research. But a review of the literature makes it clear that the two are not well integrated. Although considerable research has been focused on strategy content in terms of specific industry (Porter, 1980, 1985, 1991, 1998, 2001), or resource structures (Barney, 1991; Prahalad and Hamel, 1990; Peteraf, 1993; Wernerfelt, 1984, 1995), less attention has been devoted to how these structures arise in the first place. Similarly, while much strategy process research has examined contextual factors, decision making processes, intuitive and analytic aspects (e.g. Mintzberg, 1976; Mintzberg and Waters, 1985), less attention has been paid to specific managerial practices that determine the origins of, and the connection to, these industry and resource positions. In brief, the conceptual development at the interface between strategy process and strategy content research is at a preliminary stage (e.g. Burgelman, 2002; Schendel, 1992; Rumelt, Schendel and Teece, 1991, 1994; Chakravarthy and Doz, 1992). So it seems that there is a potential for a theoretical contribution in attempting to develop conceptually the interface between strategy content and strategy process research.

Compounding this lack of conceptual development at the interface between these two streams of thought is the apparent lack of integration within each of them. The first of the two, *strategy process research*, has seen a number of integrative frameworks (e.g. Hart, 1991, 1992; Hart and Branbury, 1994). However, these do not seem to be very influential, and the field appears to be characterized by a certain amount of terminological as well as conceptual confusion. In particular, it is not at all clear what is meant by the term 'process'. Van den Ven made a valuable contribution to strategy process research by defining 'process' in terms of a number of steps, but it is still not clear *how many* steps might be involved (van den Ven, 1992: 172; Mintzberg and Lampel, 1999; Fahey and Christensen, 1986). In addition, many authors seem to agree that, since van den Ven's (1992) major contribution, strategy process research has languished through want of attention and does not seem to have progressed much further (e.g. Hamel, 1998; Eisenhardt, 1999). So there is much to be done to integrate the diverse perspectives within strategy process research, and it seems that work to extend van den Ven's definition of the term 'process' would be particularly valuable.

The situation becomes even more problematic in the case of the second stream of thought, *strategy content research*. In contrast to strategy process research, this field has flourished over the last two decades, and has contributed considerably to our understanding of industry structures (e.g. Porter, 1980) and resource structures (e.g. Prahalad and Hamel, 1990). However, cross-fertilization between groups of scholars focusing on either industry or resource structures seems virtually absent to date (e.g. Roos and Victor, 1999; Lissack and Roos, 1999, 2001; Eisenhardt and Galunic, 2001; Priem and Butler, 2001a). In addition to this, the most recent stream of research in strategy content (typically called the 'dynamic capability approach') criticizes both the Porterian industrial economics approach as well as the resource-based approach for neglecting the tendency of industry and resource positions to erode over time (Eisenhardt and Martin, 2000; Zott, 2001; Hamel, 2000; Teece, Pisano and Shuen, 1997). It seems, therefore, that it would be useful to conduct integrative work within the three major perspectives in strategy content, particularly with regard to the industrial economics approach, the resource-based approach, and the relatively new dynamic capability approach.

In addition to insufficient integration between and within the strategy process and content realms, many authors have recently criticized strategy-making research in general for its lack of empirical grounding (e.g. Eisenhardt and Martin, 2000; Eisenhardt and Galunic, 2001; Williamson, 1999; Priem and Butler, 2001a). Scholars have explained this inadequacy by referring to the difficulty researchers typically encounter when trying to obtain access to organizations. Studying strategy-making procedures requires significant researcher commitment and extensive organizational access, and few researchers appear to have achieved this to date (van den Ven, 1992: 181, Mintzberg, 1979: 583), probably because it demands that they place themselves in the manager's temporal and contextual frames of reference, which implies costly longitudinal and real-time research (Mintzberg, 1979; van den Ven, 1992; Eisenhardt, 1989; Helfat, 2000). Nevertheless, conducting in-depth empirical and longitudinal on-site research into strategy making seems to be the only way to add valuable insights to the field.

In summary, it appears that the role of imagination in strategy making remains inadequately understood for four main reasons:

- First, the conceptual development in strategy making appears to suffer from a lack of integration at the interface between the strategy process and strategy content research realms.
- Second, the strategy process realm seems to struggle with the question of how many steps the strategy-making process involves.
- Third, the strategy content realm appears to be characterized by a lack of integration of its main constituents, the Porterian industrial economics

approach, the resource-based approach, and the relatively new dynamic capability approach.

- Fourth, strategy-making research as a whole seems to suffer from a lack of empirical, on-site research.

These inadequacies clearly evidence an acute need for a framework for crafting strategy imaginatively in order to enhance the conceptual apparatus of strategy making in a theoretically integrated and empirically grounded way.

In recognition of the theoretical and practical background to the problem, I propose in this book a framework for crafting strategy imaginatively in times of a crisis: the strategy-making matrix. This framework is an attempt to fill the identified gaps in the current theoretical debate on and business practice of strategy making. In developing the strategy-making matrix, this study assumes an empirical and longitudinal focus and approaches the research topic deductively, and with a descriptive and behavioral-based lens (in the spirit of Barney, 1991; as well as Peteraf, 1993), rather than approaching strategy making from a prescriptive, economic and formal modeling angle (e.g. Simon, 1993).[2]

RESEARCH OBJECTIVE

Should the topic of strategy making in a crisis be approached from a strategy content or a strategy process perspective? Which angle is more appropriate – the Porterian industrial economics approach, or the resource-based approach? Over several decades of strategy research and practice each of these two concepts has been emphasized at one time or another. In this study, I would like to propose that an 'either/or' approach is not appropriate. Instead, this study takes the stance that an integrated 'as well as' approach is needed if we are to understand the important task of crafting strategy imaginatively. Indeed, this study proposes that a third aspect, which will be called 'challenging imagination', needs to form part of a complete integrated framework, in order to accommodate the tendency of resources – as well as competitive positions – to erode over time.

The objective of the study is to contribute to an enhanced understanding of strategy making in general and in a crisis in particular by (a) constructing and (b) empirically validating an integrated framework for crafting strategy imaginatively.

I would like to begin by attempting to build a framework called the 'strategy-making matrix' by integrating three major perspectives of strategy content research, namely:

- the industrial organization approach (which will be likened to a process called 'descriptive imagination'),
- the resource-based approach (which will be likened to a process called 'creative imagination'), and
- the dynamic capability approach (which will be likened to a process called 'challenging imagination')

in three steps (which will be called envisaging, conceiving, and realizing) that are derived from strategy process research. After this integration it will then be possible to deduce meaningful implications from the theoretical framework for the specific empirical work.

The empirical phase of the study attempts to test the propositions comprising the integrated framework using case-study evidence from ElectroCorp. Thus, based on the theoretical framework, the empirical study endeavors to shed light on the particulars of ElectroCorp's approach to crafting strategy by attempting to answer the following research questions:

- What is the relative importance of the three imaginations in crafting strategy imaginatively?
- What is the role and importance of sequencing the steps in crafting strategy imaginatively?

DEFINITIONS OF KEY CONCEPTS

Perhaps at the outset it would be useful to provide the assumptions that underlie the key concepts on which the above theoretical framework is based.

Framework

My understanding of a strategy-making framework as a theory-building and practice-oriented tool is derived directly from Porter's conception of theory development as a choice of either limited models or comprehensive frameworks (Eppler, 2000: 8). Porter (1991) views frameworks as a legitimate form of research that can be validated through case studies. According to him,

> Frameworks identify the relevant variables and the questions which the user must answer in order to develop conclusions tailored to a particular industry or company ... [However,] *all the interactions among the many variables in the frameworks cannot be drawn*. Frameworks seek to help the analyst to better think through the problem by understanding the firm and its environment and defining and selecting among strategic alternatives available ... (Porter, 1991: 98; emphasis added)

Porter's conceptualization of what a framework in strategy entails is applicable to the present study. His conceptualization of a framework becomes even clearer when contrasted with his conceptualization of a 'model'. Porter emphasizes:

> Each model abstracts the complexity of competition to isolate a few key variables whose interactions are examined in depth. The normative significance of each model depends on the fit between its assumptions and reality. No one model embodies or even approaches embodying all the variables of interest and hence the applicability of any model's findings are almost inevitably limited to a small subgroup of firms or industries, whose characteristics fit the model's assumptions ... (Porter, 1991: 97–8)

Porter's understanding of a framework is strictly adhered to in this study. I posit that what is appropriate strategy-making behavior depends on the situation and cannot be determined in a dogmatic or peremptory fashion. Thus, with the successive arising of new situations and new realities, re-examinations of aims and measures are necessary to ensure the maintenance of an effective alignment of efforts with actualities. The understanding of 'frameworks' in this context is therefore in contrast to the focus of 'models' on a limited set of variables that are connected by causal relationships.

Overall, for the purpose of this study, Porter's (1991) conceptualization of frameworks in strategy can best be summarized by proposing that frameworks: are descriptive, rather than normative; are a legitimate form of research, subject to empirical validation; are action-oriented, i.e. they seek to provide guidance for the practicing manager; and focus both on what could be done in strategy and how this might be accomplished.

Strategy Making

Since the theoretical framework of this study focuses on strategy making, the key concept of strategy making itself deserves closer inspection.

Strategic management as a field of scholarly investigation is characterized by two key distinctions. The first is between strategy formulation (or strategy making) and strategy implementation (or strategic/organizational change). The second distinction in the literature is between strategy process (how strategies are formed and implemented) and strategy content (what the relationship is between strategic choice and performance).

Crafting strategy imaginatively, as it is seen in this study, concerns the formal processes that lead to the formulation of a strategy that is to be implemented at corporate and/or business unit level. Crafting strategy is furthermore seen as a process that involves both top and middle management. Finally, and most importantly for the purposes of this study, strategy making is seen to involve both strategy process and strategy content perspectives.

First, crafting strategy imaginatively concerns the formal processes that lead to the formulation of a strategy that is then to be implemented, without considering the strategic change processes associated with such implementation. This conjecture assumes that it is actually possible to divide strategy formulation (or strategy making) and strategy implementation (or strategic/organizational change). Indeed, the division of these two concepts seems well established in the literature and can be traced back to three works in thinking about strategy: Alfred Chandler's *Strategy and Structure* (1962), Igor Ansoff's *Corporate Strategy* (1965), and Andrews et al.'s *Business Policy: Text and Cases* (1965). In the words of Andrews: 'Strategy has two equally important aspects, interrelated in life but separated to the extent practicable in our study of the concept. The first of these is formulation, the second implementation' (Andrews, 1965, cited in Rumelt, Schendel and Teece, 1994: 20). It should, however, be acknowledged that the distinction between formulation and implementation has not gone unchallenged. As Andrews suggests above, it is not clear whether it is made for rhetorical, analytic or expository reasons. As a consequence, its sometimes vague rationale has led a number of scholars to question the division between formulation and implementation in strategy making. At the heart of this argument was the idea that while it may be analytically convenient to separate the two concepts, their distinction is often difficult to reconcile with the reality of strategy-making processes (see for example Hilb, 2001: 46; Rumelt, Schendel and Teece, 1994: 20; Schendel, 1992: 2). Nevertheless, despite or because of this criticism, the distinction between formulation and implementation seems to have flourished since its inception in the 1960s and I have adopted it for the purposes of this study. I acknowledge that, practically speaking, the making of a strategy and its implementation are interdependent processes. However, in line with the established consensus in the literature (Andrews et al., 1965: 17), crafting strategy, or the process by which a strategy is determined, is for analytical convenience seen as independent from the process of actually implementing this strategy.

Second, an important question causing considerable confusion in the literature is from where and from whom strategies emerge in a company, i.e. where do strategy-making processes evolve? More recent conceptualizations are inconsistent with the traditional view that strategy making is the exclusive province of top management (Ansoff, 1965; Andrews et al., 1965, Schendel and Hofer, 1979). Mintzberg, for instance, challenged the traditional locus of strategy making and suggested that it should be seen as a combination of deliberate and emergent decisions involving strategy makers from various levels of the organization (Mintzberg, 1978, 1994; Mintzberg and Waters, 1985; Mintzberg and McHugh, 1985). Most recently, Burgelman describes strategy making as a product of autonomous behavior located outside top management

(Burgelman, 2002). Similarly, Wooldridge and Floyd have advocated strategy making 'from the middle' (Wooldrige and Floyd, 2001), and Hilb has suggested a 'Matrioshka' approach to strategy making, which systematically involves all organizational members (Hilb, 1995). Along the same lines Fredrickson observed: 'Participation in the strategy-making process is not limited to a few individuals who are located at the very top of an organization' (Fredrickson, 1984, cited in Wooldridge and Floyd, 1990: 231).

Fredrickson (1984; Fredrickson and Mitchell, 1984), and later Wooldridge and Floyd (1990, 2001; Floyd and Wooldridge, 1996) have provided empirical evidence of the effects of the involvement of strategy makers who are not on corporate boards, but are middle managers. Most of these studies suggest that strategy making is located on two organizational levels, namely top management and middle management, and does not generally involve the entire organization. The strategy-making team, usually comprising two broad groups, namely middle and top managers (the CEO in particular), is generally seen as the focal point of this activity (Andrews, 1971). It should be appreciated that the conjecture that strategy making, while involving middle management, need not necessarily involve the entire organization, stands in contrast to strategy implementation or strategic change which, in fact, does seem to require that the entire organization be involved (e.g. Orgland, 1995; Schendel, 1992).

While the specific tasks in the strategy-making process seem to differ for the two broad groups of strategy makers (e.g. Thakur, 1998), research suggests that the key strategy makers in corporations are top management and middle management (Fredrickson, 1984; Fredrickson and Mitchell, 1984; Wooldridge and Floyd, 1990, 2001; Floyd and Wooldridge, 1996). Although strategy, at least in part, may emerge autonomously from the grass roots of an organization, it is the CEO and the strategy-making team's stamp of approval that is seen as the referent for the organization's strategy (in line with Szulanski and Doz, 1995: 19). This study therefore views strategy making as a process that involves individuals from both top and middle management. In recognition of this stance, managers from both levels were interviewed as part of the empirical study.

A third and, for the purposes of this study, most important aspect related to strategy making is the distinction between strategy process and strategy content research. This distinction seems to be as old as the concept of strategic management itself (Rumelt, Schendel and Teece, 1994), and its continued importance and relevance is suggested by the fact that no less than four special issues of the *Strategic Management Journal* were recently dedicated to strategy process and strategy content research. Similar to the division between strategy formulation and implementation, the distinction between process and content research is a contentious issue, which has not gone unchallenged. It has been called an impediment to progress in the field of strategic management (e.g. by Schendel, 1992: 2), and the coincidence of process and content has been advocated. At the heart of this argument lies the distinction's artificial nature, and the notion that process should be studied alongside, or coincidentally with, content (e.g. Eisenhardt and Zbaracki, 1992). By contrast, the distinction between the two was championed particularly because it facilitates teaching the field of strategy (see Schendel, 1992).

The objective here is not to reconcile this debate for strategic management in general but to observe that, in the case of strategy making in particular, assuming the coincidence of strategy process and strategy content is advantageous. It would appear that in crafting strategy imaginatively it is decidedly difficult to focus exclusively on *what* strategic positions of the firm lead to optimal performance under varying environmental circumstances (the domain of content research), without simultaneously considering *how* (the domain of process research) a firm's administrative systems and decision processes influence its strategic positions (see Chakravarthy and Doz, 1992: 5, for a related argument). In this study, I have therefore opted to view strategy making as an effort involving both strategy process research ('how') and strategy content research ('what').

Strategy Process Research (How?)

Process research in strategic management is concerned with *how* effective strategies are shaped within the firm and then efficiently implemented (Pettigrew, 1992: 6; Schendel, 1992: 2; van den Ven, 1992: 169). Rich in perspectives, empirically complex, and paradigmatically diverse, the field of strategy process research appears very fragmented – which several scholars regret (e.g. Pettigrew, 1992: 5; Chakravarty and Doz, 1992: 5–7). According to the literature, the reason for this fragmentation could be strategy process's drawing on a variety of disciplines, including organizational sociology, decision sciences, psychology, political science and ethics (Chakravarty and Doz, 1992:7; Rumelt, Schendel and Teece, 1994: 24–40). Perhaps due to its broad discipline base, wide-ranging efforts have been undertaken to categorize this 'crazy quilt of perspectives' (Eisenhardt and Zbaracki, 1992: 17). This has resulted in numerous, sometimes conflicting, categorization schemes, since authors delineated a multitude of 'modes' of strategy making, a stream of thought to which Henry Mintzberg is a prominent and prolific contributor (Mintzberg, 1978, 1994; and Waters, 1985; and McHugh, 1985; and Lampel, 1999).

Dissatisfaction with the individual categories of strategy making has led other observers to rearrange these categories using quite different bases for differentiating the multiple schools of strategy process research (see especially

Hart, 1991, 1992, for integrative frameworks). This has added yet another layer of complexity: categorizations are now rearranged in meta-categoriz-ations, few of which have enjoyed empirical validation. In these exercises whether such meta-categorizations are 'simple' (e.g. Lumpkin and Dess, 1995), rather than 'comprehensive' (e.g. Fredrickson, 1984) seems to have been a key question. In an apparent response to this question, Mintzberg endeavored to expand his 'modes of strategy making' from the original 'three modes' (Mintzberg, 1973a, 1979), to 'ten schools' of strategy making (Mintzberg and Lampel, 1999).

At the heart of this conceptual confusion seems to reside the question of what is meant by the term 'process'. Indeed, a careful review of the numerous process frameworks that have been proposed in the literature shows that the term 'process' has been used in many different ways. Three meanings of process seem to be particularly prominent: first, process as a logic that explains a causal relationship between independent and dependent variables, second, as a category of concepts or variables that refers to actions of individ-uals or organizations, and third, as a sequence of events that describes how things change over time (van den Ven, 1992: 169–75).

The quest to clarify the term 'process' has consequently led to the interpre-tation of it as a sequence of events, or, put differently, as distinct steps in a given course that develops over time (see especially van den Ven's seminal 1992 article). According to van den Ven, these steps can be interpreted as constituting a linear, circular, divergent or convergent process. The bottom line is that strategy process research can best be understood in terms of a sequence of events that evolves over time, and comprises several steps (van den Ven, 1992). This interpretation of 'process' is adopted for the present study, which proposes that strategy process research is primarily involved with delineating generic steps in a sequential course of action, such as: envisaging, conceiving and realizing imaginative strategies.

Strategy Content Research (What?)

The fourth key concept underlying the theoretical framework is strategy content. Content research in strategic management is concerned with *what* is decided in a corporate setting (Rumelt, Schendel and Teece, 1994: 18–20; Fahey and Christensen, 1986: 167; Schendel, 1991: 1). Whereas strategy process primarily dominated research agendas from the 1960s to the 1980s, in the past two decades strategy content research has contributed significantly to the development of the strategic management field (Eisenhardt and Zbaracki, 1992; Huff and Reger, 1987). Strategy content research does not seem as para-digmatically diverse and fragmented as strategy process research. Essentially, it appears to have provided three distinct explanations in regard to strategy making: first, the Porterian industry structure view (also called 'descriptive imagination', Roos and Victor, 1999); second, the resource-based view (also called 'creative imagination', ibid.); and third, dynamic interpretations of resource positions (also called 'challenging imagination', ibid.). This third perspective is relatively new and has been developing as an outgrowth of the resource-based view in that it represents the latter's extension into dynamic markets (e.g. Teece, Pisano and Shuen, 1997).

Strategy content theories based on the industrial organization view (Mason, 1939; Bain, 1956) explain how companies use reductions in competition in order to strengthen their positions (Schendel, 1988; Montgomery, 1988). Porter (1980) translated the concepts of industrial organization economics into the strategy field, and developed a general cross-sectional framework for explaining individual firm performance. Due to the prominence of Porter's work in this stream of research, it was often called the 'Porterian view'. Porter's work can be seen as turning classical industrial organization economics on its head: traditionally the role of industrial organization economics had been to identify socially wasteful sources of 'monopoly' profits, but Porter used the framework to develop strategies to appropriate abnormal returns which would lead to a competitive advantage for firms (Rumelt, Schendel and Teece, 1994: 22–3). Building on and extending agency theory, evolutionary economics and, more recently, game theory, industrial organization perspectives have recently been referred to as 'descriptive imagination'[3] in that they primarily focus on elucidating and apprehending the environment of the firm (Rumelt, Schendel and Teece, 1991, 1994; Nalebuff and Brandenburger, 1996). The perceived need to 'see' and describe five industry forces is a manifestation of the descriptive nature of this stream of thought (Roos and Victor, 1999: 349) which focuses on the industry 'out there' as a source of variation, rather than on the firm itself. Indeed, firm and resource homogeneity are assumed. This is in sharp contrast to the heterogeneity of firms and their resource endowments associated with the second explanation for strategy making provided by content research, namely the resource-based view.

The resource-based view, similarly to the industrial organization view, has been highly influenced by economic theory. The sub-field of transaction cost economics, developed primarily by Williamson (1975, 1985) building on Coase's seminal work (1937) is principally used as the conceptual backdrop to this approach to strategy. The focus here is on costs of transactions and suitable structures for conducting such transactions, i.e. markets or hierarchies, the reasoning being that uncertainty, idiosyncratic firm resources and opportunistic behavior lead to inefficient or unfair market prices and that firms result as a consequence of this market failure (e.g. Rumelt, Schendel and Teece, 1991, 1994; Schendel, 1988, 1991). The resource-based perspective of the firm furthermore builds strongly on Penrose's (1959) notion that firm-specific resources and capabilities, rather than industry positions, determine the direction and growth of the firm. In emphasizing firm-specific resources, this perspective is interested in delineating tools and mechanisms that can be utilized to take advantage of the most critical of firm resources (Rumelt, 1984, 1987, 1991; Wernerfelt, 1984, 1995; Barney, 1991; Prahalad and Hamel, 1990; Nelson and Winter, 1982). Knowledge resources in particular seem to be critically associated with firm success (e.g. Spender, 1996a, b; Grant, 1996, 1997; Nonaka, 1994; Nonaka and Takeuchi, 1995; Kogut and Zander, 1996). Resource-based perspectives have recently been described as 'creative imagination' in that they focus on how resource and capability endowments are created and sustained over time (Roos and Victor, 1999).

The third perspective, often called 'dynamic capabilities', can be seen as an outgrowth of the resource-based view (Teece, Pisano and Shuen, 1997: 515). To illustrate: a problem faced by the resource-based view is path dependency, which suggests that a firm's previous investments in managing and creating resources constrain its behavior and the strategic options available for investing in, and managing, new resources (e.g. Dierckx and Cool, 1989; Leonard-Barton, 1992, 1995). This observation has apparently lead to 'dynamic' interpretations of the resource-based view (see Teece, Pisano and Shuen, 1997, for their pioneering contribution). Variously referred to as 'strategy innovation' (e.g. Hamel, 2000), 'value innovation' (e.g. Kim and Mauborgne, 1999a), or 'dynamic capabilities' (e.g. Teece, Pisano and Shuen, 1997; Eisenhardt and Martin, 2000; Zott, 2000), these interpretations appear in their own right to have established themselves as a third sub-field in the most recent strategy content debate. In this emerging stream of thought writers such as Gary Hamel, Johan Roos, and Kathleen Eisenhardt, typically drawing on complexity theory (e.g. Allison and Kelly, 1999; Bar-Yam, 1997; Kauffman, 1993, 1995), challenge the established logic of doing business, and advocate questioning and re-drawing the boundaries of industries and businesses. It has therefore also been labeled the 'challenging imagination' approach to strategy content (Roos and Victor, 1999: 350).

Thus, from the above analysis, three main approaches to strategy content can be deduced from the extant literature. Likewise, this study sees strategy content research as primarily concerned with three sub-fields:

- industrial organization perspectives,
- resource-based perspectives, and
- dynamic capability perspectives.

WHAT NEXT?

In the following chapter, I hope to develop and formalize the theoretical argument. To this end I will be outlining a framework integrating prior work emanating from the strategy process and strategy content research realms. This framework, the strategy-making matrix, has been systematically deduced from an internally consistent theoretical perspective, based on these two main streams of thought. Strategy process research provides the three generic steps for the strategy-making process, which I will be calling: envisaging, conceiving and realizing. Strategy content research provides three basic thrusts of strategy making, which I will be calling: descriptive, creative and challenging imagination. Juxtaposing the three generic steps in the strategy-making process with the three basic thrusts of strategy making in a matrix format yields this study's theoretical framework, a three-by-three matrix. Earlier frameworks associated with each of the three basic thrusts of strategy making are critically discussed. Based on this discussion, a comprehensive three-step framework for envisaging, conceiving and realizing imaginative strategies can be developed that builds on the strengths of earlier frameworks, while attempting to eliminate their weaknesses.

Next, I shall be turning to the empirical part of the study. In it I shall be revisiting the theoretical framework with the objective of empirically examining the logic and soundness of its constituent propositions, and of refining them in the light of empirical evidence. For ease of exposition and for readers' convenience, the empirical part is a 'mirror image' of the strategy-making matrix. The three generic steps of strategy making (envisaging, conceiving and realizing) and the three basic thrusts of strategy making (descriptive, creative and challenging imagination), are systematically subjected to empirical appraisal. The research methodology adopted for this exercise is the single-embedded case study.

In the concluding chapter, I will be outlining the main theoretical and practical insights that have been gained throughout the entire analysis in a condensed format. For this purpose, the principal conclusions that have been gained in terms of the research objective are given first. Subsequently, the study's overall contributions are discussed, and a recognition of its limitations is provided. Finally, Chapter 4 provides implications for the development of the literatures on which the theoretical framework is based, and discusses the implications for imagining a future beyond a pending or current crisis.

NOTES

1. This study uses 'strategy making' and 'crafting strategy' interchangeably.

2. The framework presented here should be seen as descriptive in that it spells out the characteristics of the process of crafting strategy imaginatively. A review of the literature shows that descriptive conceptualizations of strategy making have often been used as a basis for normative prescriptions. The framework developed in this study does not attempt to be a normative model of strategy making for all organizations.
3. This notion of descriptive imagination should not be confused with the normative/descriptive distinction made in the objective of this study.

2. Imaginative strategy making: existing frameworks

As discussed in the last chapter, it would appear that in using imagination for strategy making in a crisis, it is difficult to focus exclusively on *what* strategic positions of the firm lead to optimal performance under varying environmental circumstances, without simultaneously considering *how* a firm's administrative systems and decision processes influence these strategic positions (Chakravarthy and Doz, 1992; Rumelt, Schendel and Teece, 1994; Schendel, 1992). My main point of departure is, therefore, the conjecture that crafting strategy imaginatively is an effort involving both strategy process research and strategy content research. The two streams of research can be thought of as the two dimensions of a matrix where the horizontal axis describes how a strategy is made and the vertical axis describes what is being imagined when crafting strategy. I envisage the question of *how* a strategy is made as a *sequential process* involving a number of process steps (see van den Ven, 1992, as well as Schendel and Hofer, 1979, for related arguments). On the horizontal axis, therefore, we find the three generic steps in the strategy-making process: envisaging, conceiving and realizing strategies. Exactly *what* is decided in this process is contingent upon an important source of such decisions: the human *imagination* (see Roos and Victor, 1999; Kearney, 1988). On the vertical axis, therefore, the strategy-making matrix argues that imaginative strategies can best be envisaged, conceived, and realized by considering all three thrusts of strategy making: descriptive, creative, and challenging imagination.

The juxtaposition of the three generic steps of the strategy-making process with the three basic thrusts of strategy making yields a three by three matrix (Figure 2.1), and this matrix brings together two distinctions that have often been made, but that, to my knowledge, have not as yet been systematically analysed in conjunction. As will be discussed, each of the nine boxes of the matrix hosts what I shall be calling three 'strategic imagination levers', which work to unleash the imagination of the strategy maker.

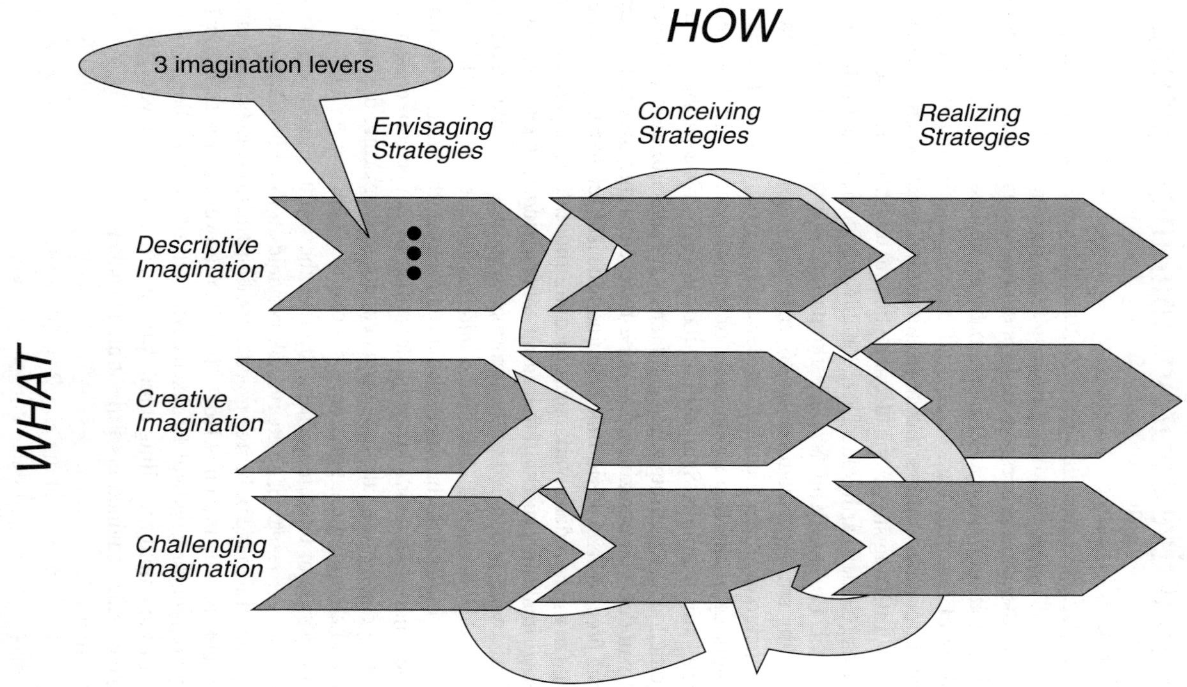

HOW

Realizing
Strategies

Conceiving
Strategies

Envisaging
Strategies

3 imagination levers

Descriptive
Imagination

Creative
Imagination

Challenging
Imagination

WHAT

Source: Author.

Figure 2.1   A blueprint for the strategy-making matrix

THREE GENERIC STEPS IN THE STRATEGY-MAKING PROCESS (HOW?)

In this study, the three generic steps in the strategy-making process (envisaging, conceiving and realizing) are derived from a review of existing work in the strategy process realm. Process research in strategic management is concerned with how effective strategies are shaped within the firm and how they are then efficiently implemented (Pettigrew, 1992: 6; Schendel, 1992: 2; van den Ven, 1992: 169; Chakravarty and Doz, 1992: 5–7). As discussed in the previous chapter, strategy process research is very rich in perspectives, as well as being empirically complex, and paradigmatically diverse.

Dissatisfaction with the field's 'crazy quilt of perspectives' (Eisenhardt and Zbaracki, 1992: 17) has led researchers to construct different categorization schemes for delineating modes, and archetypes of the strategy process (for example, Mintzberg, 1978, 1994; Mintzberg and Waters, 1985; Mintzberg and McHugh, 1985; Hart, 1991, 1992). Candidate frameworks were invariably countered by the empirical questioning of their underlying assumptions and limited explanatory power. This questioning rejected the rational explanations of strategy making, portraying it instead as incremental and distorted by partisan influences (for example, Szulanski and Doz, 1995). The essence of this seems to be the quest to define what is meant by 'process'. In a most influential article, van den Ven explained that three different usages of the term are salient: first, process as a logic that explains a causal relationship between independent and dependent variables; second, process as a category of concepts or variables that refers to the actions of individuals or organizations; and third, process as a sequence of events that describes how things change over time (van den Ven, 1992: 169–75).

According to the literature, process as a logic that explains a causal relationship between independent and dependent variables can be thought of as an input–output process model that serves to explain the relationship between observed inputs (independent variables) and outputs (dependent variables) in variance theory (Mohr, cited in van den Ven, 1992). In this usage, process is not directly observed. Instead, a process theory is used as a tool for explaining how and why an independent (input) variable exerts an influence on a dependent (outcome) variable (van den Ven, 1992: 170). Most studies that investigate the relationship between business performance and strategy-making processes, for example, fall into this category. Empirical investigations, however, have often provided conflicting evidence. For example, Fredrickson (1984) and Fredrickson and Mitchell (1984) discovered that comprehensiveness in strategic decision-making processes is positively related to performance. Eisenhardt (1989) validated this conjecture. However, Lumpkin and Dess (1995), and later Thakur (1998), found contradictory evidence. Van den

Ven and Huber (1990) and van den Ven (1992) argue that the root cause of these variations is that causation in these studies is often explained using highly restrictive and unrealistic assumptions. They therefore conclude that the interpretation of 'process' as a causal relationship is sub-optimal.

Process as a category of concepts of individual and organizational actions can be seen as the second frequently-used interpretation. According to van den Ven, communication frequency, workflows, decision-making techniques, as well as strategy formulation, implementation and corporate venturing all belong to this category. In this usage, process refers to a category of concepts that are operationalized as constructs, and measured as fixed entities (that is, variables), the attributes of which can vary on scales from low to high (van den Ven, 1992: 170). To illustrate: studies that examine how strategy-making processes influence executive understanding of cause–effect relationships involving the firm and its environment would belong to this category. Examples include scanning, analysis, and planning as methods to aid decision-making processes about the firm's alignment with its environment. However, according to van den Ven, such processes are again not directly examined. Instead, process constructs are represented as entities or attributes of reality and therefore only allow the researcher to measure if, and not how, a change occurred in a variable measured at different points in time (Abott, cited in van den Ven, 1992). This limitation leads van den Ven to dismiss the interpretation of process as a category of concepts as well.

The third, and according to van den Ven, the least understood interpretation of process, is process as a *sequence of events* or activities that describes how things change over time. Whereas the second definition of process examines changes in variables over time, the third definition of process takes a histori-cal developmental perspective and focuses on the sequences of incidents, activities, and stages that unfold over time (van den Ven, 1992: 170). Very recently, prominent strategy process researcher Henry Mintzberg, who is well-known for first categorizing strategy process research in three modes of strat-egy making (Mintzberg, 1973a), and later in 'ten schools' of strategy making, also suggested that the 'ten schools' can be usefully conceptualized as steps in a sequence of events that evolves over time (Mintzberg and Lampel, 1999). Indeed, the best-established developmental process frameworks pertaining to strategic decision-making can be seen as belonging to this third interpretation of process (for example, Mintzberg, Raisighani and Thoret, 1976; Quinn, 1980; Mintzberg and Lampel, 1999; Lorange, 1980). Several approaches have been used in these studies to infer the phases or steps in a process, including company historical self-reports or categorizing of companies into a certain number of stages or phases (van den Ven, 1992: 172).

Van den Ven and Mintzberg's succinct advocacy of the third interpretation of process is adopted in this study, not least because interpreting 'process' as a sequence of a certain number of steps that evolve over time seems intuitively and etymologically appealing.[1] More specifically, I would like to argue that in the interests of clarity, and to facilitate practical applicability, strategy-making processes can best be conceptualized using three generic steps, which I will be calling envisaging, conceiving and realizing strategies. The three generic steps in the strategy-making process are based on an extensive analysis of the most prominent strategy process frameworks. An evaluation of the similarities and differences between the major frameworks in strategy process research suggests that, while all view the strategy-making process as a sequence of events, this sequence involves a heterogeneous number of steps. For example, Lorange (1980) uses five steps whereas many other frameworks, including those that are most established (particularly Mintzberg's), use three generic steps. While terminology differs across the authors reviewed in Table 2.1, it is evident that all authors implicitly adopt the generic three steps in the strategy-making process that I would also like to take up, namely envisaging, conceiving and realizing strategies, conceptualized as follows:

- *Envisaging* constitutes the first generic step in strategy making. This step comprises determining the agenda, with issues that are currently recognized as strategic at corporate or business unit level. Research suggests that strategic issues are defined as events, developments or trends that are potentially important for the future development of the organization (Mintzberg and Quinn, 1991; Mintzberg, Quinn and Goshal, 1995; Chakravarthy and Lorange, 1991). According to Mintzberg, envisaging is first and foremost about developing a plan – some sort of consciously intended course of action, a guideline (or set of guidelines) formulated in response to a situation. By this definition, envisaging strategies have two essential characteristics: they are made in advance of the actions to which they apply and they are developed consciously and purposefully (Mintzberg, Quinn and Goshal, 1995: 13). So, the first generic step in strategy making is about determining objectives, that is, determining a strategic direction for the firm and its divisions and business environments. An example of an objective would be General Electric's intent to be the primary contender in markets in which it competes (Chakravarty and Lorange, 1991: 4).
- *Conceiving* strategies form the second generic step in strategy making, logically following on from envisaging strategies. Research suggests that if strategies are envisaged, they can also be conceived. In other words, envisaging a strategy is not sufficient; a concept is needed that encompasses the resulting behavior (Mintzberg, Quinn and Goshal, 1995: 14). To illustrate: conceiving strategies comprise the different functions of the organization necessary to produce output, that is, products or services in

one or more businesses (Chakravarty and Lorange, 1991). It should be appreciated that the verb 'conceived' indicates that the activities comprise only those activities that could actually be carried out (Mintzberg and Waters, 1985: 270). It should furthermore be appreciated that conceiving strategies are very different from implementing strategies, which are not the focus of this study. Table 2.1 indicates that the conceiving step in the strategy-making process encompasses activities such as assessing the organization's ability to implement strategy (Eisenstat and Beer, 1994; Beer and Nohria, 2000), evaluating strategic alternatives (Lyles, 1994), budgeting and establishing action programs (Lorange, 1980). Thus, while envisaging strategies focus on the intellectual activities of ascertaining what a company might do, conceiving strategies focus on deciding what a company can do, and bringing these considerations together in optimal equilibrium (Mintzberg, Quinn and Goshal, 1995: 57).

• *Realizing* strategies are particularly important but particularly problematic in situations in which the business landscape is neither stable nor predictable (Lissack and Roos, 1999, 2001). Research indicates that realizing strategies are closely related to 'organizational learning' (Senge, 1990; von Krogh and Vicari, 1993). This step in the strategy-making process encompasses 'nurturing capability for continuous innovation' (Lyles, 1994; Hart, 1991), 'energizing the organization' (Nasser and Vivier, 1995), 'sustaining formal commitment' (Quinn, 1980), and 'maintaining an entrepreneurial spirit' (Mintzberg and Lampel, 1999). Realizing imaginative strategies are about ensuring competitiveness over time. In particular, they are about ascertaining that the competitive environment and strategy do not develop in different directions. This last is a phenomenon Johnson (1988) called 'strategic drift' (see also Quinn, 1980). According to Johnson's accepted view, organizations should have formal mechanisms in place to prevent such strategic drift. Realizing strategies can therefore be seen as the logical step following the conception of a given strategy. They constitute a feedback loop and the primary purpose of this step in the strategy making process is monitoring, control and learning (Chakravarthy and Lorange, 1991: 6).

The foregoing review suggests that while all the frameworks reviewed have furthered our understanding of the strategy process considerably and, while all are based on extensive empirical work, they only seem to focus on the question of 'how' strategies are crafted (namely in three steps). However, it would seem to be decidedly difficult to focus exclusively on *how* (strategy process) a firm's administrative systems and decision processes influence its strategic positions, without simultaneously considering *what* strategic positions of the

Table 2.1 The three generic steps of strategy making

Authors and synopses of findings	Stages or steps in the strategy formulation process				
Nasser and Vivier (1995) Case studies of South African corporations gearing themselves for global competitiveness under the post-apartheid government	1. Engage the market, understand the future, create value for the customer, calculate the risk, then pre-empt: *envisaging* strategies	2. Mobilizing capability, defy the old paradigms, focus on speed, simplicity and self-confidence, create obsession for perpetual renewal: *conceive* or *realize* strategies	3. Energizing the organization, nurture competitive angst, inspire with pack leadership, manage through creative tension: *realize* or *conceive* strategies		
Hart (1992) Studies different types of strategy-making process capabilities in a sample of 285 top managers	1. Command, set strategic goals, top manager realizes control: *envisaging* strategies	2. Produce a corporate mission and vision using symbols: *envisage* strategy	3. Solidify position achieved, defend: *conceive* strategy	4. Continuously improve to realize strategic fit: *realize* strategies	5. Nurture capability for continuous innovation: *realize* strategies
Mintzberg Raisinghani & Theoret (1976) Field study of 25 strategic, unstructured decision processes	1. Identification phase, decision recognition, diagnosis routine: *envisage* strategy	2. Developmental phase, search routines, and design strategic routines: *conceiving* strategy	3. Selection phase, screen routines, establish evaluation-choice routines: *realize* strategies		
Gluck, Kaufmann & Walleck (1980) Investigation of planning and control systems	1. Basic financial planning, meet budget: *envisaging* strategy within financial constraints	2. Forecast-based planning, predict the future: *conceiving* strategy	3. Externally oriented planning think strategically: *realize* strategy	4. Strategic management, create the future: *realize* strategies	

Table 2.1 *(continued)*

Authors and synopses of findings	Stages or steps in the strategy formulation process				
Mintzberg and Lampel (1999) Meta-analysis of the last 30 years of process research	1. Analyze, learn from past then position: *envisaging the* strategy	2. Plan, implement, and execute: *conceive* envisaged strategy	3. Realize entrepreneurial spirit, learn and adapt: *realizing* imaginative strategies		
Lorange (1980) Normative framework of corporate strategic management	1. Setting objectives by evaluating relevant strategic alternatives: *envisage* strategy	2. Strategic programming, develop programs for achieving chosen objectives: *conceiving* strategy	3. Budgeting, establish detailed action program for near term: *conceiving* strategy	4. Monitoring, measure progress toward achieving strategies: *realizing* strategies	5. Rewards, establish incentives to motivate goal achievement: *realizing* strategies
Quinn (1980) Cross-case analysis of nine corporations	1. Sense need, develop awareness and understanding: *envisage* strategy	2. Develop partial solutions: *conceive* strategies	3. Build consensus, increase support: *conceive* strategy		
Lyles (2001) Inductive cross-case analysis of major multinationals, development of a strategic decision-making framework	1. Understanding strategic alternatives, delineating types of alternatives, developing alternatives: *envisaging* strategy	2. Generate alternatives, focus on obvious, creative and unthinkable alternatives, instill capacity for relentless alternative generation: *conceiving* strategies	3. Nurture organizational processes to aid alternative generation on a sustained basis: *realizing* strategies		
Eisenstat and Beer (1994) Cross-case analysis of US corporation's development of a framework for aligning the organization with strategy	1. Develop a partnership with organization members: *conceiving* strategies	2. Assess the organization's capability to implement strategy: *envisaging or conceiving* strategy	3. Orchestrate strategic initiatives that will realign the organization with its business strategy so as to stimulate learning and to build and sustain commitment: *realizing* strategies		

Source: Author.

firm lead to optimal performance under varying environmental circumstances (strategy content). It is particularly disadvantageous that none of the frameworks reviewed considers the three fundamental types of imagination, or as this dissertation has termed them, the three basic thrusts in strategy making (descriptive, creative and challenging imagination).

THREE BASIC THRUSTS IN THE STRATEGY-MAKING PROCESS (WHAT?)

Content research in strategic management is concerned with what is decided in a corporate setting (Rumelt, Schendel and Teece, 1994: 18–20; Fahey and Christensen, 1986: 167; Schendel, 1991: 1). Strategy content research is not as paradigmatically diverse and fragmented as strategy process research. Upon analysis, strategy content research has provided three distinct explanations: the first is the industrial organization view, the second is the resource-based view, and the third, emerging, perspective may be termed the 'strategy innovation' perspective. This last has developed as an outgrowth of the resource-based view in that it represents the resource-based view's extension to dynamic markets.

A careful review of the strategy content literature reveals that the essential quality of a strategy is its originality, since originality allows a firm to outperform its rivals (Roos and Victor, 1999). Originality can take the form of a first-mover advantage, a unique position in the market, a unique bundle of resources or a unique dynamic capability (for example, Eisenhardt and Martin, 2000; Zott, 2001). If that originality is hard to imitate (Barney, 1991; Wernerfelt, 1984), and is uniquely suited to external competitive positions (Porter, 1980, 1985, 1998, 2001), a strategy based on it can confer lasting competitive advantage. Conversely, without originality, a strategy is a mere commodity and may be ineffective in conferring and sustaining competitive advantage (Roos and Victor, 1999). However, recent work has found a persistent lack of originality in contemporary strategies (Hamel, 2000; Eisenhardt and Galunic, 2001; Eisenhardt and Martin, 2000; Lissack and Roos, 2001; Szulanski and Amin, 2001; Szulanski and Doz, 1995). According to Roos and Victor, the fact that a key ingredient in strategy making, namely imagination, is lacking in contemporary strategies is fundamental to this issue (Roos and Victor, 1999: 349).

Given that it is critical for crafting strategy, imagination itself therefore warrants deeper attention. The term 'imagination' has been given many different cultural and linguistic connotations (see, for example, Kearney, 1988). As two prominent strategy scholars have argued, while all share the basic idea that humans have a unique ability to 'image' or 'imagine' something, the variety of uses of the term 'imagination' implies not one, but at least three meanings (Roos and Victor, 1999; drawing on Kearney, 1988): to describe, to create and to challenge.

These three imaginations are ideally suited for categorizing extant strategy content literature. The strategy content literature can also be thought of as encompassing three main sub-fields of inquiry: the industrial organization, resource-based and dynamic capabilities perspectives, corresponding to the three forms of imagination. The parallels between the three streams of thought within the strategy content literature and the three imaginations are striking. Industrial organization perspectives seek to 'describe' the environment of the firm. This perspective's perceived need to describe five industry forces represents a manifestation of the descriptive nature of this stream of thought (Porter, 1980, 1985). Similarly, resource-based perspectives can be usefully conceptualized as 'creative' in that they focus on how resource and capability endowments are 'created' over time (Hamel and Prahalad, 1994a; Barney, 1991; Prahalad and Hamel, 1990; Peteraf, 1993; Wernerfelt, 1984). Dynamic capability perspectives can be usefully seen as 'challenging' in that they urge us to 'break out of old paradigms, challenge received dogmas' (Hamel and Prahalad, 1996: 242). Since the three imaginations in strategy making are fundamental to this study, a definition of each follows.

- Social science literature depicts *descriptive imagination* as the mind's evoking of a new understanding of a complex world. It seeks to identify patterns; it finds and labels discovered regularities in order to reduce the complexity of the world 'out there'. It can therefore be seen as essentially preoccupied with describing the world (Roos and Victor, 1998: 5–6). The recognition of a desire to describe the world is equally prevalent in the strategic management literature. Porter (1980), for instance, advocated that the need to describe the outside world in terms of industry structure and dynamics was the essence of strategy. Descriptive imagination is intrinsic in many frameworks and tools of the industrial organization view in strategic management. The literature recommends a variety of techniques to stimulate descriptive imagination through rigorous and systematic diagnostics that facilitate the diagramming and profiling of the competitive environment, with the ultimate aim of creating increasingly precise descriptions. Popular examples include value chains, Du Pont frameworks and growth share matrices (see Roos and Victor, 1998: 6–10).
- *Creative imagination* is conceptualized in the social science literature as the mind's invention of an idea that is new to the world, and it has often been confused with the definition of imagination itself, namely creativity. However, as this study, in line with Kearney, argues, creative imagination can be seen as only one of three constituents of imagination

(Kearney, 1988: 18). It seeks to evoke new possibilities through the combination, recombination or transformation of things or concepts (Weick, 1979, cited in Roos and Victor, 1999). The recognition of the need to create ideas that are new to the world is equally prevalent in the resource-based view in strategic management. Creative imagination occupies a central role in many activities such as 'creating new competitive space' (Hamel and Prahalad, 1994a), 'strategy as stretch and leverage' (Hamel and Prahalad, 1993), and creatively shaping, rather than accepting industry conditions (Hamel, 1996).

- *Challenging imagination* is described as the mind's negation of what it describes or creates, that is, of the previous two imaginations. According to the social science literature, it is typically sardonic and evokes a deconstruction of things or concepts previously held. Challenging imagination contradicts, defames and destroys the clarity generated by description and the sense of progress that comes from creativity (Kearney, 1988). As the defining characteristic of postmodern thought (Lyotard, 1984; Derrida, 1981, 1988), Foucault called challenging imagination the 'shattering truth' (see Cilliers, 1998). The recognition of the need to challenge existing descriptions and creations is particularly relevant to the extant, dynamic business environment, and it comes as no surprise that the strategy content literature has eagerly adopted the idea of challenging imagination. Concepts such as challenging of 'core rigidities' (Leonard-Barton, 1992, 1995) and 'industry revolution' (Hamel, 1996) bear witness to this exceedingly modern form of imagination in crafting strategy.

Following Kearney (1988), this study takes the stance that each of the three imaginations above plays an indispensable and complementary role in the making of a strategy. Crafting strategy imaginatively can be seen as reliant on the complex interplay of all three imaginations. As will be discussed in the next section, each of the three imaginations, while indispensable, suffers from a downside that demands the consideration of the other two.

In the work that follows, I shall be exploiting the similarity between the three streams of thought in the strategy content literature and the three imaginations to deduce the three basic thrusts of strategy making. The following three sections discuss extant frameworks and conceptual aids associated with each of the three imaginations in greater depth (see Table 2.2 for an overview). Based on an analysis of the respective similarities or differences and strengths or weaknesses of frameworks associated with each imagination, a 'new' integrated framework for envisaging, conceiving and realizing imaginative strategies that considers all three imaginations strategies can be systematically built in the remaining pages of the chapter.

EXISTING FRAMEWORKS FOR CRAFTING STRATEGY IMAGINATIVELY

To learn more about imagination in strategy making, it is important to take a look at exemplary frameworks of descriptive, creative and challenging imagination.

Major Frameworks Associated with Descriptive Imagination

Until the 1980s the dominant strategy-making paradigm focused on describing companies' environments (Spender, 1996a; Nanda, 1996; Belohlav, 1996; Teece, Pisano and Shuen, 1997). This paradigm viewed the essence of strategy making as 'relating a company to its environment. The key aspect of a firm's environment is the industry or industries in which it competes' (Porter, 1980: 4). The classic idea underlying this type of imagination is the 'mimetic impulse' (Roos, personal communication, June 2000) to mirror the world in increasingly precise descriptions on which strategic decision making can then be based. The impulse to arrive at increasingly precise descriptions seems understandable given that a lack of accurate description could lead to flawed strategic decision-making. The quest to arrive at such increasingly precise descriptions of the 'world out there' has its roots in the Renaissance and the positivist philosophy of science. When this thinking is applied to the strategy world, it entails an assumption that it is actually possible to objectively reduce the complexity of the firm's environment by using patterns, labels and regularities. This can be observed in strategy making, where industry and competitor analysis is often proposed as a structured way to evoke the strategy maker's imagination of the factors determining attractiveness and profitability of industries.

The recognition of the need to describe the world seems very prominent in strategy-making literature. Indeed, descriptive imagination can be found in many frameworks and conceptual aids of the industrial organization view in strategic management. Often this is done by way of approaches such as five forces frameworks, value chains, Du Pont frameworks, product life cycle frameworks, scenario techniques and market growth share matrices. Such frameworks emanating from the industrial organization literature have greatly enhanced our understanding of how to stimulate descriptive imagination through rigorous and systematic diagnostics that facilitate the diagramming and profiling of the competitive environment, with the ultimate aim of creating increasingly precise descriptions. A review of these frameworks of descriptive imagination in strategy making shows that several respected authors have emphasized the importance of accurate descriptions of the competitive environment (for example, Porter, 1980, 1985). This importance has also been confirmed in detailed empirical analyses, sometimes even on a global scale (for example, Porter, 1990), suggesting that the industrial organization literature has a rich tradition of sophisticated frameworks for stimulating descriptive imagination.

From this rich research tradition, I have selected for analysis a number of exemplary frameworks, based on their exposure in the extant literature and their influence on thinking in strategy making. Other than the ones I have chosen, several other frameworks exist, but I have not included them for discussion here. These fall into two broad categories. The first category includes frameworks of descriptive imagination that have been developed on the basis of Porter's well-known industry framework, but redefines industry structure using various bases of segmentation. These, generally not very influential, frameworks include 'resource-based' industry typologies (Collis and Ghemawat, 1994), and frameworks that use 'information' as the basis for such redefinition (for example, Sampler, 1998, 2001). The second category of frameworks not included focus heavily on existing product life cycles (for example, Hayes and Wheelwright, 1979), experience curve concepts (for example, Stern and Stalk, 1998), or the 'product impact on market share' (PIMS) database (for example, Schoeffler, 1977). It would appear that only thinking in terms of existing products and markets could compromise strategy making. Consistent with the definition of strategy making adopted for this study, I believe that strategy making requires imagination and originality to think beyond existing products and markets.

Three frameworks, then, best encapsulate the paradigm of descriptive imagination: Ansoff (1980), Henderson (1979), and Porter (1980, 1985, see Table 2.2).

The Ansoff (1980), Henderson (1979) and Porter (1980, 1985) frameworks seem to share a focus on the revealing of patterns, or seeing things in a new way as a key similarity. Closer analysis reveals that all frameworks reviewed seem to implicitly follow the basic sequence of the three generic steps in strategy making as they were deduced from the strategy process literature earlier in this chapter, namely envisaging, conceiving and realizing strategies.

However, the activities implied by each of the three generic steps seem to reveal a great deal of diversity. While most frameworks agree that the strategy-making process starts with a description of the competitive environment, there is considerable diversity as to the scope of environmental aspects under investigation, and the relative foci within these aspects. To illustrate: the major differences among the frameworks reviewed revolve around the translation of the steps into concrete activities. For example, the Boston Consulting Group (BCG) matrix focuses on the delineation of measures for market growth as a proxy for cash flow generation potential of the individual business units in the portfolio. Porter, on the other hand, focuses on describing a more comprehensive set of

Table 2.2   Comparison of the nine reviewed frameworks

	Ansoff (1980)	Henderson (1979)	Porter (1980)	Wernerfelt (1984)
Empirical validation	Yes, in a wide variety of industries.	Yes, in a wide variety of industries.	Yes, in a wide variety of industries in a global context.	No, conceptual paper.
Examples	Many examples are provided.	Many examples are provided in the original framework and its elaborations.	Largely absent.	Largely absent.
Unit of analysis	The firm in its competitive environment.	The multi-divisional firm and its portfolio of business units.	The industry in which a firm competes.	The firm as such.
Research method	Large-scale surveys.	Case studies based on positivist large-scale surveys.	Case studies based on large-scale surveys.	Deductive literature review.
Dominant inference patterns	Strategy making as a function of the strengths/ weaknesses of the firm relative to the opportunities or threats of its environment.	Firms can capitalize on market growth.	Competitiveness is a function of the attractiveness of the industry in which it competes.	Competitiveness is a function of its resource position, rather than its position in the industry.
Application context	Large corporations operating in a national economy.	Multi-divisional firm in a growing market.	Large, incumbent companies in established industries.	No specific application context mentioned. Generic relevance assumed.
Strategic question	How to best create fit with environment.	How best to allocate resources among competing investment opportunities.	How to achieve long-term competitive advantage.	How to configure firm resources across a firm's product portfolio.

Prahalad/ Hamel (1990)	Barney (1991)	Hamel (1996)	Evans/ Wurster (1997)	Eisenhardt/ Sull (2001)
Yes, but based on secondary case study data.	No, conceptual paper.	Yes, based on secondary case study data.	Yes, based on case study evidence.	Yes, based on secondary case study evidence.
Yes, many examples are provided.	No, largely absent.	Yes, a number of case vignettes is provided.	Yes, many examples are provided.	Yes, many case vignettes provided.
Firm resources or comptencies as such.	Firm resources as such.	Strategy making as such.	The industry value chain.	Strategy-making procedures as such.
Case vignettes based on archival analysis.	Deductive literature review.	Deductive literature review, case vignettes.	Case studies.	Deductive literature review, short case vignettes.
To the extent a firm is conceived of as a bundle of competencies, its competitiveness can be enhanced.	Resource heterogeneity across firms can lead to sustained competitive advantage.	Upsetting industry equilibrium leads to revenue growth.	To the extent information becomes a commodity, industry value chains are deconstructed.	The more dynamic the markets, the simpler the rules for competing in them should be.
Any firm in any industry, particularly in knowledge-driven industries.	Any firm, in any industry.	Any firm, implicit focus on incumbents.	Mostly information industries.	Mostly fast-moving industries.
How to identify 'core' competencies and leverage these across a firm's products synergistically.	How to differentiate critical from non-critical resources.	How to create new competitive space.	How to develop new business in a deconstructing value chain.	How to best take advantage of serendipitously emerging opportunities.

Table 2.2　(continued)

	Ansoff (1980)	Henderson (1979)	Porter (1980)	Wernerfelt (1984)
Strategic trap or risk	Industry and resource position perceived as given, and hardly changeable.	Overemphasis on large, multidivisional companies, less relevant in only moderately growing markets.	Industry boundaries are described as static.	Overemphasis on firm resource positions at expense of consideration of industry positions.
Strategic steps	Identify S/W relative to O/T.	Segment business portfolio. Balance business portfolio according to cash flow potential.	Assess attractiveness of industry. Deduce generic strategies. Configure activities along value chain.	Identify resources. Configure resourses among product portfolio.

factors that needs to be taken into account when practicing descriptive imagination. In effect, Porter's five forces framework complements the BCG framework in that market growth becomes only one component of a total of five forces defining market attractiveness (Belohlav, 1996). According to Porter: 'the growth share matrix can be one component of a competitor analysis when combined with the other kinds of analysis as described [in the five forces]' (Porter, 1980: 364).

Within this literature, it appears that the first step, envisaging, is given most attention – apparently at the expense of the other two steps (conceiving and realizing). While Porter must be credited with forwarding the value chain framework as a tool for conceiving strategies, the BCG and Ansoff frameworks appear to lack such a tool for step two. The lack of attention to concrete processes to realize strategies (step three) seems even more severe. While the general assumption (particularly in Porter's framework) is that competitive advantage is sustainable in the long run, little is said about how to actually realize strategies that confer such sustained competitive advantage into the future. Thus, in terms of similarities and differences, it transpires that most agreement seems to revolve around step one, envisaging strategies. However, steps two and three (conceiving and realizing strategies) are seen differently by the authors both in terms of relative emphasis and also in terms of activities implied. These observations seem to suggest the merits of balancing the

Prahalad/ Hamel (1990)	Barney (1991)	Hamel (1996)	Evans/ Wurster (1997)	Eisenhardt/ Sull (2001)
Overemphasis on competencies, 'competitive myopia'.	Overemphasis on resource positions, assumed resource heterogeneity.	Overemphasis on deconstruction, little emphasis on alternative truth.	Overemphasis on information as key driver for competitiveness.	Overemphasis on serendipity, firm's path dependence largely omitted from framework.
Identify core competencies. Focus on core competencies, outsource other activities. Leverage core competencies across product portfolio.	Focus on critical resources. Manipulate these resources to achieve lasting competitive advantage.	Reconception of a firm's product or service. Avoiding the tyranny of the served market. Challenging industry boundaries.	Ascertaining the extent to which the new economies of information affect a given business. Deduction of strategic imperatives.	Establishing extent of market dynamism. Creating room for serendipity. Following a number of simple rules in the pursuit of opportunities.

diverging emphases that the frameworks give to the activities implied by each of the three steps.

In terms of strengths and weaknesses, my analysis of the literature selected suggests two major weaknesses. It first and foremost transpires that a major strength of these three frameworks would be that all have enjoyed extensive empirical validation in diverse industrial settings and also in diverse countries. However, it should also be appreciated that the empirical validation was carried out mainly in the 1970s and 1980s, a period characterized by relatively stable industry environments and which lacked the highly dynamic nature of today's markets. Indeed, the current dynamism in markets characterized by blurring and even vanishing industry boundaries (for example, Sampler, 1998), would seem to call into question the relevance of strictly descriptive approaches. These tend to take a static definition, or at best, linear view of the evolution of industry boundaries as the cornerstone of strategy formulation. Such a static definition of industry boundaries therefore seems to represent a key weakness of descriptive imagination. According to Stalk, Evans and Schulman,

> ... when the economy was relatively static, strategy could afford to be static. In a world characterized by durable products, stable consumer needs, well defined national and regional markets, and clearly identified competitors, competition was

a 'war of position' in which companies occupied competitive space like squares on a chessboard ... Competition is now a 'war of movement' in which success depends on anticipation of market trends and quick response to changing customer needs. Successful competitors move quickly in and out of product-markets, and sometimes even entire businesses – a process more akin to an interactive video game than to chess ... (Stalk, Evans and Schulman, 1992: 62)

The above extract strongly suggests that the assumption of static industry boundaries could compromise the potential of the frameworks reviewed when applied to environments where such conditions do not hold. Even if the frameworks and their assumptions did hold (as indeed they do in more mature, highly asset-intensive industries, such as steel manufacturing, see Collis and Ghemawat, 1994), their explicit focus on descriptive imagination at the expense of the other two basic thrusts in strategy making, creative and challenging imagination, seems sub-optimal. This conjecture can be validated with a quote by Hamel:

The traditional 'competitive strategy paradigm' (for example, Porter, 1989) with its focus on product-market positioning *focuses on only the last few hundred yards* of what may be a skill-building marathon. The notion of competitive advantage (Porter, 1985) which provides the means for computing product-based advantages at a given point in time ... provides little insight into the processes of knowledge acquisition and skill building ... (Hamel, 1991: 83; emphasis added)

Hamel's call for more emphasis on skill and competence creation suggests that descriptive approaches to strategy making could be less effective in certain environments and clearly necessitates the inclusion of creative and challenging forms of imagination.

A *second weakness* stems from the differences in the frameworks. While all the frameworks seem to have adopted the *three generic steps* – envisaging, conceiving and realizing – they have done so implicitly only. While the generic steps are implied, the diversity of their implied actions seems to compromise their potential to make a clear link between the question of 'what' and the question of 'how'. While all frameworks implicitly follow the three generic steps in strategy making, they have lost this link explicitly. However, in crafting strategy imaginatively, it is decidedly difficult to focus exclusively on *what* strategic positions of the firm lead to optimal performance under varying environmental circumstances (content), without simultaneously considering *how* (process) a firm's administrative systems and decision processes influence its strategic positions.

Therefore, in order to mitigate the weaknesses while building on the strengths of the frameworks reviewed, I propose to cluster the activities mentioned by the authors in the three generic steps of the strategy-making process in order to make the strategy-making process more transparent.

Overall the analysis identified two key weaknesses of the major frameworks associated with descriptive imagination:

- While the frameworks seem to implicitly adopt the sequence of the *three generic steps* in the strategy-making process, the diversity of their implied actions seems to compromise their potential to make a clear link between the question of what should be done in strategy making and the question of how it is accomplished.
- While sophisticated in their descriptive power, the frameworks reviewed could suffer from a trap inherent in this same sophistication: the result could be 'a never-ending plethora of new descriptions, like different industry analyses, different SWOT analyses, and different portfolio analyses' (Roos and Victor, 1999: 349). In other words, an important *downside of descriptive imagination,* that is, the quest to develop increasingly precise descriptions seems to be the proverbial 'paralysis by analysis', which could neglect creative and challenging forms of imagination in strategy making.

Major Frameworks Associated with Creative Imagination

From the mid-1980s onwards, the so-called 'resource-based' paradigm in strategy making (for example, Wernerfeld, 1984; Rumelt, 1987; Prahalad and Hamel, 1990) challenged the descriptive orientation in strategy making. Building on Penrose's conception of the firm as a 'collection of productive resources, both human and material' (Penrose, 1959: 31), and contrary to the descriptive focus, proponents of this school have adopted a view on strategy that is essentially creative. Von Krogh and Roos explain that the resource-based approach re-establishes the importance of the individual firm, as opposed to the industry as the relevant unit of analysis (von Krogh, Roos and Hoerem, 1997).

At the core of this argument is the observation that creative imagination is the source of human invention (Kearney, 1988, cited in Roos and Victor, 1999). Associated with modernity, enlightenment, existentialist philosophy, and the constructive branch in the philosophy of science, creative imagination seeks to generate new opportunities that are implicit but unrealized in descriptive forms of imagination. The modern foundation of this form of imagination in strategy making is particularly present in the enlightenment view of the human being as an autonomous and productive individual. Less prosaic and mundane than descriptive imagination, creative imagination is often cloaked in mystery, and little is known about what stimulates it. In the strategy literature, however, this imagination has been described as a means to create and leverage firm resources and it can therefore be a source of sustained competitive advantage

(Roos and Victor, 1999; Barney, 1991; Wernerfelt, 1984; Prahalad and Hamel, 1990). Indeed, the recognition that the world should not only be described, but also created is very present in the strategy-making literature, and can be found in many frameworks of the resource-based view in strategic management. To illustrate: companies sometimes shape industry conditions, rather than take them for granted (for example, Hamel, 1996). In a similar vein firms are seen as heterogeneous with regard to their creative capabilities and resource endowments (see, for example, Wernerfelt, 1984; Barney, 1991).

Frameworks in the resource-based literature have greatly furthered our understanding of how company-specific resources and competencies can be leveraged, combined, and co-opted (see, for example, Prahalad and Hamel, 1990, also Prahalad and Ramaswamy, 2000) through creative imagination. Creative imagination therefore occupies a central role in many activities such as 'creating new competitive space' (Hamel and Prahalad, 1994a); 'strategy as stretch and leverage' (Hamel and Prahalad, 1993); and actively shaping, rather than accepting industry conditions (Hamel, 1996). In view of creative imagination's apparent relevance for strategy making, it is interesting that few actual frameworks of creative imagination in strategy making can be discerned from the literature. This might be due to the relatively recent nature of this field of research when compared to the much more established literature on descriptive imagination in strategy making. A review of frameworks of creative imagination in strategy making suggests that while several scholars have emphasized the importance of creating, rather than accepting industry conditions (for example, Hamel, 1996), the resource-based perspective associated with creative imagination is generally characterized by a lack of actionable frameworks. Along the same lines, and unlike frameworks from the descriptive imagination literature, resource-based perspectives have enjoyed much less empirical grounding (for example, Eisenhardt and Martin, 2000; Priem and Butler, 2001a).

Once again, I have selected exemplary frameworks for discussion on the basis of their exposure and influence in thinking about strategy making. The three frameworks discussed in this section are widely cited in the resource-based research field. I will not be looking at frameworks that see knowledge resources as the most critical, or 'core' resources in the organization, and that are specifically geared towards the management of knowledge (for example, Nonaka and Takeuchi, 1995; Davenport and Prusak, 1998; von Krogh and Roos, 1995, 1996; von Krogh, Roos and Slocum, 1994; Itami, 1987). While the management of knowledge undoubtedly constitutes a critical task, these knowledge management frameworks all focus on the exchange of knowledge within the organization, for example, through best practice forums, Yellow Page intranet portals, and urgent request functions (for example, Davenport and Probst, 2000). This suggests that these frameworks are more focused on operational performance improvement, than on strategy making (see Porter, 1996, for a discussion of the difference between operational management and strategy making). I will also not be including frameworks based on total quality and reengineering approaches (for example, Hammer and Champy, 1993), which focus mainly on strategy implementation, rather than strategy making. Since this study assumes that strategy making can be seen as an activity separate from strategy implementation or strategic change, I am setting aside these frameworks. The third, and probably largest set of frameworks not included, has paraphrased the articles to be discussed below, without augmenting the conceptual argument (see Priem and Butler, 2001a: 23–5 for a comprehensive overview of these studies).

Predicated on this selection process, I have identified three frameworks that best represent the paradigm of creative imagination: Wernerfelt (1984), Prahalad and Hamel (1990), and Barney (1991).

As evident from Table 2.2, the above frameworks share two main similarities. First, they seem to share a focus on creating strategies based on leveraging resources across markets, rather than focusing on positioning within a given market, as did the frameworks under the heading of descriptive imagination. Furthermore, it appears that the frameworks all focus on resources, or bundles of resources as the key interest of strategy making. One major contribution of these frameworks' focus on resource positions, rather than on product market positions, would consequently be to direct scholarly attention back towards resources as important antecedents of product market positions (Priem and Bulter, 2001a; Hamel, 1991). It seems interesting to note that in early conceptualizations of strategy making (Ansoff, 1980), scholars generally gave equivalent attention to firm strengths and weaknesses versus the opportunities and threats emanating from the competitive environment and industry structure. The publication of Porter's work (particularly Porter, 1980) then shifted the emphasis toward external, industry-based competitive issues. The common feature of the frameworks reviewed in Table 2.2 is that they seem to have served as a reminder that creative imagination 'lies at the heart of their competitive positions' (Dierckx and Cool, 1989, cited in Priem and Butler, 2001a: 23).

The second similarity is that all creative-imagination frameworks seem implicitly to follow the basic sequence of the three generic steps in strategy making as they were deduced from the strategy process literature: envisaging, conceiving and realizing. To illustrate, all the frameworks, albeit in varying degrees, suggest the differentiation between critical and non-critical resources or core competencies as a first step (envisaging strategies). This concern seems understandable from the practitioners' perspective, since, if a manager knows which components of the portfolio of organizational resources are critical from a strategic point of view, he can focus his attention on them.

Similarly, the second and third steps (conceiving and realizing) are typically seen as associated with 'bridging the gap between exploiting existing resources and building new ones' (Wernerfelt, 1984: 178).

However, the activities implied by each of the three generic steps seem to reveal a great deal of diversity. This *difference* seems particularly evident in the first step, envisaging imaginative strategies. To illustrate: different scholars seem to hold different views concerning appropriate criteria to be used to distinguish critical from non-critical resources. While Wernerfelt merely emphasizes the importance of delineating the most important resources without explicitly providing criteria, Barney (1991) proposed the criteria of value creation for the company, rarity compared to competition, as well as imitability, and substitutability. Prahalad and Hamel distinguished what they called core competencies from 'non-core' competencies as follows: core competencies should be suitable for application in many different markets, they should create a significant contribution to customer value, and consonant with Barney, competitors should have difficulty in imitating them (Prahalad and Hamel, 1990: 84). Thus, in terms of similarities and differences, it transpires that while all three steps of the strategy-making process can be delineated from the frameworks, the emphasis appears to center around step one. Steps two and three seem to be given much less attention. Moreover, despite the common emphasis on step one, this step is apparently viewed differently by the authors, both in terms of emphasis relative to the other steps and also in terms of activities implied. The observations made seem to suggest the merits of balancing the emphases between the activities implied by each of the three steps.

In terms of strengths and weaknesses it should first and foremost be appreciated that all frameworks reviewed have considerably enhanced our understanding of how to view firms from the resource side, rather than from the product market side. They have served a useful purpose in alerting scholarly attention to the importance of tending to corporate resource positions as fundamental antecedents to corporate product market positions. However, a major weakness of the frameworks would be that systematic empirical validation of this very focus seems largely outstanding (see, for example, Eisenhardt and Martin, 2000; Priem and Butler, 2001a, for the most criticism of the lack of empirical grounding). The root cause of the lack of empirical work in the field is sometimes ascribed to the tautological nature of the definition of core competencies, and the criteria used to distinguish core from non-core competencies: those resources that can generate sustained competitive advantage are identified by their ability to do so (see, especially, Priem and Butler, 2001a, b; and Barney, 2001).[2] This lack of empirical grounding was recently even described as the key impediment to progress in the resource-based research realm (Priem and Butler, 2001a, b).

A second key weakness of the frameworks reviewed would be their strong analytic emphasis on resource positions at the expense of the competitive environment (that is, at the expense of descriptive imagination). It seems interesting to note that while these frameworks have been forwarded in recognition of the simplifying assumptions underlying the industrial organization approach to strategy making (for example, that of omitting resource positions from the framework), they ironically introduce yet another set of simplifying assumptions (for example, that of omitting the competitive environment from the framework). While Wernerfelt's influential article starts with the sentence, 'For the firm, resources and products are two sides of the same coin' (Wernerfelt, 1984: 171), the frameworks reviewed do not seem to accord equivalent attention to product, or market and resource positions, respectively. It should be appreciated that the drawbacks associated with the mutual exclusion of industry and resource-positioning perspectives have been largely neglected so far, and are only now being addressed in the most recent literature (for example, Priem and Butler, 2001a, b; Barney, 2001). Two prominent scholars succinctly summarized that Wernerfelt's

> ... two sides of the coin' conceptualization has come to represent, surely in a way unintended by Wernerfelt, the separate consideration of firm resources and the competitive environment. Such mutual exclusion may reflect the state of the academic field, but is not an accurate reflection of the practice of strategic management. This artificial separation ... may be restricting out ability to fully conceptualize strategy making ... (Priem and Butler, 2001a: 64)

This inadequacy would clearly necessitate the inclusion of approaches to strategy making that explicitly describe such product market positions, that is, it would necessitate the inclusion of descriptive forms of imagination in crafting strategy.

A related, third, key weakness of the frameworks reviewed would be their failure to acknowledge the tendency of resource positions to erode over time. Yet, the tendency of resources to become obsolete relative to the competitive environment, could critically affect the competitiveness of the firm (Leonard-Barton, 1992, 1995; Gibbert, Leibold and Voelpel, 2001). It seems almost ironic that although the resource-based approach to strategy making began as a dynamic approach emphasizing the development of resources over time, for example, by advocating 'balance between exploitation of existing resources and the development of new ones' (Wernerfelt, 1984: 178), much of the subsequent literature has been static in concept (Teece, Pisano and Shuen, 1997; Eisenhardt and Martin, 2000; Priem and Butler, 2001a). This drawback would clearly necessitate the inclusion of approaches to strategy making that challenge established wisdom, path dependent behaviors, and resource positions in firms, that is, it would necessitate the inclusion of challenging forms of imagination in crafting strategy.

A fourth important weakness stems from the differences between the frameworks. While all frameworks seem to have adopted the three generic steps of envisaging, conceiving and realizing strategies, they have done so implicitly only. Indeed, while the generic steps are implied, the diversity of their implied actions seems to compromise their potential to make a clear link between the question of 'what' (pertaining to strategy content research) and the question of 'how' (pertaining to strategy process research). This can be partly attributed to the fact that the analyzed frameworks emanate from the strategy content realm, which traditionally focuses mainly on the 'what' question. Thus, while all frameworks implicitly follow the three generic steps in strategy making, they have lost this link explicitly.

Overall, analysis identified three key weaknesses of the major frameworks associated with creative imagination:

- While the frameworks seem to implicitly adopt the sequence of the three generic steps in the strategy-making process, the diversity of their implied actions seems to compromise their potential to make a clear link between the question of 'what' should be done in crafting strategy imaginatively and the question of 'how' this should be accomplished.
- While the frameworks have alerted us to the usefulness of looking at strategy making from the resource side, the frameworks reviewed could suffer from a trap inherent in just this focus on creative imagination. The result could be an inappropriate concentration on resource positions at the expense of a balancing focus that describes the competitive environment. In other words, an important downside of the focus on resource positions is the neglect of descriptive imagination in strategy making.
- While the frameworks have greatly enhanced our understanding of the processes by which resource positions are associated with competitive advantage, these resource positions seem to have largely been described in a static way. This seems understandable, since a firm's resource positions tend to be 'path-dependent', that is, a firm's investment in a set of resources could constrain its future behavior. However, to the extent to which the competitive environment changes, resource positions could deteriorate in value and even become obsolete, which demands a continuous challenging of the value of a firm's resource positions. In other words, an important downside of the frameworks' static treatment of resources is their neglect of challenging imagination in strategy making.

Major Frameworks Associated with Challenging Imagination

From the 1990s onwards, scholars started to recognize that neither descriptive nor creative approaches to imagination in strategy making were appropriate to cope with the increasing dynamism in markets. Scholars now argued that earlier, descriptive, approaches were flawed to the extent that they only described what is, and not what could be. Creative approaches were found equally flawed in that they ascribed pre-eminence to the exploitation of existing resources at the expense of the development of new ones. In short, they were criticized for assuming a static outlook on product market and resource positions, and for omitting from the framework the tendency of these positions to erode over time (for example, Priem and Butler, 2001a).

The starting point for approaches to challenging imagination is the endeavor to question existing product market and resource positions, and the conceptual backdrop for these approaches is complexity theory (Eisenhardt and Sull, 2001). Complexity theory constitutes an approach emanating from biology that seeks to explain the co-evolution of organisms and their environments (for example, Kauffmann, 1993, 1995). Challenging imagination in strategy making further seems associated with the deconstructionist philosophy of science (for example, Cilliers, 1998). Applications of this broad idea to the business environment appear to be in an emerging state. It is therefore difficult to predict their future acceptance. However contributions by strategy scholars published in highly respected journals (for example, Eisenhardt and Sull, 2001; Eisenhardt and Brown, 1999; von Krogh, Roos and Slocum, 1994), and recent special issues devoted to the topic (for example, by *Organization Science*) seem to have contributed to the acceptance of challenging forms of imagination in strategy making, and suggests it may have future potential. The recognition of the need to challenge established concepts and 'ways of doing things around here' seems particularly relevant to today's discontinuous business environment. Though less established than resource-based perspectives (creative imagination), and certainly less established than the literature on industrial organization (descriptive imagination), the strategy content literature nevertheless contributes a small selection of early frameworks that further our understanding of challenging imagination. For example, this type of imagination seems to play a central role in 'challenging core rigidities' (Leonard-Barton, 1992, 1995), bringing about 'industry revolution' (Hamel, 1996), 'being coherent, not visionary' (Lissack and Roos, 2001), 'managing out of bounds' (Hamel and Prahalad, 1996), and taking advantage of industries that are 'blown to bits' (Evans and Wurster, 1997, 2000). Overall, however, it appears more difficult to discern the most relevant frameworks in challenging imagination given the emerging nature of the field.

I have attempted to review a careful selection of frameworks that fall within the challenging category. Due to the emerging nature of this research stream, it is difficult to predict the popularity and future authority of the frameworks chosen. Frameworks that I have not included for discussion are primarily those that draw heavily on analogies from biology (Kauffmann, 1993, 1995), philosophy (Cilliers, 1998), or popular, rather than academic, sources (Peters, 1992, 1998).

Predicated on this selection process, I have identified three frameworks that might best represent the paradigm of challenging imagination: Hamel (1996), Evans and Wurster (1997), and Eisenhardt and Sull (2001).

As Table 2.2 suggests, an important similarity among the frameworks picked out above is that they seem to be characterized by a focus on evoking the negation of things previously held. In this sense, they would all focus on a kind of 'anti-imagination' – they attempt to negate, defame, contradict, and even destroy the insights gained from descriptive and creative imagination (for example, Roos and Victor, 1999). Calling it industry revolution, Hamel admonishes managers to be 'heretics', to disillusion themselves of the progress of their companies, and to challenge the established wisdom of their companies and even the entire industry (for example, Hamel, 2000). Along the same lines, Evans and Wurster advocate a 'deconstruction' of things or concepts previously held, such as industry value chains (Evans and Wurster, 1997, 1999). Eisenhardt and Sull seem to go a step even further than that and propose a 'cockroach' approach of serendipitously scurrying from one opportunity to the next (Eisenhardt and Sull, 2001: 108).

Careful analysis shows that the central theme of the frameworks reviewed is their explicit focus on dynamic interpretations of strategy as a process of continuous renewal, rather than on strategy as static positions (whether product or market or resource positions), that characterized the previous interpretations of strategy making: descriptive and creative imagination. However, beyond this fundamental similarity, few basic similarities in the individual steps that this process involves can be delineated from the frameworks. From Table 2.2, it appears that while all frameworks advocate the making of strategies that represent a radical departure from the established rules in the industry in which the company competes, the question of 'how' this should be accomplished still seems unanswered. This should come as no surprise, given the emergent nature of this stream of research. For the purposes of this study, it is therefore believed that much can be gained from crafting a three-step process for challenging imagination.

In terms of strengths and weaknesses, it must first and foremost be acknowledged that frameworks of challenging imagination in strategy making could focus our attention on a more informed and critical treatment of the concepts derived from the descriptive and creative imagination. It should be particularly welcomed that the frameworks, if implicitly, re-establish equivalent attention to product market as well as to resource positions of the firm, in that they argue that attention must be given to how resource positions develop over time relative to the competitive environment (see, especially,

Hamel, 1996, 2001; Eisenhardt and Sull, 2001). Particularly in today's dynamic markets, where resource positions can be eroded and devalued quickly, the challenging approach to strategy making could be beneficial. It must, however, also be realized that all frameworks reviewed, while sometimes building on extensive numbers of case vignettes, lack rigorous empirical validation. This weakness is understandable given the emerging nature of the topic, but could be a key impediment to the conceptual development of the field (Eisenhardt and Martin, 2000).

A second weakness of the frameworks reviewed can be seen in the inherent risk of challenging imagination: 'strategic nihilism' (Roos, personal communication, June 2000). Roos and Victor observed:

> Gary Hamel, [who] clearly uses challenging imaginations in his writings, does not show an alternative truth, he can only reconfirm what truth is not. What is Gary Hamel's prescription for strategy making? Labeled 'strategy as revolution', he asks us not to plan but to subvert the rules, overthrow the elite, rally the radicals, raise hell, take off our blinkers, and scrap the hierarchy … Yet, there challenging imagination has nothing new to put on the slate … (Roos and Victor, 1999: 350)

The very focus of challenging imagination on the negation of the sense of progress that can come with descriptive and creative imagination in strategy making could therefore also be its downside. In its quest to defame and negate, challenging imagination in strategy making could fail to provide feasible alternatives to the negation of product or market, or resource positioning. This inadequacy strongly calls for imaginations that 'describe' and 'create', rather than only defame. Indeed, the very process of falsifying and defying might require so much time and energy for its own operation that this preoccupation alone could become a motivation in itself that is powerful enough, however curtailed it may be, to turn into a compulsive mode of behavior. It would appear that the trap inherent in challenging imagination in strategy making makes the complementing of challenging imagination with descriptive and creative imagination highly opportune.

Therefore, in an attempt to mitigate the weaknesses while building on the strengths of the frameworks reviewed, the present study proposes to exploit the evidently complementary nature of the three imaginations in strategy making in one integrated framework, the strategy-making matrix.

To conclude, analysis identified two key weaknesses of the major frameworks associated with challenging imagination:

- While the frameworks seem to implicitly accept the necessity of guiding managerial action, and while a central theme in all the frameworks reviewed is strategy making as a process of continuous renewal, little is said about the individual steps comprising this process. This seems to compromise their potential to make a clear link between the question of 'what' and the question of 'how'.

- While sophisticated in their challenging approach to strategy making, the frameworks analyzed could suffer from a trap inherent in just this sophistication: the result could be an unending circle of negation and rejection. In other words, an important downside of challenging imagination, that is, of the quest to challenge the sense of progress that can come with descriptive and creative forms of imagination in strategy making, could be 'strategic nihilism' (Roos and Victor, 1999: 351), possibly at the expense of descriptive and creative imagination.

KEY SHORTCOMINGS OF EXISTING FRAMEWORKS

The previous sections have critically discussed the limitations of the individual frameworks that best encapsulate the three paradigms, descriptive, creative and challenging imagination. Here, I would like to attempt to summarize the key limitations across all frameworks discussed. An appreciation of these overall limitations of existing frameworks is fundamental to this study, since it manifests the benefits of the new, integrated framework proposed in this dissertation.

Upon analysis, existing frameworks suffer from two key limitations:

- The frameworks reviewed are often strong in one thrust of strategy making only (descriptive, creative and challenging imagination, respectively); generally without taking cognizance of the other two thrusts of strategy making.
- The frameworks reviewed are often strong in suggesting what can be done (that is, the content of a firm's strategy making), but mostly lack concrete recommendations as to how this is to be accomplished (that is, the process and constitutive process steps of strategy making).

The shortcomings of the frameworks analyzed imply the following:

- The first shortcoming could lead to inadequate conjectures in strategy making and is strongly indicative of the complementary potential of the frameworks analyzed.
- The second shortcoming is strongly indicative of the benefits of a three-step approach to aid strategy making.

In conclusion, the two main shortcomings of existing frameworks necessitate an integrated approach to crafting strategy imaginatively that addresses it as a three-step process (envisaging, conceiving, and realizing) revolving around the complex interplay of all three imaginations in strategy making (descriptive, creative, and challenging imagination).

NOTES

1. 'Process' is derived from the Latin 'procedere': to walk forward.
2. Tautological definitions are true by definition, and thus not subject to empirical testing (Williamson, 1999).

3. The three imaginations step by step

Let's turn to the individual steps of the strategy-making matrix. As discussed previously, I take a deductive approach here by drawing on, and condensing, previous process models into three generic steps.

A THREE-STEP APPROACH FOR DESCRIPTIVE IMAGINATION

Step One: Envisaging Imaginative Strategies

Defining industry boundaries

Industry analysis represents a focal concern in descriptive imagination, which seeks to describe and simplify a complex and confusing world 'out there'. As Porter emphasized, the industry or industries in which the firm competes is the single most important variable in strategy making (Porter, 1980, 1985, 2001). Industry analysis illuminates the competitive landscape in ways so as to aid strategy making. To illustrate: it can help establish whether a particular industry is likely to prove attractive to the average competitor and consequently shed light on profit differences among competitors in that industry (Collis and Ghemawat, 1994). In descriptive imagination the industry or industries in which the firm competes determine or significantly affect industry performance (for example, Porter, 1980; Bain, 1956). Put differently, the industry or industries in which the firm competes pose contingencies in terms of the types and ranges of competitive actions pursued in different contexts (for example, Datta and Rajagopalan, 1998). Before beginning to analyse an industry, it seems expedient to define the boundaries of the industry to be analysed. For the purposes of this study, industry analysis is divided into two levers: 'defining industry boundaries', which will be discussed in this sub-section, and 'diagnosing industry dynamics' which will be discussed in the next sub-section. Thus industry definition becomes the fundamental starting point in descriptive imagination.

Literature shows that industry definition is not a straightforward task, because industry boundaries can be defined along a variety of dimensions. For example, should the definition of the US automobile industry be confined to passenger cars, or should it also include light trucks, which have become an increasingly popular means of transportation? (Collis and Ghemawat, 1994). Statistical definitions such as the Standard Industrial Classification (SIC) are often used to answer these and similar questions. However, using the SIC approach can unduly limit descriptive imagination. If the SIC approach is used, the automobile industry would be defined as consisting of a fairly homogenous set of companies. Additional complexities can arise if the 'automobile industry' is more broadly conceived as the 'transport industry'. The consequent narrow conception of the automobile industry hardly captures the nature of competition occurring within it, and would preclude, for example, competition from the public transport sector. This is one reason why SIC codes have been criticized for rarely corresponding to competitively relevant industry conditions (for example, by Collis and Ghemawat, 1994).

A review of the literature demonstrates that to amend these challenges in defining industry boundaries, substitution possibilities on both supply and demand need to be identified and accounted for. On the demand side, the strategy maker should look for alternative products offered by direct competitors, as well as those competitors who currently offer products or services that might be close substitutes of their own. On the supply side, technological substitutability should be accounted for as well. In the case of the automobile industry, the advent of alternatives to the traditional combustion engine would be noteworthy, for example. Therefore, demand- and supply-side considerations usually form part of industry definitional endeavors (Abell, 1980; Collis and Ghemawat, 1994; Robinson and McDougall, 1998).

Despite the principle of substitutability, the definition of industry boundaries often remains as much 'an art as a science' (Collis and Ghemawat, 1994: 175). This is mainly due to ambiguities surrounding the various dimensions of the scope of the industry to be defined, and particularly the questions of vertical and geographic scope (Robinson and McDougall, 1998). Researchers provide answers to the ambiguities surrounding vertical and geographical scope. With regard to vertical scope, the key issue is how many vertically interlinked stages of the value chain should be identified to span it. In general, if a competitive market for third party sales exists between vertical stages, the stages could be uncoupled in defining industries. If not, they should not be linked at all (Collis and Ghemawat, 1994; Abell, 1980; Robinson and McDougall, 1998).

With regard to geographic scope, the key issue is whether physically separate markets should be treated as being served by the same industry or distinct industries. A case in point is the pharmaceutical industry, which is generally seen as a 'global' industry. This is typically ascribed to the need for amortization of tremendous research and development costs, making the pharmaceutical industry one characterized by high interdependence across national markets (Porter, 1990; Abell, 1980; Robinson and McDougall, 1998). A key criterion for deciding the geographic scope is, therefore, whether competitive positions in international markets are interdependent: the greater the interdependency, the broader the geographic scope (for example, Porter, 1994).

Diagnosing industry dynamics

Once the industry in which the firm competes has been defined, it is then expedient to diagnose the dynamics within that industry. Researchers agree that diagnosis of industry dynamics represents the most common form of strategy making in the descriptive mode (Porter, 1980, Henderson, 1979). This is not surprising, given that careful diagnosis of industry dynamics can help illuminate the competitive landscape in a way that aids crafting strategy imaginatively. In particular, it can help establish the dynamics in a given industry that affect the profitability of the firms competing in this industry. One objective of industry analysis is therefore to predict the average level of long-term profitability of a particular industry (for example, Porter, 1980). Another important objective of diagnosing industry dynamics is to gain an understanding of profit differences among competitors in the same industry. Collis and Ghemawat explain that the extent of such differences is a helpful indicator of the scope and type of the strategies that might outperform industry profitability averages (Collis and Ghemawat, 1994: 175).

Perhaps the best-known framework for diagnosing industry dynamics is that by Porter (1980). Porter employed industrial organization economics concerning market power and profitability to build a cross-sectional framework for explaining individual firm performance. This author argued that the true origin of competitive advantage may be the proximate or local environment in which the firm is based. The proximate environment will define many of the factor markets on which the firm has to draw, the information that guides strategic choices, and the incentives and pressures on firms to both innovate and accumulate skills and resources over time (Porter, 1991: 100). Until Porter, firms in strategic management had been seen as adapting to general, even rather vague, environments (for example, Rumelt, Schendel and Teece, 1994). Porter's five forces framework substituted a structured, competitive economic environment in which the ability to bargain effectively in the face of an 'extended rivalry' of competing firms, customers, and suppliers determined profit performance (Porter, 1980).

It should be appreciated that by diagnosing industry dynamics, companies attempt to achieve superior profitability relative to their competitors and despite the prevailing industry dynamics. To illustrate: traditionally the focus of industrial organization economics had been to identify socially wasteful sources of 'monopoly' profits. The diagnosing of industry dynamics, however, has a different focus. Its principal focus becomes not one of how to select antitrust and regulatory policies so as to increase consumer welfare but, rather, how to increase profits (and, if necessary, reduce consumer welfare) by containing and restricting competition (Pennings, 1985; Rumelt, Schendel and Teece, 1994; Teece, Pisano and Shuen, 1997).

Several authors agree that the key challenge in diagnosing industry dynamics is to isolate the characteristics of an industry in order to understand the contingencies in terms of the types and range of competitive actions pursuable in that industry (Rumelt, Schendel and Teece, 1994: 23). The most important characteristics include degree of capital intensity, product differentiability, and growth rate or life cycle. With regard to the degree of capital intensity, the literature generally agrees that the greater the degree of capital intensity, the greater the emphasis on efficient asset management and cost control. A firm in a capital-intensive industry is generally committed to a course of action, since capital intensity often creates rigidity in production processes to such an extent that new products and markets cannot be accommodated without incurring high costs. Capital intensity therefore logically restricts the range of new competitive actions to be pursued relative to those practiced in the past. Thus deviations from past practices are far fewer in capital-intensive industries (Ghemawat, 1991; Datta and Rajagopalan, 1998).

With regard to the second key dimension along which industry dynamics can be diagnosed, namely product differentiability, it appears that industries that are highly differentiated tend to offer more avenues for competition than industries that are less differentiated. Typically, an undifferentiated product requires firms to attend primarily to cost and efficiency factors, restricting the type and range of competitive actions. In contrast, in industries that are characterized by high differentiation, the means-ends linkages are relatively more complex, thereby offering a wider range of potential options to individual firms (Porter, 1980, 2001; Ghemawat, 1991; Datta and Rajagopalan, 1998).

Industry growth rate, or industry life cycle, is a third key dimension used to diagnose industry dynamics. Industry growth rate influences the availability of opportunities for market expansion, new product introduction and overall levels of competitive variation. High growth industries are characterized by unprogrammed decision making and poorly understood means-end linkages, again resulting in a wider variety of competitive behaviors. As an important stream of research in the industrial organization research realm, large numbers of researchers have investigated the individual stages of growth, also called industry life cycle (see for example, Fahey and Christensen, 1986 for a comprehensive review).

Typically the life cycle of an industry has been divided into stages of emergence, growth, shake out, maturity, and decline (for example, Fahey and Christensen, 1986). Maturity has to date received the most attention. The research indicates that firms pursue different strategies across different industry stages and that particular strategic behaviors are most appropriate at specific stages. The findings suggest that firms adapt their strategies as the industry evolves through its life cycle. In the maturity phase, firms tend to capitalize on their high levels of relative product breadth, relative product quality, relative quality of services offered, and vertical integration backward, for superior market share (Willard and Cooper, 1985, cited in Fahey and Christensen, 1986: 176). Furthermore, in the maturity phase there seems to be a clear relationship between efficiency and profitability. The investments required to generate growth are no longer necessary, and efficiency in the form of asset utilization, translates directly into comparative profitability. Research has shown that once the maturity phase develops into the declining phase, the most successful firms are those in industries with comparatively low exit barriers, particularly in terms of manufacturing and technology assets (Hambrick, MacMillan and Day, 1982).

A further question in diagnosing industry dynamics is the global scope of analysis. Porter's findings suggest that among the most significant influences on industry dynamism is the presence of local rivalry. A case in point is Honda, a company that faced competition from eight other Japanese auto companies, all of which competed internationally. It has been further found that firms rarely succeed abroad unless they compete successfully with capable rivals at home (Porter, 1990). It must therefore be emphasized that the scope of industry analysis needs to be broadened according to the extent that the industry or industries in which the business competes are of global scope (Porter, 1990, 1994).

Particularly noteworthy in this regard are what Porter (1990) terms 'related and supporting industries'. Such 'industry clusters' are groupings of industries linked together through customer, supplier, or other relationships at global level. As clusters form, the industries that comprise them tend to become mutually reinforcing. By implication, aggressive rivalry in one industry can spread vertically and horizontally in the cluster through spin-offs or related diversification (Porter, 1990, 1994). This conjecture seems particularly relevant given developments during the dot.com crisis of the late 1990s, where 'firms are global by birth' (Hamel, 2000; Hamel and Sampler, 1998; Porter, 2001).

Balancing the investment portfolio
Leading authors in the strategy field emphasize that ascertaining industry dynamics can provide important insights when allocating resources among competing investment opportunities, an exercise which the literature often calls 'balancing the investment portfolio' (for example, Ansoff, 1965; Porter, 1980, 1985). Balancing the investment portfolio so as to take optimum advantage of the diagnosed industry dynamics is a well-established tenet in descrip-

tive imagination in strategy making, as the two following quotes by renowned strategy scholars demonstrate:

> Strategy is the determination of the basic long-term goals of an enterprise, and the adoption of courses of action and the allocation of resources necessary for carrying out these goals ... (Chandler, 1962: 13)

> Strategic decisions resemble capital investment decisions, which deal with resource allocation ... (Ansoff, 1965: 23)

According to Rumelt, Schendel and Teece, the key tenet of balancing the investment portfolio as a fundamental lever in envisaging strategies is derived from the agency theory literature, and is primarily concerned with the design of financial claims and the overall governance structure of the firm. According to these authors, 'it is the branch which is most significant to strategic management' (Rumelt, Schendel and Teece, 1994: 28–9). The rationale behind the endeavor to balance the investment portfolio is to eradicate the problem observed by Jensen (1988), namely that in many firms managers have inappropriately directed free cash flow toward wasteful investments in the firms' portfolios. Indeed, the Boston Consulting Group offered precisely this diagnosis in its study of many diversified firms in the early 1970s. According to the Boston Consulting Group, many firms mismanaged their portfolios, misusing the funds generated by mature, cash-rich businesses, typically by continuing to reinvest in those businesses long after market-growth had slowed down (Rumelt, Schendel and Teece, 1994: 29).

The literature on descriptive imagination offers several decision heuristics that serve as decision-making tools for balancing investment portfolios. Typically, two or more attributes are used to graph the products on to a grid, and to plot different investment opportunities and their development trajectories over time. The literature suggests that the two best-known examples are those of the Strategic Planning Institute, and the Boston Consulting Group. Both tools presuppose that a firm can be subdivided into sub-units, or 'strategic business units,' which are defined in terms of external attributes such as classes of customers served, and organizations with which they compete, and which are sufficiently separate from other strategic business units for them to be treated as profit centers. The delineated strategic business units are then plotted in a matrix that serves as a heuristic for their classification into investment priorities (for example, Pennings, 1985; Belohlav, 1996).

The central feature of these decision-making heuristics is that they seek to identify likely candidates for preferential treatment in resource allocation decisions. To illustrate: excess profit from so-called cash-cows, which enjoy high market share in low-growth markets, would not be re-invested, but would be transferred to 'stars' deserving preferential treatment due to their favorable positions in high-growth markets. Decisions regarding divestitures can be taken in a similar manner. An example of divestiture would be strategic business units suffering from low market share in a low-growth market (these strategic business units are commonly called 'poor dogs'). Other examples are well documented in the literature (for example, in Pennings, 1985).

Seen from this perspective, many downsizing, de-layering, lean management and business process re-engineering endeavors can be interpreted as approaches to dovetail the potential of the individual strategic business units with market contingencies (for example, Garvin, 1998; Hammer and Champy, 1993; Davenport, 1993). The decision-making heuristics therefore seek to balance the investment portfolio by determining the inter-divisional cash flows that underlie the strategic shifts in the company's product portfolio (Pennings, 1985: 23).

Step Two: Conceiving Imaginative Strategies

Configuring value chain activities

Configuring activities along the value chain is an important technique to stimulate descriptive imagination in the phase where envisaged strategies are actually conceived. The value chain represents a rigorous and systematic diagnostic for describing the underpinnings of a firm's relative position. The value chain framework postulates that favorable positions in an industry can be described by disaggregating the value creation process of a firm into discrete activities that contribute to the firm's relative cost position and create a basis for competitive advantage (Porter, 1985). In this sense, the *rationale* for using the value chain framework revolves around its three uses: first as a template for describing cost position, second as a template for describing produce effects on the cost position of buyers, and third, as a tool for describing the added cost that differentiation might imply (Porter, 1994: 110).

Most authors in the literature agree that the activity disaggregation in a value chain must be complete in the sense that it captures all activities performed by the firm. To aid descriptive imagination in strategy making, it is important that the activity-disaggregation exercise not be too detailed, while still enabling the strategy maker to identify those activities that are strategically important. The heuristic developed by Porter for disaggregating activities suggests that the resulting activities have different economics, a high potential impact on differentiation and represent a significant proportion of cost (Porter, 1985: 39–40, 1994: 110). The value chain provides impetus to descriptive imagination by introducing a two-level generic taxonomy of value creation activities that includes primary activities and support activities. Primary activities are directly involved in creating and bringing value to the customer, whereas support activities enable and improve the performance of the primary activities. Support activities thus only affect the value delivered to customers by affecting the performance of primary activities. Primary value chain activities deal with physical products, whereas support activities deal with issues of procurement, technology development and human resource management (Porter, 1985: 38).

The concept of the value chain provides further impetus to descriptive imagination in that it aids in understanding important issues pertaining to global industries, thereby widening the focus of the value chain to include the global or transnational firm (Porter, 1990). Both domestic and global firms and industries have value chains, but the global firm would have special latitude along two dimensions: first, configuration, or where the activities in a firm's value chain are located; and second, coordination, or the nature and extent to which the conduct of dispersed activities is coordinated versus allowing activities the autonomy to tailor their approach to local circumstances. With regard to the first dimension, the international configuration of a firm's value chain should be carried out according to two criteria: choosing where to locate each activity, and deciding how many locations should be performing one activity. The rationale in adopting these two criteria is to gain competitive advantage by arbitrating comparative advantage across locations. To illustrate: many multinational software firms have located software development and program maintenance to India so as to take advantage of low-cost programmers (Porter, 1994: 112).

Several researchers agree that the second dimension to be considered when configuring value chains globally is coordination of the globally dispersed value chain (for example, Porter, 1985; Ghemawat, 1991). The way in which a firm coordinates its activities around the world determines its ability to benefit from a particular configuration (Porter, 1990). Coordination encompasses the setting of standards, the exchange of information and the allocation of responsibility among sites. Similarly, coordination that involves allocating responsibilities across countries, such as worldwide responsibility for producing particular frameworks, can unleash economies of scale. Coordination involving information and knowledge exchange is needed to foster worldwide learning (Nonaka and Takeuchi, 1995; Hedlund, 1994). Indeed, a central challenge in coordinating value chain activities is how and where information, technology and knowledge from disparate locations are integrated and reflected in organizational processes (Davenport and Prusak, 1998; Porter, 1990). Coordination of value chain activities across geographically dispersed locations involves daunting challenges, among them language, cultural differences (Hilb, 2000), and difficulties in aligning individual managers' incentives with the enterprise as a whole (Gibbert, Kugler and Voelpel, 2000). In other words, coordination allows a firm to realize the advantages of configuring value chain activities globally, while failure to coordinate lessens those advantages (Porter, 1990).

Work around the turn of the twenty-first century challenged the descriptive logic of the value chain framework, dismissing its two-level categorization and categorization approach as outdated (for example, Eisenhardt and Sull, 2001; Shapiro and Varian, 1999). The main thread of argument in these contributions revolves around the impact of the Internet on the value chain. Most authors agree that since every activity involves the creation, processing, and communication of information, information technology exerts a tremendous influence on value chain activities (for example, Evans and Wurster, 1997). It would appear that the special advantage of the Internet is the ability to interlink one activity with another, and to make real-time data created in one activity widely available both within the company and to outside suppliers, channels and customers. Multiple activities can be linked together through tools such as customer relationship management, supply chain management and enterprise resource planning systems. However, as Porter argued, the basic logic of the value chain is not distorted by enabling technologies such as the Internet (Porter, 2001: 74).

Establishing position
Once the industry or industries in which the company competes have been delineated, and the dynamics within the industry's boundaries have been ascertained, the firm needs to establish a position within the competitive context. The rationale for establishing a position distinct from its existing competitors is one of establishing and sustaining monopoly rents by momentarily inhibiting competition (Teece, Pisano and Shuen, 1994). The basic argument is that a firm with a position distinct from its competitors benefits, since it faces less competition (for example, Porter, 1980). A firm that conforms to the strategies and positions of others has many similar competitors that limit the performance of the firm (Henderson, 1979).

Establishing a position typically involves identifying a niche in the market and then exploiting it. This means that a firm establishes a position in what it *ex ante* perceives to be an unexploited or underexploited niche. Porter (1991: 102) postulated 'the firm must stake out a distinct position from its rivals. Imitation almost ensures a lack of competitive advantage and hence mediocre performance.' A distinct position enables a firm to earn higher rents, because it would face less competition and perhaps even enjoy a local monopoly (Porter, 1980, 1991).

The first challenge in establishing a position is to ascertain competitors' positions. A central tenet in the descriptive imagination literature is that the positioning of a firm in a particular industry be made relative to other players in that industry. This implies that the strategic imperative is not one of establishing absolute dominance, but of establishing a position that is better relative to the immediate competition (for example, Porter, 1985). In the words of Porter (1994):

Performance is a function of the attractiveness of the industry in which the firm competes and its relative position in that industry. The firm's relative position depends on its competitive advantages (or disadvantages) vis-à-vis its rivals. Competitive advantage is manifested either in lower costs than rivals' or in the ability to differentiate and command premium prices that exceed the extra cost of differentiating ... (Porter, 1994: 109).

In descriptive imagination, therefore, the key task for the firm is one of becoming better than its immediate competitors. This demands adequate consideration of the competitors' relative positions, and the underpinnings thereof. In descriptive imagination the approach taken to reach this end is often one of benchmarking best in class competitors. Benchmarks can be established by carefully describing traits and characteristics that make competitors successful (for example, Davenport, 1993; Hammer and Champy, 1993). David Kearns, CEO of Xerox Corporation, defines benchmarking as 'the continuous process of measuring products, services, and practices against the toughest competition or those companies recognized as industry leaders' (Kearns, cited in Hart, 1994). Indeed, when in the late 1970s Xerox compared US-made products to those of its Japanese affiliate, the company was amazed to discover that they were selling at prices equivalent to US manufacturing costs. By 1983 Xerox had incorporated benchmarking as a key element in its corporate-wide improvement effort (see Harrington, 1991: 222). The central tenet is that such benchmarks need to be realistic, even if they require a stretch to achieve, and they need to be attainable within the company's current environment (Harrington, 1991). Areas for benchmarking include, but may not be limited to: financial performance, quality, service ratings, cycle time, brand awareness and market share (Johnson, 1988, 1994).

A second key challenge in establishing a position is to deliver a value proposition, or set of benefits different from those that competitors offer. Often, in descriptive imagination, the current strategy provides the logical basis for generating value propositions for customers. As Porter (2001) admonished his readers in a more recent contribution:

Strategy requires a strong focus on profitability rather than just growth, an ability to define a unique value proposition, and a willingness to make tough trade-offs in choosing what not to do. A company must stay the course, even during times of upheaval, while constantly improving and extending its distinctive positioning. A company must define a unique value proposition that it will stand for, even if that means foregoing certain opportunities. Frequent corporate reinvention then, is usually a sign of poor strategic thinking and a route to strategic mediocrity ... (Porter, 2001: 71–2)

The above illustrates that descriptive imagination is based on the appreciation of obvious alternatives to establishing positions relative to existing competitors. These positions are obvious in the sense that they represent the types of alternatives that are aimed at long-term extension of the firm's current strategy, for example, extending its market share within both end-customer and distribution channel segments by extending its current product lines and/or penetrating existing and new customer segments. Typically such moves include six alternatives stemming from current strategy:

1. Extending the variety of models, styles or types of each product within each of the firm's product lines.
2. Adding new products to one or more of the existing product lines.
3. Making the firm's current products available to customers in new geographic areas.
4. Making additions to the current product lines or products available to customers in new geographic areas.
5. Penetrating new distribution channels with the existing products.
6. Reaching new customers within existing geographic markets (Lyles, 1994: 283–5).

General Motors provides a case in point in the literature. In the face of deteriorating marketplace performance over a number of years, the car manufacturer sought strategies that could help it regain market share and compete more efficiently. The company first changed some of its core operating processes, including forcing its internal suppliers to compete directly with outside vendors. This helped General Motors to choose among its internal and external suppliers in order to increase quality and reduce the price of its parts. This in turn led to improved product functionality and quality, and enhanced the firm's image and reputation in the eyes of existing and potential customers (*Business Week*, June 1992, cited in Hart and Branbury, 1994: 283).

Defending position
As the previous discussion illustrated, the focus of establishing position is a long-term one. The strategic logic in the descriptive mindset is one of 'fortifying and defending positions', as Eisenhardt and Sull (2001: 109) have succinctly summarized it. As was previously explained, the 'fortify and defend' logic suggests that defending a position translates into extending the current strategy that leads to a particular position (Porter, 2001: 71). The question arising from this long-term focus is how to best defend the position against competitors, so as to reinforce the position attained.

As Mintzberg and Lampel (1999) have illuminated, defending and fortifying a position once attained can be found in Porter, and it is also present in earlier analyses by the Boston Consulting Group, and can interestingly be traced back to its military origins (for example, Clausewitz, 1998). The common denominator in these contributions is that strategy making is about exploiting generic positions selected through formalized descriptions of industry structure, and that industry plays a central role in determining and limiting the latitude with which such positions can be established and defended (for example, Teece, Pisano and Shuen, 1997; Rumelt, Schendel and Teece, 1994).

As was described previously, the rents accruing to firms who succeed in staking out a favorable position in a given competitive context are 'monopoly rents'. In the descriptive mindset, firms in an industry earn rents when they are able to impede the competitive dynamics prevailing in a particular industry (in either factor or product markets). Interfering with these forces is desirable from the viewpoint of industrial economics, because perfect competition would drive economic returns to zero (Teece, Pisano and Shuen, 1997: 511).

The ultimate objective of defending position is thus to secure monopoly rents over the long term (an endeavor Porter called 'sustaining competitive advantage', see Porter, 1985). Logically, to the extent that in neoclassical economics competition would erode the extra profits earned by successful firms, leaving just enough profit to pay for factor costs calls for impediments to the elimination of abnormal returns (Rumelt, Schendel and Teece, 1994). In the literature, the most important tools suggested for achieving this end are erecting strong barriers to entry, and delineating 'generic strategies' that interfere with free competition and thus allow for abnormal profits in the long run (for example, Rumelt, Schendel and Teece, 1994; Teece, Pisano and Shuen, 1997; Nelson, 1991). The first tool for defending a position is discussed here, and the second is discussed in the section that follows.

Average industry profitability is likely to be influenced by potential as well as existing competitors. The concept typically used in the literature for describing the threat of entry is erection of entry barriers (for example, Porter, 1985). Porter describes the function of entry barriers as acting to prevent an influx of firms into an industry whenever the profits, adjusted for the cost of capital, rise above zero (Porter, 1994: 178). Entry barriers can take many different forms. Some barriers tend to reflect intrinsic physical or legal obstacles to entry. For example, the existence and efficacy of international patents on aspartame (NutraSweet®) and other artificial sweeteners can impede entry into new segments of that industry (Porter, 1994: 179).

The most common forms of barriers to entry are the type and scale of investment required to enter a particular industry as an efficient competitor. The aluminium industry is a telling example: it requires enormous capital stock to enter this industry on an integrated basis, since an efficient integrated facility would cost several billion dollars. Such a facility would only account for 5 per cent of worldwide demand, a figure low enough to have led to overcapacity and soft prices (Porter, 1994: 179). Similarly, well-established brand names can represent a formidable barrier to entry, for example, in the case of

Coca-Cola. However, it must also be appreciated that particularly in fast-moving consumer markets, established brand names can be a double-edged sword, particularly when 'kids start wearing T-shirts that say 'just don't do it', it's a bit late to think about re-vitalizing your brand' (Hamel, 2000: 55).[1] Particularly in markets where switching costs are low for consumers, deteriorating brand-awareness can be disastrous (Hamel, 2000).

Defending a position in an Internet-enabled context can be particularly daunting, if seen in the light of the Internet's effect on barriers to entry. As Shapiro and Varian (1999) elaborate, the Internet would effectively reduce barriers to entry, such as the need for a sales force, access to channels and physical assets. Similarly, it is very difficult to keep Internet applications proprietary, since imitability tends to be very high. This was echoed by Porter (2001) who argues that on the Internet, buyers can often switch suppliers with just a few mouse-clicks, and Internet technologies are systematically reducing switching costs even further. For example, companies like PayPal provide settlement services or Internet currency that enable customers to shop at different sites without having to enter personal information or credit card numbers (Porter, 2001: 68). Evans and Wurster forecast that this trend is likely to increase rather than decrease, since effectively new businesses emerge whose revenue stream is derived from providing convenient navigation, linking suppliers with customers or vice versa, through so-called 'reverse auctions' (Evans and Wurster, 2000).

Step Three: Realizing Imaginative Strategies

Discriminating generic strategies

The distinguishing feature of descriptive imagination in strategy making is its propensity to focus on a 'disciplined' extension of the current strategy in line with the descriptions of the environment gathered through experience or analysis (Roos and Victor, 1999). In Porter's words, 'Having a strategy is a matter of discipline' (Porter, 2001: 70).

According to the literature, descriptions of the competitive environment help the strategy maker clarify the range of options available. The literature of descriptive imagination in strategy making has yielded a widely accepted framework for discriminating between the range of options available (see Porter, 1980, 1985). The framework's ultimate objective is to establish and sustain the financial viability of the venture. In the words of Porter: 'The creation of true economic value becomes the final arbiter of business success. Economic value for a company is nothing more than the gap between price and cost and its reliability measured only by sustained profitability.' (Porter, 2001: 65)

In order to achieve the objective of financial profitability, Porter's framework prescribes the discrimination of so-called 'generic strategies'. The generic nature of the strategies proposed would suggest their robustness over time and across contexts. Indeed, the relevance across contexts (industries and countries) of Porter's framework for discriminating generic strategies has been established in the literature from the wide range of applications it enjoys, both in terms of different industries (as diverse as banking, shipping and hospital services, see Campbell-Hunt, 2000), and countries as diverse as Ireland, Portugal and Korea (see Porter, 1990).

The generic strategies' relevance over time is a central tenet in descriptive imagination (for example, Porter, 1985), even if less thoroughly validated empirically than the framework's robustness across contexts. As a matter of fact, research to date has produced largely equivocal results as to the durability of advantage (for example, Campbell-Hunt, 2000). Called the Law of Nemesis, economists assert that 'nothing good lasts forever', in other words that competitors will invariably find ways to share the wealth of the market leader. Overall sustainability seems to be a matter of degree (for example, Day, 1994), and would be contingent on the discriminations made among different types of generic strategies.

Several authors agree that the framework can be seen as making discriminations on four levels of analysis (see, for example, Campbell-Hunt, 2000; Porter, 2001; Robinson and McDougall, 1998). First, a differentiation is made on the basis of whether or not the firm has some distinctive advantage relative to its competitors. On a second level, a scheme is introduced for delineating the basis of that advantage (cost-based or differentiation-based). Third, a heuristic is offered for describing firms' competitive strategies according to their marked scope (focused or broad). Finally, a theoretical proposition is offered regarding the performance implications of cost- or differentiation-leadership positions: that failure to discriminate between them leads to inferior performance ('stuck in the middle').

Cost minimization, the first generic strategy, builds on a philosophy of being a lower-cost producer than one's competitors, and generating alternatives that keep the cost structure low. Increased rivalry in many industries has led many companies to pursue cost-reduction alternatives. Manifestations of this trend include, but may not be limited to, experience curve effects, total quality management, business process re-engineering and enterprise relationship planning. For example, Internet-enabled approaches to improve operational effectiveness and decrease costs by increasing the exchange of real-time information, and enabling improvements throughout the entire value chain (for example, Porter, 2001). It must furthermore be emphasized that in the descriptive orientation, 'simply improving operational effectiveness does not provide competitive advantage. Companies only gain advantages if they are able to achieve and sustain higher levels of operational effectiveness than competitors'. (Porter, 2001: 71)

Sustaining advantage based on cost minimization can be arduous, since competitors tend to emulate these through best practice benchmarking. Best practice competition can eventually undermine the profitability of an entire industry, because it could lead to strategy convergence with many firms doing the same things in the same ways (Porter, 2001; Hamel, 2000).

Indeed, due to the nature of Internet applications, sustaining cost-leadership tends to become more difficult than ever (for example, Shapiro and Varian, 1999; Hamel, 2000; Evans and Wurster, 1997, 2000). The openness of the Internet combined with advances in software architecture, development tools, and modularity (for example, Eisenhardt and Brown, 1998, 1999), tends to make the design and implementation of cost-saving applications relatively quick and easy. Porter illustrates this using the example of a US drug store chain that was able to implement a complex Internet-based procurement system in just 60 days (Porter, 2001: 71). Thus, resulting improvements in operational effectiveness tend to be broadly shared among competitors in an industry, which calls their contribution to establishing and maintaining a distinctive position into question (Porter, 2001).

As the value of cost leadership for the purpose of strategic positioning is undermined, the promise of advantage based on differentiation is accentuated. If a company finds it hard to be operationally better than its rivals, another way to generate higher levels of economic value is to gain advantage by competing on the basis of differentiation, which is the second generic strategy. Differentiation creation defines alternatives that enhance the organization's competitive posture, that is, how the company distinguishes itself from its competitors in the eyes of the customer (Porter, 1985, 2001; Lyles, 1994). The emphasis in the differentiation strategy is on identifying potential ways in which the firm can differentiate itself in each of its customer segments. The sources of differentiation vary considerably across industries and firms, and can include, but may not be limited to, unique market positions (market share as well as reputation) and unique product features. Product features have to be upgraded continuously for them to stay ahead of competitors. This is vividly illustrated by the Japanese consumer electronics market where Sony was forced to introduce 160 versions of the Walkman in order to withstand the intense rivalry in this market segment (Day, 1994: 304).

A final challenge in discriminating among types of generic strategies revolves around the assumptions that guide discrimination. An important step in assessing the feasibility and promise of a type of generic strategy would be to isolate the assumptions underlying the discriminations made. The literature provides rich insights into the biases and incomplete understanding of strategy makers (for example, Mintzberg and Lampel, 1999). For the purposes of this study, three critical habits that could lead to misguided discriminations can be delineated. The first of these habits is that selective perception occurs when people tend to structure their decision-making processes in the light of their past experience, training, and culture, and can be traced back to Lao Tse's writings ('You see what you are'). The second habit is that availability of data resources can also significantly influence decision-making processes. The third is that emphasis is usually given to facts and opinions that are easy to retrieve. Often, however, these are data about past successes, which tend to be given greater weight than future adversity (Probst, 2000). The likely result is underestimation of competitors' abilities to gain market acceptance and penetrate previously secure markets (Day, 1994; Kim and Mauborgne, 1999a)

Cultivating competitive angst

Clive Weil, former Chief Executive Officer of Game, a South African retail chain, coined the concept of 'competitive angst' to describe the way Game worries about competition (Nasser and Vivier, 1995: 101). 'Competitive angst' would seem a very apt and succinct description of the mindset underlying descriptive imagination in strategy making: 'Competitive angst resembles the fear of the hunted, the wariness of the warrior and the spirit of the underdog ... This angst is displayed in the form of a relentless drive to improve the edge over competitors...' (Nasser and Vivier, 1995: 102).

The ultimate objective of cultivating competitive angst is sustained competitive dominance relative to competitors in a particular industry, as evident in the writings of competitive strategists such as Porter (1980, 1985), and is epitomized in the concept of relative competitive advantage. The consensus among authors in the descriptive realm is that while it is tempting for companies to define the basis of their businesses' competitive advantage in absolute terms, such as selling products at the lowest price or offering the best quality service, it can obscure an important issue. What often matters in the marketplace is not how good or bad a product is in absolute terms, but whether any or all of these attributes are perceived as being superior to those offered by competitors (for example, Rumelt, Schendel and Teece, 1994; Porter, 1996).

A telling example of cultivating competitive angst can be gained from observing the struggle of General Motors against its three major Japanese competitors (Toyota, Nissan and Honda) in the 1980s. According to a ten-year longitudinal study, in 1980 General Motors had, on average, 110 problems per 100 cars compared to the 43 of the Japanese competition. By 1990 the General Motors figure had been reduced to 40 problems per 100 cars. However, in the interim, the Japanese companies had achieved a failure rate of 17. These data clearly suggest that General Motors had made a remarkable improvement, but the data also suggest that General Motors still suffered from a competitive disadvantage in relative terms (Gupta, 1994: 93). Thus the intent of cultivating competitive angst is to differentiate the firm and its product offerings from current competitors as understood and perceived by customers.

Many of the most successful companies seem to obsessively cultivate competitive angst. Jack Welch of General Electric, for instance, explained his efforts to regain competitiveness for General Electric in its key markets as follows:

> To be content to be the third or fourth position in your industry is foolish. One morning you will wake up and find that number one or two has changed the rules of the game. What use is all your effort then? You may well find that you have slid from being third or fourth to being sixth or seventh ... (Welch, cited in Nasser and Vivier, 1995: 33)

As the above quote illustrates, cultivating competitive angst implies a conscious decision to delineate: (a) areas in which the company must remain superior to competitors; (b) areas in which the company would accept the possibility of being on par with competitors; and (c) areas in which the company would accept the possibility of being at a disadvantage vis-à-vis competition. Indeed, several authors agree that it may not always be necessary for the firm to be superior to competitors in all areas (for example, Porter, 1980; Ghemawat, 1991; Porter, 2001). However, a lack of superiority in critical dimensions implies that the firm's current position is unlikely to be sustained.

Many tools and conceptual aids for cultivating competitive angst emanating from the descriptive imagination literature emphasize this point. The Boston Consulting Group growth share matrix, for example, can be seen as one tool for cultivating competitive angst among strategy makers in that firms' different relative positions in a growing market are visualized (from unfavorable positions such as 'poor dogs', to favorable ones such as 'stars', Henderson, 1979; Belohlav, 1996). Similarly, competitor benchmarking (for example, Garvin, 1998; Hammer and Champy, 1993), as well as competitive intelligence gathering (for example, Davenport and Beck, 2001), has been described as a conceptual aid compelling businesses to position their performance relative to emerging practices of industry leaders, and ultimately compelling businesses to cultivate competitive angst.

Creating a fit with the environment

One of the most widely shared and enduring assumptions in crafting strategy in the descriptive mindset is that the appropriateness of a firm's strategy can be defined in terms of its fit, match or congruence with the environmental or organizational contingencies facing the firm (for example, Andrews, 1971; Chandler, 1962; Porter, 1980, 1985; Venkatraman, 1989). Nadler and Tushman define fit or congruence as 'the degree to which needs, demands, goals, objectives and/or structure of one component are consistent with the needs, demands, goals, objectives, and/or structure of another component' (Nadler and Tushman, 1980: 40). In the descriptive orientation, fit would imply a match at a single point in time. Venkatraman, after having comprehensively reviewed research on strategic fit, concludes that 'the existing structures have focused on static, cross-sectional approaches for specifying and testing fit within strategy research' (Venkatraman, 1989, cited in Zajac, Kraatz and Bresser, 2000: 429).

Fit with the competitive environment is thus a core concept in descriptive imagination frameworks and the pursuit of strategic fit has been viewed as having desirable performance implications (Ginsberg and Venkatraman, 1985; Venkatraman, 1989; also implicit in Porter, 1985). However, despite the concept's criticality, relatively little explicit attention to the concept of fit has been found in the recent strategy process and strategy content literature. Research on 'fit' has emanated mainly from the strategic change and organizational learning literature in which it is argued that organizational contingencies have to be appropriately matched with environmental contingencies, so as to realign the organization with the prevailing realities (for example, Beer and Nohria, 2000; Senge, 1990). I found little prior research to explicitly conceptualize fit in strategy making (with the exception of Zajac, Kraatz and Bresser, 2000).

The reason for this lack of explicit attention has been mainly ascribed to the multi-dimensionality of strategic fit. As Zajac, Kraatz and Bresser discovered, methodological challenges to the study of fit abound, given that simple, bivariate techniques are ill-suited to capture the multiple environmental and organizational contingencies that can affect strategic fit. The authors conclude that the literature seems rather ambiguous in proposing that particular structures are more appropriate for given environments, and that changes in environmental conditions require a reassessment of the choice of structure (Zajac et al., 2000). What seems clear, however, is that the descriptive mindset proposes a specific causality: environmental conditions determine structure. The implication arising is that creating fit with the environment is essentially an endeavor to create accurate descriptions of the environment, and matching the structure accordingly (Zajac et al., 2000: 430).

Further insight into creating fit with the firm's competitive environment as a lever for descriptive imagination can be gained from revisiting the classic contributions by Andrews (1971) and Chandler (1962). As Zajac et al. explain, the concept of fit has theoretical roots in contingency perspectives found in both the strategy and organization theory literatures. Revisiting Andrews' and Chandler's earlier work suggests that the initial strategy paradigm was rooted in the concept of 'matching' or 'aligning' organizational resources with environmental opportunities and threats (Zajac et al., 2000: 431). Indeed, the original work by Chandler, *Strategy and Structure*, emphasizes the interdependency of structural alignment with strategy. As Miles and Snow illustrate: 'the process of achieving fit begins with, conceptually at least, aligning the company to its market-place... this process of alignment defines the company's strategy' (Miles and Snow, 1994; cited in Zajac et al., 2000: 429). In the case of a 'misfit' with the environment, the strategist is admonished to reassess the strategy against the new contingencies, and to create a new strategy better suited to the new status quo.

Finally, researchers argue that fit with the environment is typically a matter of degree and that 'misfit' is associated with undesirable performance implications (for example, Johnson, 1994). Sometimes called 'strategic drift', such misfit between the competitive environment and the firm is said to materialize when the organization's strategy gradually, and usually imperceptibly, loses its focus on the demands of its competitive environment. As Miller pointed out, the root cause of this development is that firms tend to become the victims of their own past successes. A telling example is Digital Equipment Corporation (DEC). DEC's success in the 1970s and 1980s was based on the design of its technologically sophisticated microcomputers. As a result, the company fostered an engineering monoculture in which technological fine-tuning reigned and customers' needs for smaller, more economical and user-friendly computers were ignored (Miller, 1990, cited in Johnson, 1994: 421).

A THREE-STEP APPROACH FOR CREATIVE IMAGINATION

The previous section dealt with descriptive imagination. Here, I would like to move on to discuss the second important thrust in strategy making, creative imagination.

Step One: Envisaging Imaginative Strategies

Concentrating on core competencies
Creative imagination revolves around a fundamental issue. This issue is the conceptualization of the firm, not as a collection of discrete strategic business units or product/market positions (as in descriptive imagination), but as a collection of core competencies that draw on certain common resources (for example, Wernerfelt, 1984; Prahalad and Hamel, 1990; Barney, 1991). The rationale for this conjecture is that most products require the services of several resources and most resources can be used in different product markets. This has led to the insight that by specifying the scope of the firm's activities in different product markets, it is possible to infer the minimum necessary resource commitments. Conversely, by specifying a resource profile for a firm, it is possible to find the optimal product/market activities (Wernerfelt, 1984: 171).

It is interesting to compare the conceptualization of the firm as a bundle of resources versus its conceptualization as a bundle of product/market positions. The former is the realm of creative imagination, the latter of descriptive imagination. While descriptive imagination has largely focused on developing accurate descriptions of product/market positions, creative imagination asks how these arise in the first place and focuses on antecedent organizational structures that create product market positions (for example, Barney, 1991). As Hamel illustrates, conceiving the firm as a portfolio of core competencies suggests that inter-firm competition, as opposed to inter-product competition, is essentially concerned with the acquisition and exploitation of resources, suggesting that competitive advantage would be highly associated with organizational resources. A key question therefore is to identify which core competencies the firm has and which ones it needs to develop (for example, Prahalad and Hamel, 1990).

The literature shows that answers to this question are based on the assumption that firms' resource and competence endowments are heterogeneous. Teece, Pisano and Shuen (1997) have identified reasons why this may be so. First, business development is seen as a complex and organizations may often lack the capacity to develop or acquire new competencies swiftly enough. Also, some assets such as tacit knowledge may not readily be tradable, because they are generally difficult to articulate, and as a consequence difficult to transfer and trade (Polanyi, 1958, 1966). Therefore, Teece et al. argue, resource endowments cannot equilibrate through factor input markets, hence the assumption underlying the creative approach to crafting strategy: critical resources can only be acquired partially and consequently need to be developed internally (Teece et al., 1997).

Most authors in the creative imagination realm explain that the key to understanding resource-based strategy making is to distinguish critical from less critical resources (for example, Barney, 1991). The next logical step in creative imagination is therefore to decide which resource, capability or skill may be critical in providing sustainable competitive advantage (Nanda, 1996). The strategic management field seems deeply involved in identifying those resources which would yield sustainable competitive advantage, that is, the most critical resources. This concern is understandable from the practitioner's perspective, since, if a manager knows which components of the portfolio of organizational resources are critical from a strategic point of view, he can focus his/her attention on them (Hamel and Prahalad, 1993, 1994a; Hamel, 1991).

Different scholars have held differing views on appropriate criteria to be used to differentiate critical from non-critical resources. Barney (1991) proposed the criteria of value creation for the company, rarity compared to competition, as well as imitability and substitutability. Prahalad and Hamel

(1990: 84) distinguished what they called core competencies from 'non core' competencies as follows: core competencies should be suitable for application in many different markets, they should create a significant contribution to customer value, and consonant with Barney, competitors should have difficulty in imitating them.

The answer to the question of which organizational resource accommodates these criteria, that is, which is most strategically significant, also seems to be unclear in the literature. Many scholars are ambiguous in their terminology and a review of the literature reflects considerable diversity. A plethora of phrases including 'firm resources' (Barney, 1991), 'invisible assets' (Itami, 1987), 'knowledge assets' (for example, Davenport and Prusak, 1998), and 'intellectual capital' (Sveiby, 1997) is used. The definitions are sometimes tautological; resources are defined as firm strengths, and firm strengths are subsequently defined as strategic resources.[2] In these characterizations, competencies are, by definition, those resources that yield sustainable competitive advantage. Seeing competitive advantage from a resource-based perspective presumes (core) competence, and research has shown that until the substance or nature of competence is defined, only a substitute for the idea of competence is established, not an explanation (Spender, 1996b; Nanda, 1996).

An emerging consensus among scholars (Nanda, 1996; Spender, 1996b) proclaims that the prevalent terminological ambiguity would prescribe that organizational knowledge, whether referred to as 'invisible assets' (Itami, 1987), 'absorptive capacity' (Cohen and Levinthal, 1990), 'core competencies' (Prahalad and Hamel, 1990), 'strategic assets' (Amit and Schoemaker, 1993), 'core capabilities' (Kogut and Zander, 1996), or 'organizational knowledge' (Nonaka and Takeuchi, 1995), can be viewed as the only resource that fulfils the foregoing criteria, and should therefore be seen as the most strategically significant resource. Prahalad and Hamel substantiate this view as they themselves often use core competencies and knowledge interchangeably: 'core competence does not diminish with use, unlike physical assets, which do deteriorate over time, competencies are enhanced as they are applied and shared. But competencies still need to be nurtured and protected, knowledge fades if it is not used.' (Prahalad and Hamel 1990: 82)

With the recognition of the strategic importance of knowledge as the most critical, or 'core' competence, has presumably come the acknowledgement that a new, 'knowledge based' (for example, Grant, 1996, 1997; Spender, 1996a, b), or 'organizational epistemology' (von Krogh and Roos, 1995; von Krogh, Roos, and Slocum, 1994) approach is needed to conceptualize strategy making. In this area of focus, the analysis of competitive performance is scaled down to the level of knowledge, thereby (often implicitly) assuming knowledge as the appropriate unit of analysis (see, for example, von Krogh and Roos, 1995; Nonaka and Takeuchi, 1995).

Finally, literature emphasizes that while critical, the knowledge component could represent only one of a variety of components comprising core competencies. Prahalad, Fahey, and Randall therefor emphasize that core competence is a concept that is often misunderstood (Prahalad, Fahey and Randall, 2001: 243). The key to an appropriate understanding of competence-based strategy making is that although core competencies incorporate a knowledge component, they also involve governance processes inside an organization (for example, the quality of relationships across functional knowledge domains within a business unit, or across business units in a multi-business firm, for example, Prahalad and Hamel, 1990). According to the literature, another important component of core competencies would be collective learning across levels, functions, and business units. Lastly, technology constitutes an important component of core competencies. However, core competence would only result if firms harmonize multiple technologies. For example, Sony's expertise in miniaturization requires expertise in several technologies such as microprocessors, miniature power sources, power management and user-friendly design (Prahalad et al., 1994: 262).

Propagating strategic intent
As discussed earlier, a key tenet in descriptive imagination is the quest to establish a fit between existing resources and emerging opportunities. Essentially the idea of strategic fit emphasizes the trimming of ambitions to match current resource endowments by firms. However, research has discovered that the most successful companies were those that did the exact opposite: nurturing ambitions that were out of all proportion with existing resources, and focusing on seemingly unattainable goals. This represents an orientation that was called 'strategic intent' (by Hamel and Prahalad, 1989; or 'value innovation' by Kim and Mauborgne, 1997a, 1999a, b).

Indeed, research has discovered that the most successful companies were those whose ambitions were un-constrained by their current resource endowments. To illustrate: research indicates that companies that have risen to global leadership over the past 20 years invariably began with ambitions that were out of all proportion with their resources and capabilities. Major examples cited in the literature include Toyota versus General Motors, CNN versus CBS, and Easyjet versus all major airlines (Sull, 1999; Hamel and Prahalad, 1993).

Underlying strategic intent is the core idea of 'numerator management' (Hamel and Prahalad, 1994a: 125). Numerator management refers to aspirations to increase the numerator of the return on investment (ROI) equation (that is, net income), rather than decreasing the denominator (that is, investment, net assets or capital employed). The challenge with numerator management is that it is generally more difficult to raise the denominator than it is to raise the numerator. For example, it is often considered more difficult to raise the net income of a corporation than it is to cut assets and headcount. To increase the numerator, managers must have a sense of where the opportunities lie, be able to anticipate changing customer needs and have invested in building new competencies. Therefore, under intense pressure to improve ROI, managers often turn to the denominator as a lever for achieving relatively fast and sure results (Hamel and Prahalad, 1994a: 125).

The recent infatuation of many companies with downsizing, rightsizing, de-layering, lean management, business process reengineering and total quality management can be seen as manifestations of the quest to drive down the denominator (for example, Hamel, 2000). The ultimate objective of these endeavors to reduce the denominator would be to catch up with the competition in terms of efficiency. The very essence of competitive strategy emphasizes the need for managers to work hard to achieve the competitive advantages of their next (global) rivals. Even the very vocabulary used in this stream of research seems indicative of this preoccupation (for example, 'competitive strategy', 'competitive advantage', competitive benchmarking', see Kim and Mauborgne, 1999a, b). However, several scholars have discovered that often the quest to reduce the denominator typically leads to a reproduction of the cost and quality advantages global competitors already enjoy (for example, Hamel, 2000; Hamel and Prahalad, 1994a; Kim and Mauborgne, 1999a, b). As Hamel and Prahalad put it: 'imitation may be the sincerest form of flattery but it will not lead to competitive revitalization' (Hamel and Prahalad, 1989: 63).

According to recent empirical research, Xerox was the dominant player among copier manufacturers in the 1970s, the brand name even becoming synonymous with copying itself (Hamel, 2000). Threatened by a loss of market share to Japanese competitors, Xerox benchmarked its Asian competitors, re-engineered its processes and streamlined its customer service to eventually attain radical efficiency improvements. Yet Xerox never regained its dominance in the copier market. While it nearly matched, and in some areas (for example, customer service) even surpassed, its Japanese rivals, it failed to regain its original profitability. Researchers argue that the reason for this can ironically be ascribed to exactly its success in matching its Japanese rivals: Xerox essentially got better without getting different (for example, Hamel and Prahalad, 1991: 83).

The quest to gain the efficiency, quality and cost advantages of competitors often leads to strategy convergence in an industry, that is, a situation in which many players simultaneously pursue different strategies (Kim and Mauborgne, 1999a, b; Hamel, 2000). This can have disastrous effects on profitability, because it can eventually lead to price wars (Porter, 1980). These drawbacks suggest the benefits of original strategies that focus on the numerator, rather than the denominator. Sun Tzu illuminated this point in a military context 3000 years ago: '...all men can see the tactics by which I conquer, but what none can see is the strategy from which victory is evolved' (Sun Tzu, cited in Hamel and Prahalad, 1989: 64).

Overall, the literature suggests that propagating strategic intent seeks to focus the manager to abandon the 'feasibility sieve' (Hamel and Prahalad, 1989: 66) that is usually used to match emerging opportunities with existing resources, and to nurture ambitions that are out of all proportion to the company's current resources and capabilities. Whereas denominator management focuses on establishing and maintaining a fit between opportunities and resources, propagating strategic intent focuses on the numerator and implies a sizable stretch in goals for an organization. By implication the company is forced to make the most of limited resources when focusing on stretch goals. Thus, whereas denominator management focuses on creating and sustaining a fit between existing resources and current opportunities, propagating strategic intent seeks to create an extreme misfit between resources and ambitions.

Transcending competitors
With strategic intent established, a further lever for unleashing creative imagination is to transcend competitors, rather than trying to catch up with them. As Hamel puts it, 'catching up is necessary to stay in the game but the winners invent new games' (Hamel, 2000: 11). The key in this lever is to make the competition irrelevant, rather than attempting to beat it (Hamel, 2000: 14). The Chinese military strategist Sun Tzu admirably condensed this mindset in 2600 BCE: 'To win without fighting is best. Only do battle when there is no choice' (Sun Tzu, 1997: 47).

Sun Tzu's axiom can usefully be applied to less martial endeavors in the strategy realm. Indeed, a review of the literature on strategy content as well as strategy process suggests several drawbacks associated with the focus on 'fighting' competitors. The most important being that traditional competitor benchmarking is often like a '*snapshot of a moving car...* which yields little information about the car's speed or direction' (Hamel and Prahalad, 1989: 64; emphasis added). Interestingly, the proponents of benchmarking themselves have defined the term as 'an ongoing investigation and learning experience that ensures that best industry practices are uncovered, analysed, adopted, and implemented' (Garvin, 1998: 86). Along the same lines, Hammer and Champy defined benchmarking as 'looking for companies that are doing something best and learning how they do it in order to emulate them' (Hammer and Champy, 1993: 132, cited in Orgland, 1995). However, as Hamel and Prahalad describe the results of their research, '... our most successful companies weren't obsessed with their competitors... What counted was not so much how they positioned themselves against long-standing rivals, but how creatively they used their core competencies to create entirely new markets.' (Hamel and Prahalad, 1994a: ix)

As Hamel and Prahalad's quote implies, infatuation with competitors can lead to an inaccurate reflection of reality. In anticipating the moves of existing competitors, companies focus on existing resources (human, technical and financial) of present competitors. Through this lens the only companies seen as a threat would be those with sufficient resources to erode margins and market share in the next planning period (for example, Kim and Mauborgne, 1999a, b). A case in point are the successes of nimble Japanese companies over their US rivals in the 1970s and 1980s. Research shows that in 1970 few Japanese companies possessed the resource base, manufacturing volume or technical prowess of their US rivals. Komatsu, for example, was apparently less than 35 per cent of Caterpillar's turnover, and Honda was much smaller than General Motors and had as yet not even begun exporting cars to the US. If General Motors and Caterpillar had extended their competitor analysis to include Honda and Komatsu, it would merely have underlined how dramatic the resource discrepancies were and how little threat consequently emanated from these companies (Hamel and Prahalad, 1989: 64).

Kim and Mauborgne (1996, 1999a, b) explained that the strategic imagination driven by the competition can have two latent effects that are ironically the exact opposite of what managers have in mind. First and foremost, it tends to put companies in a reactive mode. Often precious time and resources are spent in response to ongoing competitive moves. Second, it can lead to imitative, rather than imaginative, strategies. Companies accepted what competitors were doing and strove to do it better. However, according to Hamel (2000), the question is not one of getting better, but of getting different, because the result of getting better would be increasingly convergent strategies. This in turn would leave little room for differentiation from the next rival and typically leads to price wars and eroding profit margins (Kim and Mauborgne, 1999a, b; Hamel and Prahalad, 1994b).

In recognition of the drawbacks of an infatuation with competitors, a variety of authors have made a strong case for shifting the basis of strategy away from a focus on competitors to a focus on transcending competitors (for example, Kim and Mauborgne, 1999a, b; Hamel, 1991, 1996; Hamel and Prahalad 1994b). The next question then is how competitors can be transcended. To answer this question it is useful to adopt a more encompassing interpretation of the term 'competition'. Prahalad, Fahey and Randall (2001) have provided a useful framework for thinking differently about competition. Their research has shown that it is important to recognize that today competition takes place on multiple planes. For the purpose of this study, three planes can be delineated from the authors' analysis: end products, core products and core competence.

Competition on the level of core competence revolves around gaining a capacity to create new business by creatively combining core skills. The focus here should not be on catching up with existing competitors, even if they seem much more resourceful. Instead the focus should be on what customers value most. To illustrate: a focus on competitors often fails to describe the considerable successes achieved by less resourceful companies such as, for example, Honda, and Komatsu over their much more resourceful rivals General Motors and Caterpillar when creatively combining their production skills (ibid., 2001).

Competition on the level of core products revolves around a capacity to lead the development of new functionalities and the pace of product development. This often entails letting some established customers go. Indeed, Hamel and Prahalad have alerted their readers to the dangers of being led by existing customer demands (Hamel and Prahalad, 1994a; also Prahalad, Fahey and Randall, 2001). Along the same lines, Kim and Mauborgne (1999a, 2000) emphasize that while it is important to focus on customers, it is often more important to pay attention to non-customers as well. SAP of Germany is an illustrative example. It has continuously renewed its customer base by moving aggressively from mainframe users to client-server users to mid-size and small companies. Hasso Plattner, a co-founder of SAP, explained: 'non-customers often offer the greatest insights into where the market is moving and what we should be doing fundamentally different...' (*New York Times*, 29 March 1998).

Competition on the level of end products revolves around a capacity to manage what Prahalad, Fahey and Randall call the 'price/performance gap'. The key here is to focus on what Kim and Mauborgne have called 'value innovation'. These authors explain that 'value innovation makes competition irrelevant by offering a fundamentally new and superior buyer value in existing markets and by enabling a quantum leap in buyer value to create new markets' (Kim and Mauborgne, 1999a: 43). In creative imagination, it is therefore the drive offering a considerable leap in value that opens strategists' imagination to the differences between what industries are competing on and what the mass of buyers actually values. CNN, for example, decided to drop its big name anchors, even though the industry had for a long time competed for them. This enabled CNN to produce 24 hours of real-time news at one-fifth of the cost of producing one hour of CBS news (*Wall Street Journal Europe*, 6 March 1997).

Step Two: Conceiving Imaginative Strategies

Redefining industry boundaries

An important lever in conceiving imaginative strategies in creative imagination is a re-definition of industry boundaries. To recall from descriptive imagination, the industrial organization view holds that industry structure determines, or significantly affects, industry performance. For firms competing in a particular industry, this means that industry structure poses contingencies in terms of the types and ranges of competitive actions pursuable. As was discussed in the descriptive imagination lever 'defining industry boundaries', the focus of descriptive imagination is largely on defining the industry in terms of product/market positions. Thus, the US automobile industry can be defined in terms of the types of vehicles sold (for example, utility versus sports cars), suggesting that competition revolves around a fairly homogenous set of major players, including General Motors, Volkswagen and DaimlerChrysler.

However, literature shows that if the same approach is adopted to describe the credit card industry, a very different picture emerges. Increasingly, institutions other than banks are dominating the very profitable credit card market. According to Sampler (1998: 349), this trend was initiated with AT&T launching their own credit card in the mid-1980s. In the first year of operations, AT&T issued 12.5 million credit cards and became the seventh largest issuer of credit cards in the US. By 1995 non-bank credit card issuers controlled 40 per cent of the consumer credit card market, and are on average much more profitable than retail banks. This development has not been limited to the US. Indeed, in the UK, with regard to basic savings and checking accounts, retail banks are facing severe competition from retail chains, such as Marks & Spencer, Tesco and Sainsbury's, which are offering the full range of customer financial services (*Economist*, 1997, cited in Sampler, 1998).

This shows that increasing industry convergence and overlaps between industries emphasize the need to consider bases other than product/market positions to define industry boundaries. Such redefining of industry boundaries attempts to focus the imagination of the strategy maker not only on the product/market positions, but also on the antecedent organizational resources and factor inputs that lead to the product/market positions in the first place. Seen from this perspective, industry boundaries can also be (re-)defined by focusing on creative organizational processes that lead to the product/market positions. This approach is in line with new strategy content literature, which has emphasized resources as the principal driver of firm profitability and strategic advantage (Wernerfelt, 1984; Barney, 1991; Prahalad and Hamel, 1990).

In view of the emphasis on firm resources as drivers of strategic advantage, it does not seem surprising that several scholars have proposed that industry definition can also be accomplished by looking at the resource, rather than product/market side as the basis. As Collis and Ghemawat (1994) explain, the traditional approaches to industry definition can usefully be supplemented by classifying industries in terms of the resources that dominate competition within them and that are likely, therefore, to underpin firm success. It would appear that if a particular type of resource commitment is salient in a particular industry, investment in and utilization of these resources are likely to play a critical role in crafting strategy imaginatively. The critical bases for redefining industry boundaries emerging from the literature (for example, Collis and Ghemawat, 1994; Rumelt, 1987; Williams, 1992) are capacity-driven industries, customer- or service-driven industries, and knowledge-driven industries.

- In capacity-driven industries, capital investments tend to be relatively large in relation to cost or value-added (for example, in the steel industry). In such industries, competition takes place mostly on price, while expenditures on research and development are typically limited. Capacity-driven industries tend, furthermore, to be mature, commoditized and characterized by modest productivity improvement.
- Customer-driven industries tend to be characterized by relatively large investments in brands or consumer relationships (for example, the sports industry). These industries tend to be less mature, less commoditized and less static than capacity-driven industries.
- In knowledge-driven industries (for example, the pharmaceutical industry) investments in research and development tend to account for the largest part of value-added. As a rule, knowledge-driven industries tend to be at the earlier stages of their life cycles and more global than capacity-driven and customer-driven industries. Productivity typically improves very rapidly, and competitors often pay more attention to introducing new products and processes than focusing on enhancing efficiency of existing ones.

The above typology suggests that in order to define industries in terms of the resources that dominate competition within them, it could be useful to consider the ratio of physical stocks to value-added, advertising or marketing expenditures to value-added, and finally research and development expenditures to value-added. When an industry has a relatively high value-added in any of these dimensions, it can easily be defined in terms of dominant resources, which correspond to the three types of industries. Moreover, as the focus on knowledge-driven industries suggests, much research in the resource school of strategic management has recently shifted from focusing on tangible resources as a source of strategic advantage to intangible ones, which include tacit knowledge (for example, Nonaka and Takeuchi, 1995), core competencies (Prahalad and Hamel, 1990), learning (Senge, 1990), and intangible assets, such as brand image or corporate culture (for example, Itami, 1987).

Particularly important is information as a key resource for redefining industry boundaries. In a much-acclaimed contribution, Sampler (1998) made the point that in the 'Information Age' the key resource logically becomes information and knowledge. To the extent that information becomes increasingly critical in the extant industry environments, it seems promising to (re-) define industry boundaries in terms of the types of information exchanged in a particular industry (whether and to what extent information can be separated from the event generating the information). To illustrate: the SABRE airline computer reservation system represents a fundamental shift in the nature of competition among the key players in the airline industry by introducing seating and booking information. This information not only supports the transaction of booking seats, but has created an entirely new source of value by creating the basis from which airlines can effect dynamic seat pricing based on current and historical load factors (Sampler, 1998).

Overall, creative imagination proposes that industry boundaries can be redefined by looking at the resource, rather than the product/market side as the basis for the drawing of industry boundaries. The critical implication for the strategy maker is that this conceptualization suggests a very different set of competitors. In the case of the credit card business, a narrow conceptualization based on product/market positions suggests a fairly homogenous set of competitors, including American Express, Visa and MasterCard. However, when redefined, based on information as the key resource traded in the credit card business, the scope of analysis widens appropriately to include, for example, retail chains and insurance agencies as critical players (for example, Sampler, 1998; Hamel, 2000; Kim and Mauborgne, 1999a, b).

Leveraging internal resources

Hamel and Prahalad (1993) introduced a concept of strategy as 'stretch and leverage'. The main argument was the new contention that competitiveness is born in the misfit between a company's resources and its managers' goals. The concept of strategy as stretch and leverage was intended to complement what was perceived as the traditional contention of strategy as the fit between organizational and environmental contingencies (for example, Porter, 1980, 1985; Chandler, 1962). The traditionalist paradigm essentially viewed strategy as based on the relationship of the company and its competitors, and the allocation of resources among competing investment opportunities (Hamel and Prahalad, 1993: 77). This, according to Hamel and Prahalad, left many resources under-leveraged. Likely outcomes of this inadequacy were described by two prominent corporate leaders: Jerry Junkins, the late CEO of Texas Instruments, lamented, 'If Texas Instruments only knew what Texas Instruments knows' (cited in O'Dell and Grayson, 1998: 154); this was echoed by Lew Platt, chairman of Hewlett Packard, 'If HP knew what we know, we would be three times as profitable' (cited in Despres and Chauvel, 1999: 6).

In contrast, the new concept of strategy as leveraging resources already in possession of the company complements descriptive imagination in that it provides an alternative frame in which the concept of stretch supplements that of fit, and where leveraging resources is seen as equally important to allocating them. The notion of leverage – the continuous search to get the most from the existing resources – is designed to enable companies to build for consistency, while simultaneously nurturing an appetite for risk (Hamel and Prahalad, 1993: 77). Among the resources prone to leverage, many researchers emphasize knowledge (for example, Nonaka and Takeuchi, 1995; Davenport and Prusak, 1998). The reason for this seems to be the cost structure underlying the production of knowledge resources. Literature shows that the distinctive features of this cost structure become evident as one considers the implications of the so-called 'law of diminishing returns', which argues that the more a given resource is used, the smaller its incremental returns will be (for example, Stewart, 1998). Many authors argue that this law loses its relevance in many industries. By contrast, the law of *increasing* returns actually seems to be characteristic of many industries (Roos, Roos, Edvinnson and Dragonetti, 1998; Arthur, 1996).

The law of increasing returns argues that the more a given resource is used, the higher its incremental returns will be (for example, Arthur, 1996). The economist Brian Arthur ascribes this tendency to the fact that the production of knowledge-intensive products is characterized by 'up-front costs'. The costs of product development (in other words, knowledge production costs) are very high relative to marginal production costs (in other words, knowledge leverage costs), which are generally low (Arthur, 1996; Hebbler and van Doren, 1997). To illustrate: knowledge resources require early, high, fixed costs as an aggregation of data collection, assimilation, analysis and synthesis (as in software production, for example). Most knowledge resources therefore seem to be subject to economies of scale and scope. Such resources, once created, can be deployed at low marginal cost (the costs for copying the software developed to a CD, for example; see Grant, 1996; Spender, 1996a, b).

Two generic approaches to leveraging resources can be discerned from the relevant literature, namely recontextualizing resources and blending resources (see also Hamel and Prahalad, 1993). To recontextualize resources, companies need to invest in learning activities that allow them to draw from existing pools of resources inside and outside the company. Relevant elements of these pools need to be systematically identified and brokered across the contexts from which they originate. (Hamel and Prahalad, 1993: 79–83). In order to recontextualize resources, companies need to devise more efficient ways for timely extraction of a required resource from the reservoir of total resources (see, for example, Grant, 1996; Spender, 1996a, b).

The literature shows that redistributing resources among the often-discrete loci of resource production (for example, functional departments), however, is neither automatic nor easy. Particularly tacit forms of resources and knowledge often migrate slowly (see, for example, Hedlund, 1994; Nonaka and Takeuchi, 1995; Davenport and Prusak, 1998; von Krogh and Roos, 1995). In fact, some components of the corporate resource portfolio may be entirely inaccessible to such recontextualization (Winter, 1987). Many authors argue that what differentiates companies from one another may be less the relative quality and depth of their resource stocks than their capacity to draw from that stockpile (Prahalad and Hamel, 1990; Nonaka and Takeuchi, 1995). The ability to maximize, and capitalize on, these tacit insights depends on a variety of critical success factors. Major examples cited in the literature include: employees who are both reflective and well schooled in the art of problem solving; organizational forums (such as quality circles and efficient intranets) where employees can identify and communicate common problems and search for higher order solutions; an environment in which every employee feels responsible for the company's competitiveness; and continuous benchmarking against the world's best practices (Hamel and Prahalad, 1993).

A critical skill in the process of recontextualization is anticipating analogies, that is, a hidden overlap or similarity between two or more discrete resource bases. This skill may help to anticipate when resources developed and used in one area or department have value elsewhere. The difficulty with this seems to reside in recognizing when existing knowledge, in combination with other knowledge, has potential to be leveraged to a new context (Hamel, Doz and Prahalad, 1989; Hamel, 1991; Nonaka and Takeuchi, 1995; Spender, 1996a, b). Once attained, such resources would enable the corporation to build and continuously renew a repository of ideas with potential value for utilization outside the context from which they emanate.

In addition to recontextualizing resources, a second tool for leveraging resources is blending resources. Whereas recontextualization involves recognizing the value of locally created knowledge resources for later use elsewhere, blending involves the development of such resources through synergistic complementing to make them amenable to usage in a different context. By blending resources in synergistic ways, management can transform resource bases while leveraging them. Spender (1996a, b) has established that while knowledge resources are typically thought to be the property of individuals, they are often held socially in the organization, for example in the form of joint expertise in engineering departments. In this view many organizational knowledge resources seem to be inherently linked to the context from which they originate. Since the processes of creating resources are often significantly interdependent on the context from which they emanate, locally designed resources do not readily turn into something with exchange value or use value elsewhere (Nonaka and Takeuchi, 1995; Spender, 1996a).

Researchers have found that, as with recontextualizing resources, a critical skill in blending resources can be analogous thinking. Analogies often highlight non-obvious similarities between discrete resource bases, which may be indicative of potential use value elsewhere (Spender, 1996a; von Krogh and Roos, 1995). Through recontextualization and adaptation of existing solutions to fit the new problem, innovations may emerge (Nonaka and Takeuchi, 1995; Hagardon, 1998). To this day, for example, light bulbs are screwed into their sockets, because one of Edison's lab assistants systematically developed the analogies between the problems of keeping the newly developed light bulbs in their sockets and the screw-top cap of a kerosene can in front of him (Hagardon, 1998).

Building the intelligent enterprise
While the previous imagination lever focused on leveraging internal resources, the present imagination lever focuses on leveraging external resources emanating from value chains adjacent to the firm's own.

A firm's value chain is embedded in a system of interlinked value chains, sometimes called a 'value system' (Porter, 1985: 34). This value system includes the value chains of suppliers of raw materials and components (for example, Quinn, 1980, 1994), that tend to be interconnected by 'knowledge links' (Bardaracco, 1991), suggesting that the 'intelligent enterprise' focuses on developing 'best in world capabilities' in selected activities in-house (for example, core-competencies), while sourcing other, less critical activities from partners (for example, Hamel, 1991). This may be in one or more of several areas: distribution, brand name, selling infrastructure, technology, research and development (R&D) resources, or manufacturing capability. Where internal development of these activities is judged to require excessive time, energy, money and risk, partnerships in the form of joint ventures, or strategic alliances with other firms, can be a natural alternative (for example, Leibold and Slabbert, 1994). Building the intelligent enterprise through such alliances typically involves a long-term collaboration of two or more organizations to achieve strategic resource-exchange partnerships (Hamel, 1991).

Based on an extensive review of the creative imagination literature, two approaches to building the intelligent enterprise crystallize: (a) borrowing and (b) co-opting resources. The first of these two approaches, borrowing resources from other companies (Hamel, Doz and Prahalad, 1989), involves not only getting access to another company's knowledge pool and skills, but also internalizing these resources (Prahalad and Hamel, 1990; Hamel, 1991), thereby expanding the corporate knowledge portfolio. Successful borrowing would be a function of the scope and depth of the firm's level of prior related knowledge, which has been termed 'absorptive capacity' (Cohen and Levinthal, 1990). It has often been argued that companies may further enhance knowledge-borrowing processes by approaching foreign knowledge bases as 'students, not teachers' (Hamel and Prahalad, 1993).

The literature shows that a key challenge in borrowing resources revolves around a formidable balancing act between borrowing such resources and knowledge assets from partners, while protecting one's own assets (Leibold, Gibbert and Kaes, 2001). The challenge is to share enough skills to create advantage vis-à-vis companies outside the alliance, while preventing a wholesale transfer of core competencies to a partner (Hamel, Doz and Prahalad, 1989: 136). This challenge is exacerbated when borrowing resources involves collaborating with competitors. In such constellations, the danger of becoming 'hollowed out' by 'predatory alliance' partners (see for example, Hamel, Doz and Prahalad, 1989; Lei and Slocum, 1992) seems particularly evident, suggesting that appropriate steps be taken to ensure mutually beneficial borrowing. To illustrate: Phillips and Dupont collaborate to develop and manufacture compact discs, but neither side rivals the other's market, suggesting that there is a clear upstream/downstream division of effort. Each partner believes that it can learn from the other and at the same time limit access to proprietary resources and skills. And yet, many of the skills that migrate between companies are not covered in the formal terms of the collaboration, often, what gets traded is determined by day-to-day inter-actions of engineers, marketers, and product developers (Hamel, Doz and Prahalad, 1989: 136).

There are several areas in which steps can be taken to increase the prob-ability that borrowing resources will turn out to be effective, durable, and satisfying to all parties despite the potential drawbacks illustrated above. Leibold and Slabbert have divided the areas of focus into four categories (Leibold and Slabbert, 1994: 2):

- *Motivationally* the alliance must be well conceived so that there is a genuinely shared objective. Synergistically there must be an effective mesh of assets and skills to mutual benefit.
- *Structurally* there must be proper controls in place to afford fair protec-tion of respective contributions and assets, to monitor progress and to ensure that the performance proceeds on tracks compatible with the original rationale behind the borrowing of the resources.
- *Developmentally* there must be a provision for the alliance to change over time, since environments to which the borrowing arrangement responds may not remain static, suggesting that insufficiently flexible alliances are doomed to fail.
- *Politically* there must be a good rapport on a human level in areas such as policy, vision, and management style.

While borrowing resources is designed to enlarge the in-house resource stock, the second approach to building the intelligent enterprise, co-opting resources, is designed to economize on the in-house resource stock. In the literature, co-opting resources is intended to complement the borrowing resources in that it offsets the latter's focus on integrating and accumulating resources. Indeed, a central question in building the intelligent enterprise would be whether to increase the in-house resource pool, or whether to spin-off selected components in order to source them from the world's best suppliers through collaborative arrangements (for example, Quinn, 1994).

Resource and knowledge discrepancies have often been recognized in strategic management research as a motivator for such collaboration (Lei and Slocum, 1992; Bardaracco, 1991; Leibold and Slabbert, 1994). In these analyses, a distinction has often been made between the process of acquiring skills in the sense of merely gaining access to them (for example, by taking out a license, or utilizing a subassembly supplied by a partner), and internalizing them to make them a permanent component of the corporate knowledge pool (for example, Hamel, Doz and Prahalad, 1989; Hamel, 1991). Hamel referred to the first process as 'quasi internalization' and to the latter as 'de-facto internalization' (Hamel, 1991).

Building the intelligent enterprise by borrowing would be an approach for de facto internalization of resources from outside sources, thereby expanding the corporation's own resource pool. In borrowing knowledge, the goal is to absorb a partner's knowledge and make it one's own. Co-option of resources by sourcing knowledge assets from adequate partners can provide an alternative means for the corporation to consolidate its knowledge pool, and would be akin to quasi-internalization. In co-opting resources the goal is to economize on knowledge through well-managed external partnerships (for example, Hamel, 1991; Hamel and Prahalad, 1993). While both processes, borrowing and co-opting, are valuable approaches to leveraging corporate knowledge portfolios by systematically tapping outside sources, a singular focus on either seems inappropriate. This suggests that companies need co-option as a balancing process to borrowing and vice versa.

A key challenge in consolidating resources is to decide which resources to maintain in-house and which ones to source from collaborative arrangements. Many companies have had the experience that valuable resources have left the company through management practices such as lean management with its unavoidable discharges and outsourcing activities (Nasser and Vivier, 1995). In an attempt to recapture the valuable resources thus dismissed, companies frequently need to buy back expertise from expensive consultants – ironically often the same ones that advocated lean management and outsourcing earlier. To amend this drawback in building the intelligent enterprise, the literature suggests that core competencies be distinguished from non-core competencies using the processes described in the imagination lever ('concentrating on core competencies'), and that only non-core competencies be co-opted.

Step Three: Realizing Imaginative Strategies

Introducing multidimensional performance goals

A review of the literature reveals that the current business environment is characterized by a broad-based tendency towards knowledge-based business (see, for example, Toffler, 1990). This could result in a modification of performance objectives (see, for example, Sveiby, 1997; Edvinsson and Malone, 1997; Hilb, 1998). In particular, the tendency towards being knowledge-driven evidences the need to introduce multidimensional performance objectives, that is, performance objectives that consider intangible as well as tangible assets. One particularly important area deserving explicit attention is the phenomenon of 'intellectual capital' (see, for example, Stewart, 1998).

The acute need for multidimensional performance objectives becomes evident from the countless expressions used for the knowledge-driven tendency in the literature. Authors in academia and business practice alike describe an emerging 'dangerous society, age, or era' (Sveiby, 1997). Expressions utilized range from 'Third Wave Economy' (Toffler, 1980), 'Information Age' (Kaplan and Norton, 1996a, b), to 'Knowledge Economy' (Stewart, 1998). In this knowledge economy, which seems characterized by 'future shock' (Toffler, 1990) and 'smart machines' (Zuboff, 1988), the potential impact of knowledge on a wide variety of industries seems of such a magnitude that some observers refer to it as the 'knowledge revolution' (Stewart, 1998; Bardaracco, 1991).

Possibly as a result of the trends towards knowledge-intensive products and services, 'wealth creation is now [becoming] a mental event' (Edvinnson and Malone, 1997). Indeed, the momentum behind the proliferation of interest in intellectual capital may be attributable to the fact that it represents an increasingly large component of a company's overall market value. In many instances, intellectual capital even supersedes corporate book values. This difference between corporate market and book values is commonly referred to as the 'value gap' (see for example, von Krogh and Roos, 1996; Sveiby, 1997). It does not seem surprising that a consensus has arisen among many observers in academia regarding the significance of tending to intellectual capital. It is widely agreed that the value gap between market and book value is becoming too wide to be ignored by managers (Roos, Roos, Edvinsson and Dragonetti, 1998; Stewart, 1998; Sullivan, 1998). This suggests an intense need to introduce performance goals that take cognizance of intangible, as well as tangible assets.

Interestingly, while the importance of intellectual capital seems widely acknowledged, no consolidation in scholarly thinking has as yet evolved concerning the anatomy of this phenomenon. Different definitions of intellectual capital (Edvinnson and Malone, 1997; Stewart, 1998; Roos and Roos,

1997) as well as approaches to the categorization thereof (Saint-Onge, 1996; Edvinnson, 1997; Sveiby, 1997; Sullivan, 1998) are offered in the literature.

Fortunately there are identifiable similarities between these approaches. Leibold, Kaes and Gibbert (1999), in an extensive review of the literature, have proposed a tentative framework for synthesizing the various perspectives on intellectual capital. Drawing on an analysis of the building blocks of intellectual capital as forwarded by the most pertinent authors in the field, the tangible and intangible dimensions of intellectual capital were categorized into several building blocks. Their analysis has shown that while the authors reviewed are not terminologically congruent, conceptual commonalties seem to make the approaches amenable to synthesis. Research has suggested that intellectual capital is best divided into three main building blocks (Leibold, Kaes and Gibbert, 1999: 25):

- human capital (the skills, capabilities and competencies of the corporate workforce),
- internal capital (internal governance mechanisms and organizational culture, 'what is left when the employees go home'), and
- external capital (customer relationships and networks with relevant business partners and organizations in the non-profit and public sectors).

Drafting unique selling propositions

Research has found that the drive for innovation leads to a remarkable difference between what companies are competing on, and what buyers actually value. For example, Hamel found that often the drive for innovation pushes companies to 'over-engineer' products and services (for example, Hamel, 2000). The VCR industry offers a telling illustration. Companies in this industry competed on the basis of increasingly sophisticated (but similar) technical features that eventually lead to technically complex, but difficult to operate, VCRs. However, what customers apparently valued most was a machine that was easy-to-use (Kim and Mauborgne, 2000).

This chasm between the basis of competition in an industry and what customers really value seems particularly evident in innovation-driven industries such as mobile telephony and personal computers (for example, Kim and Mauborgne, 2000), but also in more established industries such as banking and the hospitality industry (for example, Hamel, 2000). The problem seems to be that many companies tend to focus on upgrading the basis of the competition in an industry so as to outperform competitors (for example, adding increasingly sophisticated technical features to VCRs), rather than concentrating on the buyer's perspective (for example, the desire for ease of use). This difference in perspective is noteworthy, because it suggests that creating value for the customer is less a function of a technical product feature than of its utility to customers (for example, Hamel, 2000; Kim and Mauborgne, 2000; Nonaka, Reinmoeller and Seinoo, 1998).

Seen from the perspective of the customer, it often appears that the basis of competition in an industry is highly dysfunctional, and should be re-thought. The question therefore is: how can a unique selling proposition be drafted? A review of the literature suggests a considerable variety of perspectives. Some scholars focus on differentiation versus cost advantage (for example, Porter, 1980). From this viewpoint it is advocated that customer value can be created by positioning products along a trade-off between differentiation and low cost (and hence, low price). These two options have been created in the light of the prevailing industry growth rate and the company's share of that industry.

However, knowing how to position a company in a known market often confers little insight into what it is that customers actually value. As the VCR example demonstrates, it is often not expedient to pose the question 'what shall we do to improve performance in the light of the industry?', but 'what should we do to offer customers a leap in value?' Recognizing this difference in perspective, other scholars have advocated a focus on 'creating buyer utility' (for example, Kim and Mauborgne, 2000). From this viewpoint, creating value for the customer is seen as focusing on a customer's experience with a given product. Creative imagination draws on this, second, stream of thought and attempts to aid in rethinking the basis of the competition in a given industry by focusing on the customer's perspective.

Research has demonstrated that a customer's experience can usually be broken down into two bases of appeal, the functional and the emotional, suggesting that competition in many industries converges on one of these two bases of the buyer experience (for example, Kim and Mauborgne, 2000; Hamel, 2000). Some industries compete principally on functional performance (for example, the VCR example). Other industries compete primarily on emotional appeal (for example, the motorcycle industry). The problem is that industries driven by a functional appeal tend to be commoditized in their product and serviced offerings, which lead to eroded profit margins due to higher competition (Kim and Mauborgne, 2000).

Literature also shows that the products and services within a given industry are intrinsically and unalterably functional or emotional. Companies can inadvertently drive their industries in one of these directions, thereby unconsciously educating their customers about what to expect. Indeed, a 2000 article argued that a reinforcing cycle occurs between companies' behaviors and customers' demands (ibid., 2000: 133). It was furthermore discovered that bases of appeal differ within industries as much as they differ across industries (Hamel, 2000: 66–9). To illustrate: in the motorcycle industry, BMW is usually associated with a functional appeal, whereas Harley Davidson is typically perceived in a more emotional fashion (ibid.). To quote Hamel, '...it's one thing for people to buy your products. It's quite another for them to tattoo your name on their bodies. BMW makes awesome motorcycles, but when have you last seen a biceps that read "Bayerische Motorenwerke"?' (ibid.: 68).

As Hamel's quote implies, in drafting unique selling propositions, it is often expedient to shift the basis of appeal from functional/rational to emotional. This is generally accompanied by focusing on offering a complex solution, rather than simply selling the product, and thereby increasing value for the customer. A case in point is Starbucks coffee. In the late 1980s, Procter & Gamble, General Foods, and Nestlé held 90 per cent of the US coffee market. When Starbucks entered the industry, all three companies viewed coffee as a commodity: generic beans bought from roughly equivalent producers, roasted using similar techniques and packed using standard containers. As in most commodity-driven industries, the basis of competition was on cost cutting and fighting for market share to spread costs. While the big three sold coffee as a commodity, Starbucks added emotional appeal. This was done through focusing on a complex solution: a retailing concept including the coffee bar, offering relaxation and conversation, and drinks made with frothy and flavored milks, creams, syrups and ices. In what was once an industry characterized by fierce price competition, Starbucks was able to charge premium prices and became an important chain in the US within less than ten years (*Wall Street Journal*, 27 July 2001).

Creating new market space
Creating new market space is a term introduced by Kim and Mauborgne (1999b). A review of the literature reveals that creating new 'market' space is related to the concept of creating new 'competitive' space introduced earlier by Hamel and Prahalad (1994b). Careful analysis further reveals that these authors' definition of new competitive space, while terminologically different, seems very similar conceptually to Kim and Mauborgne's creating new market space. The term new 'market' space is used in this study, because it terminologically emphasizes that creating new market space focuses on avoiding head-to-head competition. Thus, creating new market space, as it is viewed in this study, refers to the generation of value for the company not by matching or beating rivals in existing markets, as in the competitive strategy orientation characteristic of the descriptive imagination literature, but by looking for entirely new business opportunities (a contention in line with Kim and Mauborgne, 1999b: 83). In creating new market space, the goal is not to extend current expertise or to better satisfying the customer than the competition would. Hence the attribute 'competitive' was deemed to inappropriately reflect the rationale of the concept, and 'creating new market space' was adopted.

While terminology sometimes differs, many authors provide convincing empirical evidence for the conclusion that creating new market space is likely to be a key value generator for companies. To illustrate the significance of creating new market space: based on an extensive analysis of Fortune 500 companies between 1975 and 1995, Kim and Mauborgne discovered that 60 per cent of these companies were replaced. Irrespective of their industry, what was common to the new entrants was that they either created new markets or recreated existing ones. In contrast, the companies that were replaced were all competing for a bigger share of the existing market (Kim and Mauborgne, 2000). A case in point is Callaway Golf, a US golf club manufacturer. This company launched the so-called 'Big Bertha' golf club series, which proved to be extremely successful in the very competitive golf club market. However, competition in the market was centered around making sophisticated enhancements that were designed to hit the ball further, and with greater accuracy. Callaway realised that the act of hitting the ball with a little golf club head was too daunting a task for many amateur sportsmen. Recognizing a potentially lucrative new market space, Callaway went on to introduce a club with a larger head that made the game less difficult (Kim and Mauborgne, 1999b: 43).

If creating new market space is a key value driver, the next question is: how can creation of new market space be achieved? As the Callaway example illustrates, creating new market space requires a pattern of strategic imagination that is different from describing competitive dynamics within the accepted boundaries that define how players in a given industry compete. According to research results, understanding how to position a company in a known market against existing competitors provides little insight into how to create new market space, (for example, Kim and Mauborgne, 1999b; Hamel, 2000). Literature shows that the key question therefore becomes how to aid the strategist in creatively looking at established dynamics in a new way. A review of the literature suggests a variety of approaches that can be taken to stimulate such creative imagination. The following two pointers were gained through an extensive review of other work, and provide, in a condensed format, an overview of the approaches that were most widely cited in the literature.

First and foremost, the inevitableness of industry conditions can be rethought. Most companies seem to take industry conditions as a given. Such thinking, however, can severely restrict the range of strategic actions. It must be appreciated that companies not only compete with their rivals in their own industry, but also with those from substitute industries that produce similar products or services. Indeed, in making purchase decisions, customers tend to weigh up substitutes, often unconsciously. Consequently firms wanting to create new competitive space may look across substitute industries. As a result, a far wider range of strategic options can be explored. This can increase the creative scope of companies wishing to create new competitive space. It can further lead to the consideration of ideas that rivals in the same industry cannot consider (for example, Kim and Mauborgne, 1999a, b; Hamel, 1996).

The key question that companies aspiring to create new market space seem to ask themselves is therefore not what it takes to gain and sustain a competitive advantage in a given industry, but what the key discriminating factors are that lead buyers to trade across substitute industries. Based on these insights, the distinctive strengths of both industries can be combined and exploited (for example, Hamel, 2000; Hamel and Prahalad, 1994a). Southwest Airlines, for example, effectively created new market space, the short-haul air transport, by recognising that for short-haul flights transportation by car was a substitute for flying. Southwest Airlines combined the key discriminating factors leading to the purchase decision, namely the speed of flying and lower cost coupled with flexibility (Kim and Mauborgne, 1999b: 84).

Second, looking across complementary products and services, in addition to looking across substitute products and services is an important pointer (for example, Kim and Mauborgne, 1999b; Hamel and Prahalad, 1994a, b). It does not seem surprising that most companies focus on maximizing the value of products and services in their own industry. However, new market space can be created by looking across complementary products and services from other industries, and exploring the interface between the two industries. The key in exploring this interface seems to be to focus on the total solution that buyers seek when they choose a product. The question here becomes how to shed more light on the individual components comprising the total solution. Kim and Mauborgne suggested that an effective, if simple, way to focus on the total solution that customers seek is to imagine what happens right before, during and after a product or service is used. German air carrier Lufthansa, for example, made ground transport an integral part of the package offered. In this manner new competitive space can be created by widening the scope of the products and services offered (Kim and Mauborge, 1999b: 89).

A THREE-STEP APPROACH FOR CHALLENGING IMAGINATION

While the previous two sections focused on descriptive and creative imagination, this section takes a look at challenging imagination.

Step One: Envisaging Imaginative Strategies

Ensuring coherence
According to an article by Lissack and Roos, coherence is psychologically the concept of 'holding together' and of self-recognition of the boundary of self,

and acts to tie the levels of organizations together, much like the role of the unified electro-magnetic weak–strong nuclear force in physics (Lissack and Roos, 2001: 16).

Ensuring coherence is often contrasted with establishing a vision. According to the strategy process and strategy content literature, many executives feel the need to articulate an ideal end-state for their organizations – often in the guise of a corporate vision (for example, Porter, 1980; Mintzberg and Lampel, 1999). Authors explain that striking the balance between novelty and believability of such an ideal end-state is often exceedingly difficult, and empirical evidence shows that managers are satisfied with neither the vision, nor the visioning process (Lissack and Roos, 2001: 1; see also Oliver and Roos, 2000; Hamel, 2000; Eisenhardt and Sull, 2001). This argument serves the authors to conclude that the very idea of having a corporate vision is of limited use in today's complex business landscapes. Lissack and Roos (2001: 1) emphasize that once the world is seen as unstable and unpredictable, what matters is being coherent rather than being visionary.

Research into ensuring coherence in current complex business environments, inspired by complexity theory, is emerging as an intensely topical concern among scholars and practitioners of strategy (see, for example, Lissack and Roos, 1999; Cilliers, 1998; Kaufmann, 1995; Beinhocker, 1997). These authors point out why executives need to replace visioning efforts with a focus on how to become and remain coherent throughout the organization as well as offering a few guiding principles on how to do this in practice. While the literature review found that terminological and conceptual consensus has yet to be established, it is still possible to define ensuring coherence as acting in a manner that reinforces what an organization stands for, given the current environment (Lissack and Roos, 2001: 1–4).

Why, then, is the traditional concept of vision seen as unduly limiting in the challenging imagination literature? Research shows that the problem with visioning processes is that they are based on what we know about yesterday, while the strategy maker is not only trying to envision tomorrow, but some medium-term future as well. Authors agree that by naming it 'vision' (an outcome), there can be a danger of reifying the past and in doing so preclude changes in it (for example, Lissack and Roos, 2001; Beinhocker, 1997; Eisenhardt and Sull, 2001). Lissack and Roos explain,

> Having locked in an outcome (i.e. the predictable future), it is all too tempting to work backwards from it not focusing on the potential interactions that could happen along the way. The very process of working backwards, of needing to have a defined game plan for achieving set goals, will restrict your 'possibility space', and may interfere with your ability to adapt to changes going on around you and seize new opportunities when they arise … (Lissack and Roos, 2001: 4)

The next question regards the arenas of ensuring coherence, that is, it asks where coherence can be ensured. A review of the literature suggests that tending simultaneously to two arenas of corporate involvement, namely the external and the internal, can ensure coherence (for example, Hamel and Prahalad, 1993; Eisenhardt and Brown, 1998).

First, the corporation should ensure that coherence prevails internally among disparate knowledge bases. A certain synthesis or synergy of the knowledge bases has to be ensured despite the ambition to leverage knowledge from various sources inside and outside the company in a given industry. If coherence is lost and cannot be re-established by enhancing the co-ordination of internal practice, the company may need to divest certain knowledge bases until it achieves coherence again (Brown and Duguid, 1998). Indeed, the competitiveness of companies appears in part to be a function of their success at achieving collective coherence among their various internal communities of practice (Teece, Rumelt, Dosi and Winter, 1994).

Second, a company needs to ensure coherence in the external arena. Relevant in the external arena seems to be the extent to which a firm manages its long-held orthodoxies, that is, the extent to which it ensures coherence of internal practice with competitive environments (for example, Leonard-Barton, 1995). This appears to be of critical importance in view of the tendency of such orthodoxies to depreciate over time relative to the competitive environment. It is therefore critical to guard the corporation against incremental reapplication of dated concepts. Lissack and Roos (2001: 9) have identified three key assumptions leading to dated concepts:

(a) The world is stable enough for changes that may occur to be foreseeable.
(b) Prediction is possible.
(c) Boundaries are clearly defined.

Lissack and Roos explain that the focus in ensuring coherence in the external arena, instead of relying on the above, dated, assumptions,

> is on who am I, what do I see as adjacent 'possibles' in the current environment (for we can only move to the next step one at a time), are those possibilities consistent with my sense of identity and boundary (are they coherence preserving)? And for 'I' in the previous sentences one can substitute the team, the group, the unit, and the company. Action across all those scales is what the company is all about. And guiding coherent action is the key task of management ... (Lissack and Roos, 1999: 23)

The above quote leads to the next question: how can coherence be ensured? According to Hamel and Prahalad (1993), ensuring coherence in the internal and external arena can be achieved through, first, converging and, second, focusing organizational competence and knowledge assets. Ensuring coherence requires what Hamel and Prahalad refer to as industry foresight, that is, a strategic focal point on which the efforts of individual employees, organizational functions and businesses can converge over time (see also Hamel and Prahalad, 1994a, b). Convergence requires an intent that is sufficiently precise over time to guide corporate decision making, while at the same time leaving enough space for ideas to evolve freely. With convergence preventing the diversion of knowledge over time, focus is designed to prevent the dilution of knowledge at any given time (Hamel and Prahalad, 1993: 80). As Hamel and Prahalad (1994b) have emphasized, industry foresight requires an understanding of the trends and discontinuities that can be used to transform industry boundaries and create new business opportunities quicker than competitors. Industry foresight can give a company the potential to stake out a sustainable leadership position and control the evolution of its industry. This foresight seems to require a continual breaking of established managerial frames, and deep-seated assumptions about the core business of a company need to be challenged continuously (Hamel and Prahalad 1994a, b; Nasser and Viver, 1995).

Other researchers have emphasized that while it may be easy to grasp the above suggestions intellectually, acting on their implications in a knowledge leverage context could be much more difficult, since ensuring coherence may require acting against the very knowledge integral to corporate identity. In the current business environment, it no longer suffices to concentrate on corporate core competencies, because it may be these very core competencies, often central to a company's identity, that the knowledge era turns obsolete (for example, Leonard-Barton, 1992, 1995).

As Evans and Wurster have emphasized, 'new economics of information' are likely to transform the structures of businesses or industries, thereby shifting traditional sources of competitive advantage. Information businesses, where the cost of physical distribution is high, are likely to be affected soonest and most severely. Evans and Wurster believe that incumbents could easily become victims of their physical infrastructure and their long-held managerial frames (Evans and Wurster, 1997). According to Evans and Wurster, the case of the Encyclopedia Britannica provides a useful illustration. The publisher experienced a near demise, because it failed to understand that its customers were 'buying Britannica less for its intellectual content, but out of a desire to "do the right thing" for their children. Today when parents want to do the right thing, they buy their children a computer' (ibid.: 71). As a result of this misplaced perception, the publisher seemed to have interpreted CD-ROMs, which deliver the same intellectual content much more cheaply, as nothing more than an electronic version of inferior products. The way the Britannica editors appear to have seen it, the CD-ROM version was not an encyclopaedia at all – it was a toy. Britannica's customers, however, perceived the CD-ROM version of the printed product as much more than a toy (ibid.: 71–4).

Overall, recent research evidence suggests that companies should, by ensuring coherence, continuously seek to understand what its customers are actually buying and define their core business accordingly. The current business environment drastically transforms the process by which core competencies were once defined (the realm of creative imagination), or the processes by which industry positions were defended (the realm of descriptive imagination) and imposes new variables to be considered. Ensuring coherence is therefore intended to help the corporation rigorously align its definition of core competencies with the new competitive dynamics of the knowledge age. As shall be discussed in the two sections that follow, this effort requires the defying of old paradigms, and fostering a culture of constructive dissent.

Defying old paradigms

Defying old paradigms represents a central tenet in challenging imagination that seeks to disconfirm, defame and dispute the established wisdom. Defying old paradigms can be defined straightforwardly as 'questioning answers, rather than answering questions' (see Hamel, 2000: 145). It is about re-thinking 'the way we do things around here'. Hamel emphasizes that heretics, not prophets, are required for defying old paradigms in order to sustain company growth in the long term. According to Hamel, the real issue in crafting strategy is not about the present versus the future, but the orthodox versus the heterodox, the reason being that there tends to be an enormous danger in viewing 'what is changing through the looking-glass of what already is...' (ibid.: 60).

The literature amply emphasizes the importance of defying old paradigms, and abounds with examples of companies that, when faced with crucial signs of changes in the environment of the firm, tended to interpret these changes consistent with the existing organizational paradigm (see Johnson, 1994, for a comprehensive review). Similarly, the dangers of path-dependent behavior that turns core competencies into core rigidities (Leonard-Barton, 1992, 1995) are well documented and validate the importance of defying old paradigms. While there are many areas where paradigms can be defied, the literature shows that defiance of industry paradigms seems to be the most salient (for example, Nasser and Vivier, 1995). Research furthermore points out that the greatest impediment to revenue growth is getting locked into the industry paradigm. Defiance of old industry paradigms is quite different from defining industry boundaries (as in descriptive imagination), and it seems also to be quite different from re-defining industry boundaries (as in creative imagination). To illustrate with a provocative quote by Hamel:

> It's not easy to grow the top line with a strategy that's 'more of the same'. For some years, McDonald's growth in the US has been sputtering. The company introduced

a new cooking system that ... promised hamburgers even quicker from the grill. Will this solve McDonald's growth problem? It might, but maybe McDonald's should ask itself if Americans are already eating as many hamburgers as they're ever going to. Maybe Americans have reached their cholesterol limit ... (Hamel, 2000: 12)

In surveys across as many as 20 different industries, Kim and Mauborgne (1999a, b), corroborating Hamel's findings, have found that surprisingly few companies were able to grow revenues above industry average. In the case of McDonald's, as well as in the case of many other industries, Kim and Mauborgne found a strong association between unsatisfactory revenue growth rates and the inability to break out of the industry paradigm. As Hamel puts it, for some companies, 'industry is destiny' (Hamel, 2000: 12).

The most important area of application of defying paradigms therefore seems to be the dogma prevalent in the industry or industries in which a company competes. The idea here is to break out of industry dogmas, and to think across industry boundaries (rather than defining or re-defining them) in order to imagine opportunities for achieving revenue growth at the confluence of two or more industries (Hamel and Prahalad, 1996: 240). Various authors have advocated the importance of looking across industry boundaries for the purposes of identifying growth opportunities. Lissack and Roos (2001) have shown the perils of being preoccupied with mission statements that are grounded in the prevailing industry definition. Eisenhardt and Brown (1998) have pointed out the benefits of 'competing at the edge of chaos' between two or more industries, and Eisenhardt and Sull advocate opportunity-driven strategizing at the interface between two or more industries using a 'cockroach approach' (Eisenhardt and Sull, 2001: 108).

The question arising from these contributions is: how to defy paradigms? For the purposes of the present study, the above stream of thought, while still evolving, can be crystallized by a number of pointers that may help managers understand how paradigms can be defied. Synthesis of the above contributions suggests two areas of intervention for managers: first by challenging industry orthodoxies, and second by taking the perspective of the customer, and/or the competitor.

First, companies need to look for disconfirming evidence by asking the ten things a customer would never say about an industry. For example, Hamel found that few customers would say 'the airline treats customers with dignity and respect' (Hamel, 2000: 64). According to Hamel, defying old paradigms from the customer perspective can reveal deep 'customer-dissing orthodoxies', that is, ways in which the company inadvertently irritates or annoys customers (ibid.: 138). Key in defying old paradigms from the customer's perspective is to play a game of perpetually asking 'why', and 'what if', and even 'to celebrate the stupid', (meaning those who lack industry knowledge (ibid.: 138). Indeed, lack of industry knowledge can be helpful in re-conceiving orthodoxies in an industry. The goal is to look for aspects that do not fit the established wisdom. As the airline example above suggests, defying old paradigms by asking the ten things a customer would never say about an industry is imbued with irony, if not sarcasm. These two forms of humor can form a critical role in the defiance of old paradigms (Eppler and Kuepers, 2001), mainly because humor tends to lower resistance to changing from the old paradigm to a new one.

Second, strategy makers can ask, 'what are the ten things that all major competitors in the industry have in common?' (Hamel, 2000: 64). Research shows that the healthcare industry, for example, thinks of the sick as patients, not consumers. And yet, particularly in the healthcare industry, there seems to be enormous potential for rethinking the beneficiary of healthcare services. Such benefits include learning and relationship building in order to promote wellness, rather than cure illness (for example, Prahalad and Ramaswamy, 2000: 87). As with the first area of intervention, which attempts to defy old paradigms by looking at them from the customer perspective, looking at old paradigms from the competitor perspective is also prone to irony and cynicism, albeit to a lesser degree. The idea here is to deconstruct the individual components of a belief system in an industry and to invert them (Hamel, 2000; Eisenhardt and Sull, 2001).

Overall, the practice of inverting the belief system in an industry can be particularly effective if strategies in an industry tend to converge. To illustrate: a survey by Kim and Mauborgne (1999a) found that the strategies of Fortune 500 companies in many industries tended to converge, leading to perfect competition. The result of perfect competition is well documented in neoclassical economics: to the extent that companies follow identical strategies and are endowed with similar resources, profit equals cost. The implication is that 'best practice transfer', trying to benchmark best in class competitors and attempting to do better are inclined to turn companies into industry laggards. In contrast, defying old paradigms by looking at the belief system in an industry from competitors' perspective can help the strategy maker maintain the competitive differentiation necessary for sustained revenue growth (Hamel, 2000; Kim and Mauborgne, 1999a, b; Nasser and Vivier, 1995).

Fostering a culture of constructive dissent

Fostering a culture of constructive dissent is about purposefully challenging one another's thinking in the strategy-making process. It can be defined as the endeavor to develop a more complete understanding of the choices at hand, to create a richer range of options, and ultimately make the kinds of effective decisions necessary in today's competitive environments. As Eisenhardt et al. have succinctly put it: 'the absence of conflict is not harmony, it's apathy...' (Eisenhardt, Kahawajy and Bourgeois, 1997: 77).

Several authors stressed the importance of fostering a culture of constructive dissent. Kim and Mauborgne (1997b) have advocated practicing 'fair process' in strategy-making, Eisenhardt (1999) has alerted her readers to unleashing collective intuition, accelerating constructive conflict, and maintaining decision pacing. Hamel empirically confirmed the importance of fostering a culture of constructive dissent in detailed analyses across 20 industries (Hamel, 2000). Hamel also emphasized the need to 'develop corporate activists' that rebel against 'corporate apparatchiks' (ibid.: 145). Along the same lines, Leavitt and Limpan-Blumen (1995) have investigated 'hot groups' as the locus where such constructive dissent is practiced, and have also linked these groups to the performance implications of constructive dissent. The authors' findings demonstrate that constructive dissent is associated with desirable performance implications. In a well-known article, Mintzberg (1994) investigates the 'fall and rise of strategic planning', concluding that strategy makers should act as catalysts who support strategy making by aiding and encouraging managers to think strategically (1994: 108).

Unhappily, fostering a culture of constructive dissent is fraught with pitfalls. Empirical analyses find that top managers are often obstructed by the difficulties of managing conflict, associated with fostering a culture of constructive dissent. Research shows that managers do seem to know that conflict about issues is natural and even necessary, suggesting that reasonable people are likely to have disagreements about the best path for their company's future (Eisenhardt et al., 1997: 77). However, a healthy conflict can quickly become unproductive. The literature has found that the key reason for this inadequacy is that personalities frequently become intertwined with issues. To illustrate: insights from psychology suggest that a comment meant as constructive criticism can be easily interpreted as a personal attack (for example, ibid., 1997: 78; Eisenhardt, 1999: 65). According to recent empirical research, strategy makers seem particularly prone to this inadequacy, since executives often pride themselves on being rational decision makers, finding it difficult to acknowledge, let alone manage, this irrational and emotional dimension of their behavior (for example, Eisenhardt et al., 1997: 78).

The challenge of fostering a culture of constructive dissent – encouraging strategy makers to argue without destroying their ability to work as a team – is compounded by the preconditions to ignite dissent. The reviewed strategy literature gives sparse recommendations regarding such preconditions, which include diversity, frame breaking tactics and creating multiple alternatives (for example, ibid.: 69-70):

- The first, and foremost, precondition for igniting dissent is diversity. Such diversity can focus on age, experience, cultural background and professional background (Hilb, 2000).

- The second precondition that was found in the literature was frame-breaking tactics that create alternatives to obvious points of view. The traditional way to generate new alternatives to obvious points of view is the scenario-planning technique, which serves to systematically consider strategic decisions in the light of several possible future states (Eisenhardt et al., 1997: 69).
- Third, giving multiple alternatives can be a precondition for dissent. According to Eisenhardt et al. (1997: 69), multiple alternatives are frequently the most prevalent precondition for dissent. Key in giving multiple alternatives is to design alternatives as quickly as possible so that the team can simultaneously work with an array of possibilities. Indeed, Eisenhardt et al. have found that strategy makers considered it entirely appropriate to advocate options that they may not prefer, simply to encourage debate (ibid.: 70).

While these preconditions are important stimuli for constructive dissent, they are frequently also prone to dysfunctional dispute and heated discussions. The key question therefore becomes how fostering a culture of constructive dissent can be kept from deteriorating into *dysfunctional personal conflict*, how to encourage strategy makers to argue without destroying their ability to work as a team. While the psychology and social psychology literatures seem replete with approaches to manage conflict, the literature on strategy interestingly remains relatively silent as to measures that can be taken to foster a culture of constructive dissent. An exception is Eisenhardt's work in this realm (ibid., 1997; Eisenhardt, 1999; Eisenhardt and Brown, 1998), which was also widely referenced in the literature. For the purpose of this study, her suggestions for fostering a culture of constructive dissent can be summarized in two main points.

First, strategy makers should focus on issues, not personalities. Empirical evidence shows that management teams troubled by interpersonal conflict rely more on 'hunches and guesses' than on current data. Eisenhardt explains that when management teams consider facts, they are more likely to examine a past measure, such as profitability, which is both historical and highly refined. These teams favor a culture of debate that is based on extrapolation and intuitive attempts to predict the future, neither of which was found to yield current or factual results. In Eisenhardt's research, the most successful companies evidenced a direct link between reliance on current, as opposed to historical, facts, and low levels of interpersonal conflict. The authors cite from their interview data of high conflict teams, where interest in current numbers was 'minimal', and goals were described as 'subjective', or driven by 'self-aggrandizement'. By contrast, low conflict teams featured members that interviewees described as 'the pragmatic numbers guy' (Eisenhardt et al. 1997: 79).

Second, decisions need to be framed as collaborations aimed at the best possible solution for the company. According to Eisenhardt, the key here is to rally around goals, while avoiding politics. However, research has found that many managers believe that politics is a natural part of strategic choice (for example, Leonard-Barton, 1995; Eisenhardt, 1999). Managers frequently see crafting strategy as involving high stakes that compel them to lobby one another, manipulate information and form coalitions. More effective strategy makers, however, seem to focus on diffusing politics by creating common goals. These goals were found not to imply homogenous thinking, but rather to suggest that managers have a shared vision of where they want to be. The most successful way found to defuse politics and institute a shared vision was through a balanced power structure in which each key decision maker has a clear area of responsibility, but in which the leader is the most powerful decision maker. Paradoxically, the clear delineation of responsibility was found to make it easier for managers to help one another, since each manager operates from a secure power base. According to one of Eisenhardt's interviewees, 'we just don't worry much about an internal pecking order' (Eisenhardt, 1999: 71).

Step Two: Conceiving Imaginative Strategies

Deconstructing value chains

According to the Boston Consulting Group (BCG) consultants Evans and Wurster (1997, 2000), the extant 'information revolution' materializes in a deconstruction of value chains: a separation of business, and even entire industry, value chains into individual components, each of which could become a business in its own right. The reason for the deconstruction of value chains is mainly seen in the de-coupling of the flow of information goods from physical goods in virtually any industry (Evans and Wurster, 2000: 13). To illustrate, physical goods and information goods are based on fundamentally different economic logics. Evans and Wurster explain these different economic logics as follows:

> When a thing is sold, the seller ceases to own it; when an idea, a tune, or a blueprint is sold, the seller still possesses it and could possibly sell it again. Information can be replicated at almost zero cost without limit; things can be replicated only through the expense of manufacture ... (Evans and Wurster, 2000: 15)

According to the authors, the different underlying economics of physical and information goods call for different management approaches. The economics of physical goods are subject to the law of decreasing returns. The law of decreasing returns suggests that, once sold, a physical product incurs the expense of manufacture, that is, it incurs marginal cost. By contrast, information goods are subject to the law of increasing returns, particularly in information- and R&D-intensive industries such as software and pharmaceuticals (for example, Hebeler and van Doren, 1997; Arthur, 1996). The problem is that in most value chains physical goods and information goods are still inextricably linked, 'each is prevented from following its "pure" logic by the bond tying it to the other' (Evans and Wurster, 2000: 16). This linkage compromises the potential of each good to follow its pure logic, and hence compromises business performance:

> The economics of information and the economics of things have been tied together like participants in a three-legged race. Every business is consequently a *compromise between the economics of information and the economics of things*. Separating breaks their mutual compromise and releases enormous economic value ... (Evans and Wurster, 2000: 17; emphasis added)

The authors explain that the link between information and its physical carrier can be broken. This unbundling of information from its physical carrier entails a number of fundamental implications for crafting strategy imaginatively. In particular, the new economics of information would deconstruct existing value chains. This deconstruction results from the 'separation of the economics of information from the economics of things' (Evans and Wurster, 1997: 77). The authors argue that given the fundamental differences in the economics underlying physical goods and information goods, there is no longer a need for the individual components of a business structure to be integrated. As a result, value chains should be deconstructed and their individual constituents should be recombined into new businesses, in order to take optimum advantage of the separate economics of physical and information goods (Evans and Wurster, 2000: 19).

The next question is, how can the deconstruction of value chains be accomplished? According to prominent scholars, the key here is to ascertain where the interface between physical goods and information goods resides, and to break this connection: to deconstruct a given industry or business value chain. The authors demonstrate that at least two approaches to deconstruct value chains at the interface between information goods and physical goods are useful: competing on reach and/or richness (Evans and Wurster, 1997, 1999).

Competing on reach centers around access and connection. It refers to the number of customers with whom a business can connect and the number of products it can offer to those customers. Reach represents the most critical difference between physical and Internet businesses. In fact, reach is a key value proposition for companies such as Amazon, which epitomize the far greater reach afforded to Internet businesses, once the information good (for example, the book catalog) is separated from the physical good (for example, the inventory). Another illustrative example that is frequently cited in the literature is EveryCD, a company specializing in selling music compact discs, which was so confident of its ability to compete on reach that it offered prizes to customers who could prove that their catalog was incomplete (Evans and Wurster, 1999: 88–9).

Competing on richness centers around the depth and detail a company can offer its customers as well as the depth and detail it can collect about its customers. When competing on richness, the objective is twofold: to collect rich customer information and to collect rich product information. The first objective, collecting rich customer information, enables companies in the retail and hotel industries, for example, to offer customized products and services (for example, Hebeler and van Doeren, 1997). Approaches frequently used to this end include data mining and data warehousing (for example, Evans and Wurster, 1999: 91). The second objective is competing on rich product information. According to Evans and Wurster, it is generally difficult for manufacturers to use rich customer information, since retailers tend to be closer to customers, and hence better positioned to compete on rich customer information. However, manufacturers can develop distinct advantages in the realm of product information. In the music industry, for example, most of the major companies such as Sony, Universal and Warner, are developing information-rich performer biographies, recording history, chat rooms and discographies (ibid.: 92).

Co-opting customer competence

As the boundaries of the firm's value chain become deconstructed and more imprecise, so do the boundaries of managerial control (Hamel and Prahalad, 1996: 239). This poses the question of how managers can 'control' resources when those resources are outside their firm or their business units. One such resource, and an extremely important one, is the customer.

Prahalad and Ramaswamy illustrate the importance of the customer as an organizational resource by drawing an analogy. According to them, doing business used to be a lot like traditional theater. On stage, the actors had clearly defined roles, and the customers paid for their tickets, sat back and watched the show passively (Prahalad and Ramaswamy, 2000: 79). However, the roles between customers and the company are often difficult to define formally. Major discontinuities, such as deregulation, globalization and the rapid diffusion of the Internet, are blurring the roles that companies and their consumers play (for example, Sampler, 2001: 138).

Researchers are in consensus that mainly due to the Internet, consumers are now 'empowered' to engage in an active dialogue with the company (ibid.). As one observer insightfully commented: 'armed with perfect information at zero search costs, consumers are going to weed out mediocrity, hype, and inefficiency with a vengeance' (ibid.: 139). Co-opting customer competence suggests mobilizing customer communities to stimulate knowledge creation and innovation. It further suggests widening the concept of constructing value propositions to include customers as integral players in such value construction processes. Individual consumers can either address and learn about companies on their own, or through other customers' collective knowledge (Prahalad and Ramaswamy, 2000).

The critical observation is that such empowered customers can now initiate dialogue with the company – they have moved, as Prahalad puts it, from the audience on to the stage. Customer competence can be *defined* as corporate customers' knowledge relevant to the firm's operations. For example, Amazon's publishing of customers' book reviews online is one way of collecting and disseminating customer competence. By using online book reviews, for example, Amazon is able to profile its customers and provide them with personalized reading recommendations. It should also be appreciated that customer integration is different from customer relationship management. Whereas the latter focuses on gaining knowledge about the customer, customer integration suggests gaining the knowledge of the customer (ibid.).

Recent research argues that the distinguishing feature of this new scenario is that consumers become a source of knowledge for the corporation. Thinking about the customer as a source of knowledge requires a shift in mindset: it means treating the consumer as a source of value for the company, not simply as a recipient of products and services. Knowledge has long been recognized as the primary value-generator for cutting-edge companies. But this knowledge was largely sought within corporate boundaries (for example, Davenport and Prusak, 1998). The shifting mindset enables companies to look outside corporate boundaries for valuable knowledge. As a matter of fact, the very locus of knowledge seems to shift from within to outside corporate boundaries, as recent strategy literature evidences (Prahalad and Ramaswamy, 2000).

The important questions become: to what ends can customer competence be co-opted? and how can customer competence be co-opted? Regarding the first question: it would appear that the most important and also the most challenging purpose of customer integration, is the development of new products and services, that is, constructing new value propositions. This requires the emancipation of customers from passive audience to co-creators of organizational value. Based on a review of the still evolving literature in this realm, two basic ways in which such empowerment can be achieved are first through physically working with the customer, and second through virtual interaction (for example, Gibbert, Leibold and Voelpel, 2001).

Approaches of physical interaction exist where customers are actively involved in product testing. Companies are now moving beyond the testing of products in usability laboratories and are starting to test them in customer environments. For example, more than 650 000 customers tested a beta version of Microsoft's Windows 2000 and shared their ideas for improving some of the product's features with the software giant. The idea of the customer as part of an enhanced value-creation network envisions them as co-developers of personalized experiences. This would further help customers understand how the tested product could benefit their businesses. Many were even prepared to pay Microsoft a fee for this experience. The value of the collective R&D investment by Microsoft's customers in co-developing Windows was estimated at more than $500 million worth of time, effort and fees (Prahalad and Ramaswamy, 2000).

With the help of the Internet, co-opting customer competence can also be by way of virtual interaction. Software development is a case in point. At Microsoft, customers act as product testers in their native environments. Internet giants Cisco and Dell computers go one step further. These two companies give their customers access to their information and knowledge repositories through an online service that enables Cisco's customers to engage in dialogue. In this way, Cisco's customer community jointly solves the problems encountered by other customers and each customer has access to Cisco's knowledge base and user community (Sampler, 2001; Prahalad and Ramaswamy, 2000).

Co-evolving with the knowledge landscape
James Moore popularized the concept of co-evolving with the knowledge landscape. In his book, *The Death of Competition*, Moore wrote that 'companies need to co-evolve with others in the environment, a process that involves cooperation as well as conflict. It takes generating shared visions, forming alliances, negotiating deals, and managing complex relationships...' (Moore, 1993 cited in Lissack and Roos, 2001: 15).

The term co-evolution originated in biology. It refers to successive changes among two or more ecologically interdependent but unique species so that their evolutionary trajectories become intertwined over time. In other words, as these species adapt to their environment, they also adapt to one another. The result is an ecosystem of partially interdependent species that continuously adapt to one another. This interdependence is either symbiotic (each species helps one another), or commensalist (one species uses another, Eisenhardt and Galunic, 2001: 92).

The concept of co-evolution has been translated from biology to the strategy realm. Moore (1993) was among the first to develop a new ecology of competition, building on predator and prey analogies. Lane and Maxfield (1996) explained how co-evolutionary views could help explain the phenomenon of collaborative relationships in business, that is, such relationships that are mutually reinforcing. Along similar lines, a number of authors were found to be drawing on complexity theory to explain co-evolutionary phenomena in business (for example, Kauffman, 1995). More recently, Eisenhardt's work in the field of co-evolution has come to prominence (for example, Eisenhardt and Sull, 2001; Eisenhardt and Galunic, 2001; Eisenhardt and Brown, 1998).

The common denominator among these contributions is that they view firms not as a member of a single industry, but as part of a business ecosystem that crosses a variety of industries. In a business ecosystem, capabilities co-evolve around new innovations and technologies. Moore has found that in business ecosystems, firms work both collaboratively and competitively to support new products, satisfy customer needs, and eventually incorporate the next round of innovations (Moore, 1993: 76; also Nalebuff and Brandenburger, 1996). Typically, such ecosystems revolve around the exchange of knowledge, resulting in so-called 'knowledge landscapes' (Oliver and Roos, 2000).

Knowledge landscapes are particularly prevalent in technologically advanced fields, such as biotechnology (for example, Powell, 1998), or in the semiconductor and electronics field (for example, Grindley and Teece, 1997). However, co-evolution in knowledge landscapes does not seem restricted to technologically advanced fields, and appears to assume wide applicability to a range of industries (Stewart, 1998). For example, Apple Computer can be seen as the leader in a co-evolutionary process that crosses at least four major industries: personal computers, consumer electronics, information and communications. Co-evolution with the knowledge landscape surrounding Apple Computers encompasses an extended web of suppliers that includes Motorola and Sony, and a large number of customers in various market segments (Moore, 1993: 76).

The next question becomes: how can companies co-evolve with the knowledge landscape? The literature in the realm of co-evolving with knowledge landscapes is itself in an evolving state, and concrete recommendations and their discussion should therefore be done carefully. However, based on her exposure to current thinking, it seems safe to consider Eisenhardt's work as a standard reference. The key idea in her work is the pursuit to capture cross-business synergies across individual units in an ecosystem. This approach has been referred to as 'patching' (Eisenhardt and Brown, 1999, drawing on the work of the complexity scientist Kauffman, 1995).

Eisenhardt coined the term 'patching' to illustrate co-evolutionary processes in co-evolving with the knowledge landscape (Eisenhardt and Brown, 1999; Eisenhardt and Sull, 2001). Patching is the frequent re-mapping of businesses in a corporation to fit changing market opportunities. Eisenhardt describes the process of patching as follows:

> With patching, corporate executives set the lineup of businesses with the corporation and keep it aligned with shifting markets ... In turbulent markets, business and

opportunities are constantly falling out of alignment. New technologies, novel products and services, and emerging markets create fresh opportunities. Converging markets produce more. And of course, some markets fade. As a result, the clear-cut partitioning of businesses into neat, equidistant rectangles on an organizational chart becomes out of date as opportunities come and go, collide, and shrink. In this landscape of continuous flux, corporate level strategists must continually re-map their businesses to market opportunities … (Eisenhardt and Brown, 1999: 75–82)

Eisenhardt further describes patching as involving at least two diametrically opposed approaches: first 'splitting', and second 'combining' businesses within the corporation. Dell Computers was cited as an example of using splitting to focus more closely on target markets. In 1994, Dell Computers split into two segments. The transaction segment dealt with the customers who bought equipment in quantities of one or two. The relationship segment catered to customers who bought in greater quantities, from 50 to 1000 machines. By 1996, Dell's managers had split the company into six segments. According to Eisenhardt and Brown, the Dell company had in the interim announced a new split on a near-quarterly basis (Eisenhardt and Brown, 1999: 75).

Eisenhardt and Brown describe combination as the second approach to patching. Combining is the exact opposite of splitting, but it was observed to perform very well, especially at the interface between two or more industries. Hewlett Packard provides a case in point. According to Eisenhardt and Brown, Hewlett Packard's managers have relied on a wider repertoire of patching maneuvers than most managers in other firms. In one move, managers combined a new networked laser-jet printer business (based on an emergent technology for an established market) with another printing business (based on an established technology). The rationale was twofold: to transfer market knowledge from the older business unit to the new one, and to fund the new business so that it could take advantage of the emerging opportunity in the marketplace (ibid.: 76).

According to Eisenhardt and Brown, a critical variable in enabling co-evolution through patching is the size of the individual patches, the logic being that the more dynamic the market, the smaller the patch. Eisenhardt explains:

> The uncertainty of the market also affects optimal patch size. As a rule of thumb, more turbulent markets favor focus and agility – and hence small size – whereas more static markets favor economies of scale and hence large size. … The more uncertain the market, the smaller the chunks … (ibid.: 76–8).

Step Three: Realizing Imaginative Strategies

Following simple rules
Several authors have emphasized that simplicity is vital for good strategy (for example, Burgelman, 2002; Eisenhardt and Sull, 2001; Porter, 2001).

Paradoxically, the more complex the business environment, the simpler the rules:

> When the business landscape was simple, companies could afford to have complex strategies. But now that the business is so complex, they need to simplify. Smart companies have done just that with a new approach: a few straightforward, hard-and-fast rules that define direction without confining it … (Eisenhardt and Sull, 2001: 107)

Simple rules are derived from complexity theory's 'simple guiding principles' (for example, Kauffman, 1995), which suggest that complex systems tend to evolve by following surprisingly simple principles. Eisenhardt and Sull maintain that the same applies to a business environment that is fast changing, and unpredictable. The success of companies in such environments usually defies common wisdom of strategy making. A case in point is Yahoo! The Internet company enjoyed 1999/2000 annual sales growth approaching 200 per cent, and a market capitalization that has exceeded that of the Walt Disney Company. However, the success of Yahoo! is not easily explained using descriptive imagination (for example, Porter, 1980). To illustrate, Yahoo!'s success cannot be attributed to an attractive industry structure, quite the obverse: intense rivalries, instant imitators and price-conscious customers, who often refuse to pay at all, frequently characterize the Internet's competitive dynamics. Similarly, it seems difficult to explain Yahoo!'s success from the resource-based perspective (that is, from the vantage point of creative imagination). Yahoo's founders disposed of little more proprietary and difficult-to-imitate resources than a computer and an entrepreneurial spirit when they started the company (Eisenhardt and Sull, 2001: 107–8).

So the question becomes: how can the successes of companies such as Yahoo! be explained? Eisenhardt and Sull elucidate that in such markets crafting strategy should be opportunity-driven. They further explain that in fast changing, complex markets, companies can learn much from entrepreneurs, who typically use an opportunity-driven approach to strategizing. The rationale is that companies who want to succeed in such markets need a mindset that is geared towards capturing unanticipated, fleeting opportunities (ibid.: 108; Eisenhardt and Brown, 1998: 76).

Another important question that managers should ask themselves is whether following simple rules is applicable to all industries in which they compete. According to Eisenhardt and Sull, the approach of following simple rules is applicable across all industries, but the authors mostly cite examples from the high-tech industries. Evidence of the applicability of simple rules across industries was given in a letter to the editor of the *Harvard Business Review* that followed up on Eisenhardt and Sull's original article in the same journal (Campbell, 2001: 149), in which it was contended that simple rules do not only apply to start-up companies operating in fast-moving, high-tech environments. 3M's '25 per cent margins, or 15 per cent of time for skunk works', seem to validate the relevance of simple rules for mature companies as well, Campbell explains. Perhaps the best-known example of a mature company that operates in a relatively mature market is General Electric. General Electric's former CEO Jack Welch's simple rules approach calls for 'speed, simplicity, and self-confidence'.

Given their relevance across industries, the next question becomes how simple rules can be operationalized in any given industry. For the purposes of this study, Eisenhardt and Sull's original shortlist of five exemplary simple rules can be condensed into three main rules that focus on different stages of pursuing a given opportunity.

- The first main rule is that 'boundary rules' focus managers on which opportunities can be pursued and which lie outside the scope, and which apply to the initial stage of opportunity capturing. An example of a boundary rule cited by the authors is Cisco's acquisition rule that decrees that companies to be acquired must have no more than 75 employees, 75 per cent of whom need to be engineers.
- The second main rule is that 'timing rules' are designed to synchronize managers with the pace of emerging opportunities in the market. Timing rules apply to the stage when an opportunity has been observed and is being realized. An example of timing rules was Nortel, which decreed that product development teams must know when a product has to be delivered to the leading customer to win, and that product development time must be less than 18 months.
- The third main rule is that 'exit rules' help managers to decide when to pull out of yesterday's opportunities. An example of exit rules is Oticon's rule for abandoning projects in development: if a key member leaves the project to work for another company, the project is discontinued (Eisenhardt and Sull, 2001: 110–12).

The question of what exactly simple rules actually are becomes even more important in view of the fact that some companies that apparently used simple rules were not at all successful. An example of a company that failed disastrously using a simple rule approach is AT&T's corporate diversification only into 'computers and telecom' (Campbell, 2001: 149). What simple rules are not should therefore also be appreciated. According to Eisenhardt and Sull, simple rules must above all not be broad or vague. Rather than applying simple rules across the board from purchasing to product innovation, they should be tailored to a specific process. At AT&T, for example, simple rules were designed to apply to a very specific part of the company's operations, such as customer care. Thus simple rules must not be confused with mission or vision statements (Eisenhardt and Sull, 2001: 112).

Focusing on heedful interaction

Heedful interaction is a term coined by the Imagination Lab Foundation in Lausanne, Switzerland, building on earlier work by Weick and Roberts (1993). Organization scientists Weick and Roberts developed the concept of 'heedfulness' to explain organizational performance in situations requiring the collaboration of individuals with diverging goals, hence the need for heedful, or careful interaction by the parties within a corporation. The authors built on the work of social psychologist Gilbert Ryle to define the notion of heedful interaction:

> The word 'heed' captures an important set of qualities of mind that elude the more stark vocabulary of cognition. These nuances of heed are especially appropriate to our interest in systems preoccupied with failure-free performance. People act heedfully when they act more or less carefully, critically, consistently, purposefully, attentively, studiously, vigilantly, conscientiously, pertinaciously ... (Ryle, 1949, cited in Weick and Roberts, 1993: 361)

Weick and Roberts are careful to distinguish heedful interaction from habitual interaction. In habitual interaction, each performance is a replication of its predecessor, whereas in heedful performance, each action is modified by its predecessor (ibid.: 362). Weick and Roberts also link heedfulness in interacting with firm performance. If heed were to decline, the authors maintain, performance would decline too: performance would then become unmindful, unconcerned and indifferent (ibid.: 362).

In a research project at the Imagination Lab Foundation, the notion of heedful interaction was translated from the level of the individual in an organization to the level of organizations and their interaction with key stakeholders, including customers, suppliers, and the wider social and political realm. This research found that on the level of organizations interacting heedfully, a key challenge faced is to purposefully manage knowledge flows between the key stakeholders involved. Managing such knowledge flows across corporate boundaries becomes particularly important in contemporary business landscapes, which are frequently characterized by complex structures of interwoven knowledge networks of work group relationships, strategic alliances and customer networks (Lissack and Roos, 2001: 4; Bardaracco, 1991: 1).

However, the mobility of the knowledge asset exchanged in these networks need not necessarily be viewed as desirable. Teece (1998) observed that there is a simple but powerful relationship between the codification of knowledge and the cost of its transfer. Simply stated, according to Teece, the more a given item of knowledge has been codified (made explicit), the more economically it can be transferred, but also imitated (Teece, 1998). It would appear that the more explicit and codified knowledge is, the more economically it can be imitated, unless proper protection mechanisms are in place (von Krogh and Roos, 1995; Polanyi, 1958, 1966).

The key challenge in heedful interaction is to manage the ambiguous features of knowledge. To illustrate: among the most important peculiarities of knowledge as an organizational resource is the fact that controlling the mobility of knowledge assets is decidedly difficult to maintain because features restraining involuntary transfer tend to inhibit voluntary transfer. Likewise, the very properties that make knowledge difficult to imitate often also make it difficult to impart within the corporation (Spender, 1996a, b; Grant, 1996). Some sources of competitive advantage may even be so complex that the firm itself, let alone competitors, has difficulty in understanding them (Teece, 1998). On the one hand, heedful interaction therefore requires protection mechanisms to inhibit knowledge imitation by competitors, while, on the other hand, effective value extraction from knowledge requires the firm itself to be capable of replicating it domestically and in strategic partnerships with key stakeholders (Teece, 1998).

Managing the 'appropriability' of knowledge has been suggested as the solution to the challenge in heedful interaction. Appropriability refers to the ability of the owner of a resource to receive a return equal to the value created by this resource (Grant, 1996; Teece, 1998). Knowledge appears to be subject to unique problems of appropriability, because the features that make it easy to transfer also make it easy to imitate. In an attempt to come to terms with the strategic implications arising from this difficulty, scholars generally agree that appropriability should be seen as dependent on the purposeful management of, first, internal and, second, external replication (for example, Nelson and Winter, 1982; Winter, 1987; Teece, 1998).

Internal replication involves re-deploying knowledge from one concrete economic setting to another within corporate boundaries. Researchers agree that often, but not always, such redeployment crosses functional boundaries within the firm. Since individuals need to specialize in knowledge acquisition, and if producing goods and services requires the application of many types of knowledge, production must be organized so as to assemble these many types of knowledge, while preserving specialization by individuals. The firm is then an organization which has to resolve this problem. It permits individual employees to specialize in developing particular expertise, while establishing mechanisms through which these individuals can integrate their different, and often discrete, knowledge bases (Grant, 1996; Spender, 1996a, b; Nonaka and Takeuchi, 1995). Research has shown that while a discrete, functional, departmentalized division of labor may encourage local innovation, it tends to encourage the formation of localized codes of conduct and procedures as well, thereby making sharing of knowledge across functional boundaries difficult (for example, Spender, 1996a, b). Scholars conclude that the internal replication of knowledge can be handicapped by traditions of intra-organizational groupings. Schonberger, for instance, alerted management to the fact that functional organizational groupings representing, for example, production and distribution, may in fact be like 'castle walls': thick and resistant to interaction. A communicative dysfunction between the supply or production 'castle' and the marketing or distribution 'castle', for example, may often be major causes of problems such as misguided product decisions, and poor service to the best customers (Schonberger, 1996; Grant, 1996). Thus, managing internal replication can be seen as the purposeful process of coordinating internal knowledge practice with the aim of achieving high replicability of relevant knowledge inside corporate boundaries.

External replication also involves the deployment of organizational knowledge assets from one concrete economic setting to another, but across, rather than within, corporate boundaries. Research shows that external replication is distinctly different in its general mindset than that required from internal replication, since involuntary external replication, otherwise called imitation, is encouraged by voluntary external replication, such as in the case of technology sharing in strategic alliances (for example, Teece, 1998). Unlike internal replication, knowledge in external replication typically crosses corporate, rather than functional, boundaries. Due to the contextual dependence of much organizational knowledge assets, it may be easier to share knowledge across corporate boundaries simply because such disclosure does not usually cross functional boundaries (Brown and Duguid, 1998). To illustrate: when the knowledge-sharing parties 'talk the same language', spreading ideas may, in fact, be easier between the same department of different companies in different firms (for example, in the case where engineers from one partner assimilate the process technology of engineers from the other partner in a strategic alliance), than between different departments in the same company. In such conditions, practices are often fairly similar, and so barriers between different units may be relatively low (Hamel, Doz and Prahalad, 1989). Indeed, in this scenario it may be more difficult to stop ideas from spreading than to spread them. Knowledge that is 'sticky' (relatively non-fluid) inside the company can become remarkably fluid outside.

Overall, therefore, heedful interaction denotes the purposeful act of achieving high replicability in selected and appropriate circles of organizational influence (particularly internally), while limiting, or controlling, the flow of knowledge in others (particularly externally).

Building shared identity
While the previous imagination lever focused on the interaction of companies

with one another, this lever focuses on the interaction of companies with its stakeholders and shareholders. Oliver and Roos explain that an important source of stability in our increasingly complex business environment is our identity (Oliver and Roos, 2000). Recent research shows that this identity, however, is no longer restricted to the individual company, but includes the company's relevant partners: when companies co-evolve with knowledge landscapes and focus on coherence, shared identity emerges, particularly between players such as the company itself, its customers, the public and its employees (Hilb, 1997). What are the drivers for shared identity? Consonant with Kim and Mauborgne (1999a, b), as well as Hamel (2000), Leibold explains that we no longer live in an era of competitive strategy, one that only produces win or lose scenarios. Instead, it is argued that we now live in an era of cooperative strategy.

> Even in a cooperative environment, parties divide up the wealth to create win/win. The pie, however, often remains the same. With a collaborative approach, symbio-sis creates a larger pie to share and more pies to divide. Alliances of every dimen-sion are the natural order of the day in realization that go-it-alone strategies are almost always sub optimal … (Leibold, 2001: 7)

The need for cooperative strategy is accentuated by the convergence of industries (Hamel and Prahalad, 1996: 240). In cooperative strategy, it will become increasingly common to join hands with former competitors, former adversaries and former customers, who were previously considered to have interests different from ours. Indeed, much of the recent literature has either implicitly or explicitly tackled the issue of building shared identity, as evidenced by articles emphasizing broadened collaboration by 'bringing Silicon Valley inside' (Hamel, 1999), 'judo strategy' (Yoffie and Cusumano, 1999), 'fair process' (Kim and Mauborgne, 1997b), and the dismissal of the traditional 'predator and prey' notions of interaction among businesses (Moore, 1993). Such broadened collaboration manifests itself in blurring boundaries – between nations, between industries, between sectors of the economy, between organizations, and between functions inside an organiz-ation (Leibold, 2001: 12).

According to recent research evidence, blurring boundaries causes identi-ties to coalesce into what is called 'shared' identity (for example, Oliver and Roos, 2000). An important final imagination lever in realizing challenging strategies therefore is to focus on building shared identity with all relevant parties, in order to 'create a larger pie for everyone'. Issues such as respon-sible competition, creativity and innovation to avoid head-to-head competition need to be addressed when building shared identity. Furthermore, moral issues need to be incorporated into the debate. Most importantly, trust becomes a precious value. With the emergence of interdependent economy, collaborative faith is essential (Oliver and Roos, 2000; Nalebuff and Brandenburger, 1996; Moore, 1993).

The next question becomes: how to build a shared identity? Eisenhardt and Brown (1998), as well as Lane and Maxfield (1996), provide useful pointers that can serve as a framework for building shared identity. First, it is emphasized that building shared identity cannot be controlled or planned. It is not about planning an approach and predicting how it will unfold. The future, the authors argue, is too uncertain for pinpoint accuracy. Instead, and consistent with other work by prominent strategy scholars (for example, Mintzberg and Lampel, 1999), serendipity in building shared identity is advocated: 'it is about making some moves, observing what happens, and continuing with the ones that seem to work' (Eisenhardt and Brown, 1998: 8).

It must, second, be appreciated that building shared identity is not necessarily efficient in the short term. Indeed, it may often involve accepting inefficiency in the short term. Eisenhardt and Brown elucidate that building shared identity 'is about stumbling into the wrong markets, making mistakes, bouncing back, and falling into the right ones. It is about duplication, misfit and error' (ibid.: 8).

Microsoft is an illustrative example of inefficiency in building shared identity. Eisenhardt and Brown explain that the firm wasted resources on developing a proprietary version of the Microsoft Network, a misstep that ultimately cost Microsoft millions. Money was spent on technologies that were later bought from other companies and on promoting products that were eventually dropped. According to the authors, Microsoft passed up acquisitions that were later far more expensive when they had to be purchased as licensing arrangements (ibid.: 10).

Third, Lane and Maxfield emphasize that building shared identity requires heterogeneity. This means that participating agents have to differ from one another in key respects. They may have different competencies, or access to particular networks or other agents. Lane and Maxfield explain that combining different competence bases can generate new kinds of competence that reside in the relationship itself, rather than in its constituent agents. They call this process bridging 'structural holes' (Lane and Maxfield, 1996: 228).

Fourth, mutual directedness was found to be strongly associated with the building of shared identity. Lane and Maxfield make it very clear that mutual directedness goes beyond common interests and different perspectives. They must also seek one another out and develop a recurring pattern of interactions from which a mutually reinforcing relationship emerges. Lane and Maxfield also found that the willingness of the interacting agents to do this depends on the knowledge each has of the other's identity. Trust has been found to be a key ingredient in fostering this relationship. An interesting finding by Lane and Maxfield is that this trust, rather than being a precondition, is often an emergent property of building shared identity: it grows as participants become aware of the unforeseen benefits that the relationship is generating (ibid., 1996: 228).

NOTES

1. The original slogan, by the US sports apparel manufacturer Nike, proclaimed: 'Just Do It!'
2. See the heated debate between Priem and Butler, and Barney on the tautology issue (Priem and Butler, 2001a, b; Barney, 2001).

4. The three imaginations in practice

Chapter 3 looked at a theoretical framework for crafting strategy imaginatively, called the strategy-making matrix. The matrix integrates the three major perspectives of strategy content research (descriptive imagination, creative imagination and challenging imagination) in three steps derived from strategy process research (envisaging, conceiving and realizing). The next stage is to validate the matrix empirically.

In order to shed more light on the various elements of the strategy making matrix, I adopted the single-embedded case study as the research strategy of choice (Gibbert, Ruigrok and Wicki, 2008; Yin, 1994). My subject? ElectroCorp, is a major firm in the electronics and electrical engineering industry.[1] As I shall outline further on, at the time of the research, ElectroCorp was operating under difficult economic conditions. The way in which ElectroCorp used imagination may therefore hold important lessons for other crises.

My primary research objective was to empirically validate the logic and soundness of the theoretical propositions comprising the strategy-making matrix by answering the question: how does ElectroCorp craft strategy using the three imaginations (descriptive creative, and challenging) and the three steps (envisaging, conceiving and realizing)? Based on the theoretical framework developed in the previous chapter, then, the empirical study endeavors to shed light on the specifics of ElectroCorp's approach to strategy making by attempting to answer two further questions: (1) what is the relative importance of the three imaginations in crafting strategy imaginatively? and (2) what is the role and importance of sequencing the steps in crafting strategy imaginatively?

RESEARCH METHODOLOGY

At the inception of any empirical study of this nature it is important to consider carefully the choice of research method and design, the choice of research site, and factors limiting the study. The choice of method is critical because it impacts on the approaches and techniques for collecting and analysing empirical data (Denzin and Lincoln, 1994). This study uses a specific research design, the single-embedded case study (Yin, 1994), to learn more about ElectroCorp's strategy-making behavior.

Advantages of Studying Strategy Making at ElectroCorp

This section gives the rationale for the selection of the research setting, ElectroCorp.

A key question to be answered is: why is ElectroCorp a particularly appropriate setting for studying strategy making? Several methodology scholars have emphasized that the most important aspect of case study is the identification of the research setting, and the quality of the analysis and findings depends on choosing this setting carefully (Stake, 1995: 243). This endeavor is commonly referred to as 'theoretical sampling' (for example by Denzin and Lincoln, 1994), suggesting that the choice of a particular research setting for the case study needs to be based on systematic selection criteria, which need to be explicitly stated (for example Yin, 1994; Stake, 1995; Miles and Huberman, 1994). Four features in particular made the company very attractive as a research site from both the theoretical and practical perspectives:

- First and foremost, the period of the field study was a very opportune time to study strategy-making endeavors at ElectroCorp, since the company was busy with a major strategy-making program (the Business Excellence Program), and two embedded sub-projects (the Portfolio Optimization Program, and ICS 2003) in an attempt to deal with the crisis around the turn of the millenium. It should be emphasized that this was very fortunate, since it allowed the researcher the opportunity of studying strategy making in real-time, thereby enhancing construct and internal validity of the strategy-making matrix by avoiding problems stemming from retrospective data such as post-event rationalizations. I will go on to discuss construct validity and internal validity in greater depth later.[2]
- Second, convenience of access constitutes a rationale for selecting a research site. Indeed, as discussed in Chapter 2, scholars have criticized strategy-making research for its lack of empirical grounding (for example Eisenhardt and Martin, 2000; Eisenhardt and Galunic, 2001; Williamson, 1999; Priem and Butler, 2001a). This inadequacy is typically explained by the difficulty researchers have in obtaining access to organizations. In the case of this study, my contact with ElectroCorp was formal (part of the funding of this research was granted by ElectroCorp), and this greatly facilitated access to the research site.
- Third, ElectroCorp, being a multidivisional firm, is involved in all the activities associated with a large manufacturing firm (research, product development, manufacturing, marketing and sales). Furthermore, these activities in ElectroCorp's business units span a wide variety of industries, including telephony, electronics, medical solutions, transportation

systems, automation and control, and consulting. Such diversity offered the potential for levels of complexity in the data that are not usually available in other studies of strategy making, which in general focus exclusively on one industry (see, for example, Burgelman, 2002; Lovas and Goshal, 2000; Eisenhardt and Brown, 1998). This is highly advantageous, because it is conducive to the generalizability of the research findings (Eisenhardt, 1989; Stake, 1995; Denzin and Lincoln, 1994).

• Finally, although headquartered in Germany, the company is transnational in that it has subsidiaries in most developed markets in the world. This introduced another element of complexity, with the resulting possibility that the findings from the study could be more relevant for other firms (Denzin and Lincoln, 1994; Lovas and Goshal, 2000).

RESEARCH PROCEDURES

So what were the techniques employed for data collection and analysis, and what measures were taken to maximize the validity and reliability of the research findings?

Data Collection

Methodology scholars agree that the case study methodology's unique strength is its ability to deal with a wide range of data sources (Yin, 1994: 84; Eisenhardt, 1989: 533). This study gathers data collected from four sources: interviews, direct observation, participant observation, and documents/archival records. The majority of the data came from the first of these sources, formal interviews. The archival data and observations were, in general, used to corroborate the interview data. The majority of data was collected between November 2001 and March 2002. The four sources of data used in this study yielded 611 A4 pages of typewritten transcripts and summaries (these are available from the author for the purposes of academic research, provided a confidentiality agreement has been signed with ElectroCorp).

Interviews

A consensus in the literature emphasizes qualitative interviews as the single most important data-collection technique in the social sciences (see, for example, Foddy, 1993; Rubin and Rubin, 1995; Denzin and Lincoln, 1994; Yin, 1994: 88). In line with this, the majority of the data used in this study came from interviews. Managers from different levels in the organization, different functional groups, and different businesses, who had been involved in the three key projects investigated, were formally interviewed. All in all, 40

ElectroCorp managers,[3] and one external consultant with in-depth knowledge of the company were formally interviewed. Many of the managers previously interviewed were contacted again to clarify differences and discrepancies in the interview accounts. Thus, many managers were interviewed several times, amounting to 51 interviews, and yielding a total of 344 typewritten A4 pages of interview summaries. I conducted most of the formal interviews myself (35 interviews). In addition to this, particularly in the case where interviewees were board members, I made use of existing interview data from the *Financial Times*, the *Wall Street Journal*, and a bi-monthly ElectroCorp internal publication (16 interviews).

To ensure validity and reliability of the interview data, all except one interview (a business lunch with the head of corporate strategy) were tape-recorded.[4] Furthermore, reflective summaries were used in strategic places during the interviews. In the reflective summaries, I produced a short verbal wrap-up of what I understood to be the main line of argument, in order to check for misunderstandings (see also Orgland, 1995: 200–201). This technique was welcomed by interviewees, who saw it as a form of 'active listening'. Indeed, the present study has taken the notion of active listening one step further. Within 24 hours of completing an interview, a typewritten summary of the conversation was made. These interview summaries were sent to the interviewees to check within three working days as a way to further ensure validity and reliability of the data (see also Orgland, 1995; Burgelman, 1994).[5] The response rate for the interview summaries was 100 per cent.

Direct observation

Stake characterized qualitative case study work as the researcher spending substantial time on site, being personally in contact with the activities and operations, and as reflecting, and revisiting, the meanings of that which is occurring (Stake, 1995: 242). Observational techniques, whether participant observation or direct observation, are common approaches to this end. Direct observation is widely considered in the literature to be a worthwhile source of data for case studies (see, for example, Yin, 1994: 91–2; Denzin and Lincoln, 1994: 203). For example, Foddy (1993: 3) noted that the relationship between what people say they do in interviews and what they actually do, is not always very strong. Pettigrew (1990: 277) and Lovas and Goshal (2000) have observed the same tendency in their studies. This suggests direct observation as a convenient method for checking interview data. This approach can also be instrumental in improving construct validity, as will be described further on.

In order to ensure the reliability of the data, only those direct observations that were videotaped are cited in this study. A total of 11 direct observations were made, including presentations given at the annual shareholders' meetings and business conferences, as well as internal presentations. Such videos provide an excellent opportunity to corroborate interview and other data. In addition to this, using videos as a data source ensures the reliability of the research findings: it would be possible for any interested person (who has signed a confidentiality agreement with ElectroCorp) to view the films and ascertain the accuracy of the direct observations cited.

Participant observation

Participant observation is a special mode of observation in which the researcher is not simply a passive observer as in direct observation, but is actually involved in the events being studied (Yin, 1994: 92). Participant observation has been noted to involve major trade-offs between the opportunities this data collection method provides, and the problems it poses (Yin, 1994: 94). Important opportunities include access to events or groups otherwise inaccessible to scientific investigation (Lovas and Goshal, 2000: 877). In the present study, the fact that I was employed by ElectroCorp for three years greatly enhanced my ability to actually view the object of study from the 'inside', thereby gaining access to data only available to insiders. For example, interviewees were willing to respond to certain questions and enter into a discussion on certain subjects, simply because I was seen as an ElectroCorp 'insider'. On the other hand, it is precisely this 'intimacy' of the participant observer with the object studied that potentially distorts the data by introducing bias.

During the study, I rigorously followed Yin's advice to carefully balance the trade-offs involved in participant observation (Yin, 1994: 41–3, 94). I took great care to ensure construct and internal validity, and to minimize researcher bias through the use of techniques such as data triangulation for the purposes of achieving convergent validity. Probst (2000: 252) has noted the value of devil's advocacy in the process of case study research and, in certain instances, I deliberately adopted the devil's advocate position by challenging the consensus during meetings and get-togethers. This technique was found to be very useful in maintaining and reinforcing my role as an external observer. It was also much appreciated by participants who found that this challenging of their ideas enhanced their thinking. Overall it was found that the opportunities presented by participant observation outweighed the problems mentioned in the literature by far, possibly because great care was taken to eliminate a potential bias as far as possible.

Documents/archival records

Documents and archival records were the fourth source of evidence consulted. This documentation was supplied by the corporate library, the public relations department and the corporate communication department. The documents and archival records that were eventually used in the present study are all located in the case study database, which amounts to a total of 13 lever-arch files. The data include documents such as official company press releases, internal communication such as company magazines, speeches and presentations by ElectroCorp executives, and internal training material. To gain the maximum value from these sources, great care was taken to follow Yin's advice to consult documents and archival records as a 'vicarious observer', so as not to accept documents as if they contained the 'unmitigated truth' (Yin, 1994: 87). In the present ElectroCorp case study, documents were therefore used in conjunction with other sources of information, such as interviews and observations. Only when all of the evidence produced a consistent picture was it assumed that an event had occurred in a certain manner.

RESEARCH FINDINGS

Company and Industry Situation at the Time of the Field Study

At the relevant time, ElectroCorp's business portfolio comprised the following business areas:

- Communications solutions (focusing on the communications industry, including wireline and wireless networks and devices as well as business consulting).
- Automation (offering solutions in the field of production and logistics automation).
- Energy solutions (covering a broad array of energy solutions, including power generation, transmission, and distribution from power plant to consumer).
- Automotive and rail (focusing on automotive electrics, and the rail industry),
- Healthcare (providing a broad spectrum of products, solutions, and services for integrated medical care, such as technologies for diagnosis, and therapies, which minimize patient discomfort).
- Lighting systems (specializing in lighting sources and the associated electronic control gear).[7]

The company and industry situation at the time of the field study can most succinctly be described by comparing two statements, made exactly 18 months apart, by ElectroCorp's CEO and its CFO.

Just after we announced our preliminary figures … [in 1999], I read a newspaper article titled 'ElectroCorp: *Star of the stock market*.' It really dawned on me at that moment how times have changed. The former 'widows' and orphans' stock has been transformed into an attractive, fascinating stock that is outperforming Germany's DAX index. While the German market barometer rose slightly over 25 per cent in our last fiscal year ... ElectroCorp's stock surged over 90 per cent. And this trend has continued in the past few weeks. From October 1, 1998 to November 30, 1999 ... the DAX rose 44 per cent, while ElectroCorp soared 47 per cent ... (CEO, speech, Annual Press Conference, December 1999, emphasis added)

The party is over! This is true for the capital market bubble, which burst spectacularly as expected. And a number of our important competitors are feeling the hangover. Many companies, in fact, but especially, and naturally, those in the information and communications industry. But old economy companies also have to deal with the consequences of the exaggerated equity evaluations. Nor can ElectroCorp escape these effects and their resulting pressures ... (CFO, speech, June 2001, emphasis added)

As can be seen from the two quotes above, the company and industry situation at the time of the research was changing dramatically from 'the most successful year of the company's recent history' (CEO, speech, February 2001), to 'numerous challenges' that necessitated 'a firm foundation to lead our company successfully into the future' (Chairman of the Supervisory Board, speech, June 2001). The company started the fiscal year 2001 with great confidence after the excellent fiscal year 2000, expecting double-digit growth and earnings growth to outpace sales. The reasons were the generally favorable market conditions (Chairman of the Supervisory Board, speech, June 2001) that were mainly due to: a flourishing world economy; a technology, media and telecom boom in the US; and a weakened Euro.

In the course of the second quarter of 2001, however, 'dark clouds gathered over the global economy' (Chairman of the Supervisory Board, speech, June 2001). The most important reasons were (Chairman of the Supervisory Board, speech, June 2001; CEO, speech, June 2001): the world economy declined in the aftermath of September 11; the 'dot-com euphoria' subsided; forecasts for the sales of mobile phones were cut by half in less than six months; most telecom operators were struggling with considerable financial debt; and numerous industries (particularly the automotive industry and the field of information and communications) were drastically cutting their investment activities.

These generic elements of the crisis led to increasingly differentiated developments in the company's portfolio. In summer 2001, the group's performance could be divided into three categories (Chairman of the Supervisory Board, speech, June 2001; CEO, speech, June 2001; *ElectroCorp Today*, vol 4, 2001; CEO, speech, January 2002):

- First, Automation and Lighting Systems. These business units were sharply affected by the general economic downturn, particularly in the

US. The difficult situation with automotive customers and the enormous surge in energy costs had negatively affected the development of this category. Both groups, however, had reached a high level of profitability and demonstrated how a business unit can survive business cycles without deteriorating profits (CEO, speech, June 2001).

- Second, former 'problem children' (CEO, speech, June 2001) Healthcare, Energy Solutions, and Automotive and Rail had developed into strong performers following their turnaround. This turnaround was mainly ascribed to the rigorous application of the so-called Business Excellence instruments (to be discussed shortly).
- The third category was comprised of the other eight groups that, at the time of the research, were coping with challenges of varying degrees. This was particularly true for the two large groups in the Communications Solutions area. Communications Solutions Mobile was in the red due to a dramatic downturn in the mobile phone market. Communications Solutions Networks was affected by a shift in technology, from the separate transmission of voice and data to a convergence of voice and data. In addition, this group was suffering from the weak investment activities of enterprise customers. The third Communications Solutions group, ElectroCorp Business Services, traditionally a technology consultant, was focusing on e-business consulting, but its earnings were unsatisfactory (Chairman of the Supervisory Board, speech, June 2001).

In order to arrive at an encompassing picture of ElectroCorp's approach to strategy making in the crisis, business units from all three categories were included in the analysis, as will be discussed in the next section.

Level of Analysis: Corporate and Business Unit Level

This study looks into the issue of crafting strategy imaginatively in the diversified firm, i.e. a large corporation that is active in various, if related, industries (see Chandler, 1962). This focus suggests two basic levels of analysis: the corporate level and the business unit level. The main level of analysis was the corporate level, and the main research questions remain at corporate level. To arrive at an encompassing picture of ElectroCorp's approach to strategy making, the business-unit level was included as a sub-level of analysis. Here, a carefully selected sample of six business units was analysed (Communications Solutions Networks, Communications Solutions Mobile, Automation, Automotive and Rail, Healthcare, and Energy Solutions). Three selection criteria informed this sampling decision:

- First, the wide variety of industries covered by ElectroCorp's business units offered the ideal opportunity to choose business units in different industries, so as to ensure the generalizability of the research findings (Yin, 1994: 38; Campbell, 1985, cited in Stake 1995: 238).
- Second, it was possible to select business units that represented 'extreme cases' in that their performance was highly differentiated, and even diametrically opposed, so as to ensure the internal validity of the research findings (Campbell, 1985, cited in Yin, 1995: 238; Miles and Huberman, 1994).
- Finally, resource constraints in terms of time and money limited the range of relevant business units.

Unit of Analysis: Key Projects Investigated

There is widespread consensus in the literature that defining the unit of analysis is vitally important (for example, Denzin and Lincoln, 1994; Yin, 1994). Yin, for example, emphasized that:

> No issue is more important than defining the unit of analysis. 'What is my case?' is the question most frequently posed by those doing case studies. Without ... an answer, [one] will not know how to limit the boundaries of [one's] study ... The entire design of the case study as well as its potential theoretical significance is heavily dominated by the way the unit of analysis is defined ... This stage can assume a major proportion within the broader study [and can consume up to] 20 per cent of the study's overall resources ... My recommendation is that investigators spend intensive – even compulsive – effort at this stage ... (Yin, 1994: 10, 12, 110)

In line with Yin's admonitions, considerable time and effort were spent in defining the unit of analysis. The first ten months of the research were devoted to screening candidate cases on corporate level as well as on business unit level at ElectroCorp. Parts of the results of this screening process were eventually published in book format (see Davenport and Probst, 2000). The selection of units of analysis finally considered most appropriate for the purpose of this study adheres to the logic of the single-embedded case study: the present strategy-making case study involves several sub-units of analysis under an umbrella project, which constitutes the main unit of analysis.

This single-embedded case study involves three units of analysis: three major corporate level strategy-making projects that were underway at the time of the field study (2000–02). The umbrella project was called the Business Excellence Program, which, as might be expected, included measures to ensure excellence in business. In addition to the Business Excellence Program, two sub-projects were investigated. The first of these sub-projects was a major initiative to achieve sustainable growth in the company's profitability. This project involved ten measures to optimize the company's portfolio, and improve its capital structure, and was called the Portfolio Optimization Program. The second sub-project was specifically geared to improve the profitability of the Communications Solutions sector in order to achieve the medium-term profitability objectives set for 2003 and was termed CS2003.

The idea behind the umbrella project, the Business Excellence Program, was business excellence by focusing on the three so-called 'Business Excellence fields': productivity, innovation and growth. ElectroCorp made considerable progress in the three top fields after the implementation of the Business Excellence Program. In terms of the first Business Excellence field, productivity, the company had generally achieved productivity gains of between 3 and 4 per cent a year before the program was conceived. Since the implementation of the Business Excellence Program, however, the company accumulated productivity gains totaling nearly 40 per cent (CEO, speech, February 1999). In terms of the second Business Excellence field, innovation, the company also made considerable progress. In the early 1990s, ElectroCorp registered an average of 3000 inventions per year. At the time of the field study, the number had grown to more than 8000 per year (Corporate Technology Officer, interview, December 2001). In terms of the third Business Excellence field, growth, the company saw new orders climbing by 20 billion Euros to nearly 60 billion Euros (CEO, speech, February 1999; CEO, speech, June 2001).

However, these successes had not been matched by vigorous growth in the company's earnings. The reason for this was seen in the tougher competitive area forcing ElectroCorp to give up the largest share of its productivity gains to lower customer pricing. In recognition of this drawback, the Business Excellence Program was made more 'business-specific and binding' (CEO, speech, February 1999). The motto of the Business Excellence Program reflected this rationale by outlining three steps to achieve this goal: clear goals, concrete measures and rigorous consequences. To make Business Excellence more business-specific and binding, two main measures were designed. The first measure was the introduction of a new performance yardstick against which performance was gauged consistently throughout the entire company. This performance yardstick was economic value-added.[7] Introducing economic value-added as the standardized performance measurement yardstick helped ElectroCorp to foster transparency and consistency among its units and local companies. In order to remain competitive in the future, all groups within ElectroCorp therefore had to constantly increase their economic value-added. The second measure continued to center on innovation and growth, but defined clearer goals and pilot projects as to how the company intended to proceed. Five key leverage points were identified: portfolio optimization, reduction of tied-up assets, earnings-oriented sales, cost reduction and quality (CEO, speech, February 1999).

The idea behind the second key project that was investigated for the present study, the Portfolio Optimization Program, was to achieve sustainable growth in the company's profitability. The strategic magnitude of the Portfolio Optimization Program was illustrated at the end of ElectroCorp's Annual Press Conference in December 1998, when the CEO said: 'When we have implemented this package of measures [the Portfolio Optimization Program], ElectroCorp will be a different company from the one you have known' (CEO, speech, December 1998).

The Business Excellence Program had been approved in July 1998, and included measures to enhance the company's portfolio and improve its capital structure. Specifically, it included ten action items (CEO, speech, February 1999):

1.   Stabilize semiconductors. The semiconductor market was characterized by strong cyclical fluctuations and highly volatile earnings, something the company wished to avoid over the long term. ElectroCorp publicly listed its semiconductor group as Semiconductor Technologies on the Frankfurt and New York Stock exchanges in March 2000. At the time of the field study, ElectroCorp held a majority stake (56 per cent in July 2001), but intended to reduce its stake to below 51 per cent.

2.   Accelerate the Business Excellence Program. Since 1 October 1998, economic value-added had been the binding yardstick for all ElectroCorp groups. Every business unit had its own, specific, economic value-added target and was measured in terms of its contributions to increasing company value. In fiscal 2000, ElectroCorp posted a positive economic value-added for the first time – a year earlier than planned.

3.   Divestments. In divesting businesses, the company pursued its aim to avoid unstable markets. First, it withdrew from volatile businesses (such as the semiconductor business), which did not fit the risk profile of ElectroCorp investors. Second, it sharpened the focus of its portfolio by selling marginal businesses (such as defence electronics).

4.   Strengthen the portfolio. The idea was 'to bring the businesses into leading market positions. If a business is weak, there are five options for reaching this goal: fix, buy, cooperate, sell or close a business. I have always made it clear that the first option is the best: fix that which isn't working' (CEO, speech, June 2000).

5.   Reorganize business segments. Reorganization centered on the communications and information segments, where the company consolidated its Communications Solutions business area to form Communications Solutions Mobile in order to meet the demand for new technologies and mobile phone activities.

6. Reduce tied-up capital. Reduction of tied-up capital was done by focusing on asset management (the management of investments in property, plant and equipment, working capital and real estate). Asset management was one of the company's most important levers for improving economic value-added by reducing tied-up capital on which interest must be paid.
7. Improve capital structure, through the introduction of no-par-value shares and registered shares, share re-purchases, and stock option plans. These measures were approved at the Annual Shareholders' meeting in February 1999.
8. Convert accounting system to US GAAP standard. Conversion to US GAAP accounting and financial reporting standard was completed by the end of the fiscal year 2000, in order to become more transparent to international investors.
9. Listing on the New York Stock Exchange. ElectroCorp successfully applied for a listing on the New York Stock Exchange. The first ElectroCorp shares were traded in March 2000.
10. Focusing on restructuring costs. An extraordinary charge of 2 billion Euros for restructuring, as posted in the fiscal year 1998 balance sheet, was used for measures in the semiconductor and the Communications Solutions business segments.

The third key project investigated, CS2003, involved ElectroCorp's response to the market challenges present at the time of the field study. Despite a difficult business environment, ElectroCorp intended to increase earning. At the company's annual press conference at ElectroCorp headquarters in 2001, the CEO expressed confidence that the company had identified the appropriate strategies and would achieve clear successes in the fiscal year 2003 (hence the title, CS2003). In fiscal 2001 (ended 30 September 2001), ElectroCorp reported net income of 2.088 billion Euros. This was considerably lower than the previous year's record earnings and was ascribed to restructuring measures and special charges. The CEO said that the company's earnings target for the fiscal year 2003 nevertheless remained unchanged (CEO, speech, December 2001). This meant maintaining the company's medium-term goals for 2003, which had been set in December 1999. These goals, measured as a ratio of earnings before income tax to sales, had envisaged a trend of plus 20 per cent a year (press release, December 2001). The commitment to these earnings before income tax margins was strong at the company. In the words of the CEO:

> We stick to our goals, we do what we say. It must be made clear that we stick to the 2003 medium-term goals ... No matter how difficult this may be, we must take these steps regardless of the overall economic situation ... It is all about achieving sustainable growth and profitability ... (CEO, speech, June 2001)

ElectroCorp was therefore undertaking measures in view of the weakening economy, particularly in the areas of Communications Solutions, where the focus was on a more rigorous application of the Business Excellence Program (CEO, speech, June 2001; *ElectroCorp Today*, vol 4, 2001; Head of Corporate Development, interview, September 2001). More specifically, CS2003 comprised measures in four main areas of intervention (press release, December 2001):

1. Restore profitability in the Communications Solutions area. In the fiscal year 2001, Communications Solutions Networks was adversely impacted by cuts in investment by telecommunications operators and decreasing demand for enterprise telecommunications and networks systems. CS2003 was also taking hold at Communications Solutions Mobile. At the time of the field study, the mobile phones division was close to breaking even.
2. Business Excellence US Business Initiative. The US, where ElectroCorp, with the exclusion of Semiconductor Technologies, had sales of almost 20 billion Euros, became the company's biggest single market. The Business Excellence US Business Initiative had been launched to substantially boost the profitability of ElectroCorp's American businesses. The initiative was concerned with the strategies and business processes at ElectroCorp's individual operating companies as well as with the improved utilization of synergies across the entire company.
3. Focus on asset management. For 2001 as a whole, ElectroCorp posted 7 billion Euros in free cash flow from operating activities.
4. Cut central costs. The 2002 budget for corporate units had been reduced by some 15 per cent. A cut of at least the same volume was planned for fiscal 2003. Similar measures were planned to cut overhead costs at the operating units and regional companies. By the end of the fiscal year 2002, ElectroCorp expected to realize savings in this area of some 100 million Euros.

DESCRIPTIVE IMAGINATION IN STRATEGY MAKING AT ELECTROCORP

The first main 'thrust' as outlined in Chapter 2 derives from what I have termed 'industrial organization perspectives' in the strategy content literature. Industrial organization perspectives, it will be remembered, seek broadly to describe the environment in which the business is situated.

Step One: Envisaging Imaginative Strategies

The strategy process literature outlines three generic steps in strategy-making – envisaging, conceiving and realizing. The first, envisaging imaginative strategies, can best be described in general terms as determining the agenda by looking at strategic issues that may be potentially important for the future development of the company. When this step is combined with the descriptive imagination thrust, it can be seen to consist of three separate activities (or levers): defining industry boundaries; diagnosing industry dynamics; and balancing the investment portfolio.

Defining industry boundaries

The umbrella project, the Business Excellence Program, started with a strong commitment to delineate the boundaries of the electrical engineering and electronics industry, and for ElectroCorp to operate within these boundaries. The company's CEO made this very clear at the 1999 Annual Shareholders' Meeting:

> We are – and will remain – an electrical engineering and electronics company. At the same time, we have never been driven by the false ambition to cover all sectors in this dynamically growing business. We will continue focusing our activities on a manageable number of business segments in which we can maintain or achieve a strong competitive position. (CEO, speech, February 1999)

ElectroCorp focused on two key dimensions when defining industry boundaries: customers, and competitors. The most important of these dimensions was the customer. ElectroCorp was convinced that in defining industry boundaries, the fundamental starting point was the customer (Former Head of Communications Solutions Networks Sales (retired), interview, December 2001; Head of Business Excellence Program, Healthcare, interview, December 2001; direct observation, employee forum, October 2001). As part of the Business Excellence Program, ElectroCorp had established a sophisticated approach, called 'Visions of Tomorrow', to define industry boundaries using the customer dimension (*Visions of Tomorrow*, vol 1, October 2001). Visions of Tomorrow were detailed studies presenting ElectroCorp's visions of the five key corporate areas (Communications Solutions, Automation, Energy Solutions, Automotive and Rail, and Healthcare). The complex future scenarios developed by ElectroCorp had two things in common: first, they illustrated the extent to which information and communication technologies would impact all areas of life in the future, and second, they were all associated with a high level of networking and reciprocal influence with ElectroCorp's other corporate areas (Corporate Technology Officer, interview, 6 December 2001).

This meant that in defining industry boundaries from the customer perspective, ElectroCorp sought to gain a deep understanding of how information and communications would impact the consumer's life, whether in the home, in the healthcare sector, on the move, during leisure time, or in the industrial sector. Interviewees were convinced that the boundaries between the five key corporate areas, Communications Solutions, Automotive and Rail, and Automation industries would blur, and that there would be an increasing overlap with the information and communications industry (Vice President and CS CEO interview, November 2001; Member of Corporate Executive Committee, interview, *ElectroCorp Today*, June 1999). There was a significant consensus among interviewees that, whether in Automation, Automotive and Rail, Healthcare or Energy Solutions, it was always telecommunication technologies that intelligently link, monitor and control the components, systems and devices (Corporate Technology Officer, interview, December 2001).

It was very interesting to observe that ElectroCorp's approach to defining industry boundaries from the customer perspective led to new products and services at the intersection between its five key business areas. To illustrate: at the time of the field study, ElectroCorp was busy developing an electronic bus and train ticket, called 'The Card', which was intended to replace the paper ticket invented more than 160 years ago. The idea behind The Card was to enable those in possession of one to use all forms of public transport without having to buy and stamp different paper tickets every time. During the trip, the card would be detected by radio signals after every station, even through passengers' pockets and purses. A radio unit installed in every bus or train would then communicate with both the card and a computer that processed the data. Since detection occurred only en route (the radio transmitter only had a range of several meters), cardholders were not billed unless they traveled. Depending on their preference, customers either received a normal bill, or would have their charges debited from a pre-paid credit balance (Department Head, Strategic Marketing, interview, December 2001).

In an effort to gain a deep understanding of industry boundaries, ElectroCorp also focused on the competitor dimension, looking at both existing and potential competitors. Several interviewees noted that what separated ElectroCorp from other companies was that all the building blocks of the 'global information village' (Member of Corporate Executive Committee, interview, *ElectroCorp Today*, June 1999) were located under one roof, the ElectroCorp company. In defining industry boundaries using the competitor perspective, ElectroCorp was therefore able to develop a sophisticated picture of current and future competitors that could be offering alternative products. This approach to defining industry boundaries helped the company to take advantage of a multitude of opportunities for exploiting synergy potential and for generating new business by means of interdisciplinary solutions, while at the same time bearing potential competitors in these new industries in mind. Interviewees consistently cited two examples of interdisciplinary solutions that helped to envisage potential competitors (*Visions of Tomorrow*, vol 1, October 2001; Department Head, Strategic Marketing, interview, December 2001; Corporate Technology Officer, interview, December 2001):

- Software agents, independently acting and communication program units. These would not only support users when it came to finding information online, they could also help them by optimizing power network utilization, communications networks capacity and travel route planning.
- Automation systems, originally developed for the manufacturing industry by ElectroCorp, are currently needed for building management and the efficient operation of pharmaceutical plants, oil refineries or mail sorting centers.

Diagnosing industry dynamics

Prior to the announcement of CS2003, ElectroCorp had diagnosed industry dynamics. Diagnosing industry dynamics focused mainly on the very cyclical information and communications industry, which accounted for one-third of ElectroCorp's overall volume (CEO, speech, Annual Shareholder's Meeting, February 1999). A member of the board diagnosed the dynamics in this industry as follows:

> The global electrical and electronics market is growing at a rate of between 7 and 8 per cent each year, making it the *world's most dynamic large-scale industry*. It is an industry characterized by constant technological and structural transformation. The pace of progress in microelectronics and software development remains high, and product and system cycles are becoming ever shorter. New products and services, price pressures, globalization, more customer focus and e-business – these are the challenges we now face … (Member of Corporate Executive Committee, in *Visions of Tomorrow*, October 2001, emphasis added)

Due to the intimate connection of the information and communications industry to the other industries ElectroCorp was competing in, the large-scale technological changes in ElectroCorp's most important industry had ripple effects in the other industries in which the corporation competed (Automation, Energy Solutions, Healthcare, and Automotive and Rail). The company therefore also made a conscious effort to diagnose the dynamics in the industries in which it was competing, in terms of the most important technological trends and discontinuities in information and communications that affected the company's other industry dynamics (Vice President, CS CEO, interview, November 2001). Industry dynamics were clustered into so-called 'Innovation

Fields'. A senior manager at the corporate technology department explained in an interview that:

> ... [i]nnovation fields at ElectroCorp mirror the five main areas in which ElectroCorp is active ... These innovation fields are nevertheless more than simply reflections of ElectroCorp's corporate structure ... The rationale for structuring innovation fields consistent with ElectroCorp's portfolio is simple: you need a deep understanding of the industry in order to extrapolate trends. To offset this intra-industry focus, corporate technology then suggests an alternative view, one from an external observer, if you wish ... (Department Head, Strategic Marketing, interview, December 2001)

While ElectroCorp conducted a comprehensive overview of technological trends affecting all its areas of operation, the following account focuses on the evidence relating to the business units that are within the scope of analysis of the study: Communications Solutions Networks, Communications Solutions Mobile, Automation, Automotive and Rail, Healthcare, and Energy Solutions.

The Communications Solutions Networks and the Communications Solutions Mobile business units were most strongly affected by technological trends. The first of these trends was that the boundaries between information, communications and entertainment technologies were becoming increasingly blurred. The Internet Protocol was to become the most common standard, bandwidths and security problems would be overcome. This development of bandwidths would eventually open up virtually unlimited access to information of all kinds, at any time and with any type of end-user terminal or content. Moreover, voice, gesture and mimic recognition would make devices and applications easier to operate. In particular, software agents would become familiar with their users' preferences and guide them through a massive amount of data (Corporate Technology Officer, interview, December 2001; *Visions of Tomorrow*, Volume 1, 2001).

The Automation business unit was characterized by globalization of its markets, ever shorter innovation cycles and progressive, worldwide networking, which brought decisive change in production and logistics. In particular, the 'transparent factory' (Corporate Technology Officer, interview, December 2001) would be born. In the transparent factory, information and communications technology would make it possible to network business processes between all its production levels, especially in industrial manufacturing. Those employees with proper authorization would be able to obtain an overview of all processes and also control them, while a global data network would extend the entire value chain. Furthermore, a variety of intelligent sensors would increasingly decentralize automation solutions in both industrial plants and buildings, while tele-service as well as remote maintenance and diagnosis would become increasingly commonplace. Finally, software tools for forecasts, simulations (for example, virtual engineering and virtual production) and augmented reality (that is, the merging of computer and real images) would support decision making (Corporate Technology Officer, interview, December 2001).

The dynamics in the transportation industry would be characterized by more efficient means of transport, from which less noise and pollution would be produced. This would be made possible by innovations such as rapid valves for direct fuel injection, new catalytic converters, lightweight materials, new methods of vibration reduction, and software for low energy or automatic operation of vehicles (for example, streetcars or subways). Particularly important for ElectroCorp at the time of the field study was the trend towards new means of transport such as the magnetic levitation (Mag-Lev) train. This form of transportation was designed to compete with aircraft for medium-distance travelers. In addition to this, intelligent methods of payment (such as The Card) would make public transport much more convenient for travelers. Finally, situation-based driver assistance systems would increase comfort and safety in terms of parking, collision warnings, (semi-) automatic driving, multimedia entertainment, plus office and Internet access in vehicles (*Visions of Tomorrow*, 2001: 12; Head of Automotive and Rail Quality Management, interviews, December 2001 and January 2002).

In the Healthcare industry, improved technology would make it possible for medical doctors to obtain an increasingly detailed look inside the bodies of their patients. Various imaging systems that can be linked to computers could serve to service detailed, high-resolution images and improve diagnostic accuracy. These systems would use simulations to make subsequent operations safer for patients. Specialized analysis software would assist doctors in decision making (computer-aided diagnosis). In an interview, the head of the Business Excellence Program at Healthcare illustrated that computer-aided simulation could furthermore lead to minimally invasive techniques and could consequently reduce physical strain for patients. Healthcare systems of the future would form a network centered around the private living area of the individual and integrating payer institutions, hospitals, medical practices and pharmacies. Information and communications technology would provide the necessary requirements to offer medical care and assistance at home. This would enable people suffering from chronic diseases, or those dependent on special care after cardiac infarction or a stroke, to live at home and to feel safe there, while sensors worn directly on the body would monitor vital functions such as pulse, respiratory rate and blood pressure (Head of Business Excellence Program, Healthcare, interview, December 2001; published corporate technology report, 2001).

Finally, the energy industry was characterized by a massive deregulation of the energy markets. This was bringing unprecedented structural change to every aspect of the power industry, from generation and transmission of electricity to consumer sales. As with the other industries in which ElectroCorp was competing, information and communications technology in all its forms was assuming a key role in the structural change in the power industry. In particular, energy supply and associated services would no longer be coming from a single source. While transmission and distribution would continue to be monopolistic because of existing networks, generation and sales were under pressure to cut costs as a result of increased competition (published corporate technology report 2001; Vice President Corporate Technology Strategic Marketing, interview, November 2001). On the other hand, energy providers would transform themselves into multi-service companies offering not just gas and electricity, but also telephone and Internet services plus garbage disposal (*Visions of Tomorrow*, 2001).

Balancing the investment portfolio

The company at the heart of the crafting strategy imaginatively study referred to itself as 'a paragon of portfolio strategy' (direct observation, employee forum, October 2001); all key projects investigated displayed an explicit focus on balancing the investment portfolio. To illustrate: the Portfolio Optimization Program featured a separate point dedicated to 'strengthening the portfolio' (CEO, speech, February 2001). Similarly, CS2003, with its focus on 'strengthening the Communications Solutions business' demonstrated ElectroCorp's clear commitment to balance the investment portfolio (*ElectroCorp Today*, vol 4, 2001).

The most illustrative example of balancing the investment portfolio was found in the Business Excellence Program. The Business Excellence Program featured a special section on portfolio management, and the program itself was frequently, if not officially, referred to as 'rigorous portfolio policy' (for example, CEO, speeches, February 1999 and February 2001). Four principles to balancing the investment portfolio were most often encountered in the interviews and the archival material. First, ElectroCorp would continue focusing its activities on a limited number of businesses. These businesses would be within the electrical engineering and electronics industries, which include complex systems technologies, and the solution and software businesses (CEO, speech, February 2001).

The second principle for balancing the investment portfolio demanded a weighted risk structure. Thus, ElectroCorp strove to achieve: 'a healthy mixture of businesses in both attractive growth markets as well as in established markets. Only then can we tolerate high risks in young markets and in new, strategically important business fields' (CEO, speech, February 1999).

Various media throughout the case-study evidence emphasized that the relative strength of ElectroCorp was that it operated in a range of different businesses, subject to different economic cycles, as well as spreading its activities internationally so as to have a balanced portfolio of national economic cycles (*Financial Times*, January 2002).

The third principle for balancing the investment portfolio concerned the relative competitive position of the individual business units to the competition. The axiom here was that 80 per cent of the business activities should achieve number 1 or 2 rankings worldwide. At the time of the empirical analysis, ElectroCorp had achieved this in 60 per cent of its business activities (CEO, speech, February 2001).

The fourth, and final, principle for balancing the investment portfolio at ElectroCorp was generally considered 'especially important' (for example, CEO, speech, February 1999), and demanded that each business prove its ability to sustain long-term profitability on its own. In other words, no cross-subsidies were allowed among the business units in the portfolio. This meant that all businesses had to earn at least their capital cost (CEO, speeches, February 1999 and February 2001). The Business Excellence Program demonstrated that each business must benchmark itself against the best in its industry. If it could not achieve the corporation's goals within a set time limit, other solutions were considered, including cooperation or divestment. According to the CEO, 'there are no exceptions to this rule' (CEO, speech, February 1999). On the occasion of the 1999 annual ElectroCorp press conference, the CEO emphasized:

> We want ElectroCorp to have a balanced business portfolio. We need cash cows in mature business fields. We also need activities in growth fields that initially require upfront investments, but will ultimately secure future opportunities. Our portfolio has to be balanced to ensure that each business profits from the synergies and financial strength offered by the company without burdening the units ... (CEO, speech, December 1999)

In various media consulted for the field study, it was repeatedly emphasized that ElectroCorp had adopted a new approach to balancing the investment portfolio. The new approach envisaged only retaining those businesses in the portfolio whose market cycles are accepted by the ElectroCorp investors. This was seen as 'management becoming more aggressive' (for example, direct observation, employee forum, October 2001). The basic four options were 'fix, sell, buy or cooperate' (Head of Corporate Development, interview, September 2001). This new and more aggressive approach to balancing the investment portfolio was often given as the reason for the step-by-step exiting from the manufacture and marketing of semiconductors, which were handled by a separate company, Semiconductor Technologies (direct observation, employee forum, October 2001; Member of Corporate Executive Committee, interview, June 2001).

The new approach to balancing the investment portfolio at ElectroCorp furthermore foresaw that every business was measured against the global market. Previously it had been customary to measure performance of the individual businesses in the portfolio in terms of a predefined 'relevant market'. However, this was often only a niche market in the actual playing field. This practice tended to place market share and market position in a much more favorable light than applicable. Evaluation in terms of the global market provided the company with a more rigorous and accurate picture of the competitive position, and it also made it easier to identify the businesses that required additional action (CEO, speech, February 2001).

The new approach to balancing the investment portfolio at ElectroCorp was informed by a clear commitment to the corporate conglomerate structure in order to foster synergies among the individual businesses. ElectroCorp had grown with the industry it has helped to shape for more than 150 years, the head of corporate strategy summarized in one interview (September 2001). Starting from its founder's innovations, such as advanced telegraphic equipment, ElectroCorp had developed into a highly integrated technology and sales network. The value of the conglomerate form was emphasized in various media (for example, CEO, speeches, February 1998 and February 2001; Head of Corporate Development, interview, September 2001). The common denominator was that while some analysts had thought that the sum of the value of individual businesses in the corporate portfolio might be higher than the market value of the company as a whole:

> ... [t]his kind of calculation is hypothetical. It is not at all clear, for example, whether ElectroCorp's individual parts could survive on their own. If, for example, their sales organizations were broken up or their know-how drained off. ElectroCorp is a living organism, and you can't just cut off a leg to see if it can run around on its own. (Head of Corporate Development, interview, September 2001)

Precisely this focus on synergies represented an unexpected new insight. In the case-study evidence there was a clear commitment to developing and exploiting synergies as the key criterion for making portfolio decisions. This is very interesting given that the traditional measure for making portfolio decisions is cash flow, suggesting that the basis for decision making is the synergies, not the cash flow:

> While we continue to expand our business in certain groups, we are encountering limits in others. We can't do everything ourselves. This is particularly true when we see no synergies, yet there is an obvious need for substantial investments and new know-how. In such cases, *we pull out of the business, even if it's profitable* ... There are also cases where we recognize that we can gain no competitive advantages from technologies, marketing or costs, and even have disadvantages as a large company. (CEO, speech, February 1998)

Step Two: Conceiving Imaginative Strategies

Conceiving strategies logically follow on from envisaging strategies. When linked to the first thrust of the strategy-making matrix, descriptive imagination, we find in the literature levers such as: configuring value chain activities; establishing position; and defending position.

Configuring value chain activities

While emphasis on the configuration of value chain activities was implicit in the Portfolio Optimization Program and CS2003, strong explicit evidence was found in the Business Excellence Program, which focused on asset management, as well as the configuration of activities along a so-called 'Total Solution Value Chain'. The Total Solution Value Chain will be discussed next, followed by an appraisal of the Business Excellence tool 'asset management'.

The configuration of value chain activities in terms of the Total Solution Value Chain represents a most interesting example of ElectroCorp's approach. A key learning in the Business Excellence Program was that the knowledge assets of the company became increasingly important as the key value-adding activity. In recognition of this insight, ElectroCorp Communications Solutions Networks started configuring value chain activities by mapping them in terms of the knowledge required for each element. By mapping the value chain in terms of knowledge, the decisions that have to be made at every step of the process, the problems that employees have to solve, the types of knowledge necessary to make those decisions in an informed way, or to solve those problems effectively and efficiently, ElectroCorp could identify the key employees, make their tacit knowledge explicit (to the degree possible), and create a context or structure for their interaction in terms of three key activities: business development, customer planning and bid preparation:

1. Business development included the questions: What are the competitive and regulatory trends in the market? What are the technology and innovation trends in the market? Where are customers currently focusing?
2. Customer planning included the questions: What is the competitor focus and its offerings? What is the competitors' relationship with the customer? What is the customer setup and decision making environment?
3. Bid preparation included the questions: What technical solution components need to be integrated to create value for the customer? Which complementor products can be integrated? What is the relationship with the customer?

To configure value chain activities in terms of the Total Solution Value Chain, ElectroCorp Communications Solutions Networks started off by creating a team to address the basic question 'how do we sell?' Members of this team included some of the company's most experienced salespeople, the heads of the key country organizations, and representatives from markets around the world that covered the full spectrum of business situations that the company faced. An interesting new insight that emerged was that by involving the company's customers in the configuration of value chains, valuable new inputs could be gained. In one case for example, a sales team in an Asian country had bid on a project only to have its pricing structure rejected by the customer as 'too high'. The reason for this was that since the Asian telecom was partly owned by the company's home country customer, it had access to the supplier's home market pricing, which was knowledge that the local sales team in Asia did not have.

Thus, partly aided by the input of the company's customers, the team developed a high-level map of the solutions-selling process and identified broad categories of business-relevant knowledge necessary for each step (business development, customer planning and bid preparation). The team then used the framework to analyse a representative selection of recent sales projects. Traveling around the world, members conducted workshops to map each project with relevant sales teams. The workshops helped the teams to understand how its general view applied to specific situations. With this detailed knowledge, the team was able to refine its Total Solution Value Chain and to specify in fine-grained detail the question salespeople need to answer in order to develop appropriate solutions for their customers and then win the contract.

In addition to the approach of the Total Solution Value Chain, ElectroCorp configured its value chain through a clear commitment to asset management (Head of Business Excellence Program, interview, November 2001). Indeed, the Business Excellence Program was committed to configuring value chain activities through the special module 'asset management'. The idea behind asset management was to deploy assets in the best possible way, that is by reducing them and keeping them as low as possible. Of the assets considered, working capital received specific attention.[8] The asset management component of the Business Excellence Program involved optimizing the following key processes:

- the process from formulation of an order through order progressing to receipt of payments (the 'order to cash' process)
- the process by which materials flow through the company, from storage and production to shipment (the 'total supply chain' process)
- the process from selection of suppliers through purchase orders to receipt of goods and payment of the suppliers (the 'purchase to pay' process).

For example, the regional company in Hungary used a system of metrics to track the progress of asset management. The assets of individual cost centers were monitored on a monthly basis in terms of criteria such as the days sales outstanding, the days inventory outstanding, the days payables outstanding, the days of working capital, and age of receivables. In order to ensure ongoing improvement in asset management, the incentive system was also modified. To encourage managers to minimize current assets, bonuses did not only reflect business profitability, but they were also based on a positive cash balance (Head of Top Plus Program, interview, November 2001).

In configuring value chain activities, the global configuration was an important aspect in the case-study evidence. The founder of ElectroCorp hinted at the importance of configuring the value chain globally: 'since I was a boy, I have been infatuated with founding a worldwide business à la Fugger' (ElectroCorp Founder, 1966). The founder's vision had been steadily pursued, and by 1850 the percentage of revenues generated outside Germany was more than 50 per cent. (ElectroCorp Founder, 1966). At the time of the field study, the importance of the earnings contributed by non-German business was illustrated by the fact that they comprised three-quarters of ElectroCorp's entire volume (Head of Corporate Development, interview, September 2001). Furthermore, major steps were taken to ensure that the company put the 'centralist viewpoint of the German headquarters' in the proper perspective:

> Let me point out just two examples here. First, the establishment of our network of global centers of competence, which are managed from locations outside of Germany. This move has helped us make progress in adjusting regional value chains to the regional business structure. And second, the process of regionalization, or having regional companies take over business responsibilities across national borders ... We will continue to expand this strategy around the globe ... (CEO, speech, June 2001)

The global configuration of ElectroCorp's value chain activities was further emphasized in an interview with its CEO:

> We have 470 000 employees in 190 countries, less than half of these, about 180 000, in Germany, all of which are internationally networked. And our global brand opens doors. Who is more global than ElectroCorp? Perhaps CocaCola – I'll accept this as a possibility ... (CEO, interview, June 2001)

The need for a 'glocal' approach (that is an approach that is both global and local) in configuring value chain activities was illustrated by a member of the corporate board:

> Within our global context, our regional companies represent one thing above all, proximity to the customer! A Spanish power utility is certainly not going to be

happy receiving its support from a British sales engineer. Within the context of internationally successful business activity, it is essential to take proper account of cultural and linguistic diversity ... [This] will only be successful in the long term if proper account is taken of the regional needs and special circumstances of our customers. For us, it's a fact that all global business is local ... (Member of the Corporate Board, interview, February 2001)

Establishing Position

As part of the Business Excellence Program, ElectroCorp had developed a sophisticated benchmarking technology in order to establish its position relative to its main competitors. Since the Business Excellence Program was the umbrella project for the Portfolio Optimization Program and CS2003, all three projects reflected the importance of benchmarking in establishing a position relative to competitors (Head of Business Excellence Program, interview, November 2001). In the words of the CEO,

> We have ... introduced obligatory and ongoing benchmarking, which entails a rigorous comparison of our own situation with that of the rest in the world. Concrete programs are then derived from these benchmarking surveys to indicate how we can close the gap with the world's best performers, and how long this will take ... (CEO, speech, February 2000)

In establishing position, ElectroCorp differentiated between benchmarking in competitor benchmarking and that of process benchmarking. One interviewee noted that this differentiation was one of the most important differences between successful businesses and unsuccessful ones (Head of Competitive Intelligence, interview, November 2001). Competitor benchmarking centered on looking into the cost position, and into the innovation position of the relevant competitors in the same industry (Head of Business Excellence Program, interview, November 2001). By contrast, process benchmarking looked into the sophistication of ElectroCorp's production processes relative to competitors in the same industry and also in other industries.

Competitor benchmarking   In the Business Excellence Program framework, a competitor obtaining higher profit margins prompted questions such as: How does he accomplish this? Is his performance based on superior cost position, products, or pricing? If it is cost position, how large is it and from where does it stem? Does he get lower prices from suppliers or are his sales processes more efficient? And, in particular, how far is his unique selling proposition different from ours? (Head of Business Excellence Program, interview, November 2001). To illustrate: in the fiscal year 2000, the business unit Energy Solutions (which was producing steam turbines and generators) carried out a competitor benchmarking study. The result of the study revealed a substantial cost gap to the main competitor, General Electric. The unit management therefore successfully set the goal of closing this gap through product standardization and supply chain management (Head of Business Excellence Program, interview, November 2001).

Process benchmarking   The second form of benchmarking at ElectroCorp, *process benchmarking* was different from competitor benchmarking, in that it benchmarked best practice across industries, rather than benchmarking relative to a competitor in the same industry. The rationale was that even if a business unit of ElectroCorp was already ahead of its direct competitors, it could still improve its processes by benchmarking them with companies that are well-known for their best practice across industries. The head of the Business Excellence Program explained in an interview:

> In the Business Excellence framework, benchmarking does not happen within a single industry only. Business Excellence provides suggestions on the methodology of benchmarking, but what is to be benchmarked is up to the individual units ... If our mobile phone division benchmarks its processes against Nokia or CocaCola, it is up to them. In competitor benchmarking, the benchmark partner is the direct competitor ... (Head of Business Excellence Program, interview, November 2001)

When using process benchmarking, the first step was to analyze and prioritize the processes to be benchmarked. This was often done by choosing the processes that were relevant for differentiating the unit from its competitors, and that had a significant potential for improvement. In a second step, the best-in-class benchmarks were identified. During benchmarking visits, questions were answered like: How does this company handle the process we want to improve? What conditions do they have to cope with? How is this process integrated? (Head of Business Excellence Program, interview, November 2001). It was interesting to note that the case-study evidence made it clear that, unlike in competitor benchmarking, the benchmarked business was quite open to such questions, since the benchmarked business was typically not a direct competitor and could even benefit and learn from the process benchmarking endeavor (Head of Business Excellence Program, interview, November 2001).

An interesting new insight that emerged in the case-study evidence was that the benchmarking process not only helped in ascertaining the cost position, but also helped in stimulating innovation (Head of Business Excellence Program, interview, November 2001; Chief Knowledge Officer, interview, November 2001). To cite a senior manager in the Automotive and Rail business unit:

> Benchmarking projects not only helped to identify cost and productivity gaps, but also supplied valuable new insights and business ideas. To illustrate: by ascertaining what the benchmarking partner did in terms of services, the profit potential of

putting greater emphasis on services became evident. (Head of Automotive and Rail Quality Management, interview, December 2001)

Defending position

The theoretical framework highlighted the establishment of entry barriers such as superior quality, favorable cost positions or a well-established brand name as the main points of leverage for defending a company's position. Specifically, ElectroCorp focused on three key areas when defending its position relative to competitors: quality, the ElectroCorp brand name and cost.

The Business Excellence Program had a special commitment to quality. The Business Excellence team found that after years of moderate returns and a reasonable degree of satisfaction with quality output, ElectroCorp had to take a fresh look at its established processes and needed to re-assess them in the light of quality management principles (Head of Automotive and Rail Quality Management, interview, December 2001; Head of Business Excellence Program, interview, November 2001). The key to success was found to lie in mastering processes and establishing continuous process improvement. The Business Excellence quality initiative focused on two aims, namely: reducing non-conformance costs, and increasing customer benefit.[10]

In order to achieve these two objectives, the Business Excellence methodology provided a six-step approach:

1. defining improvement objectives
2. determining main problem areas
3. identifying improvement levers
4. defining measures
5. implementing results
6. monitoring progress.

In October 2000, the Energy Solutions Division started a Business Excellence quality project, strictly adhering to the above six-step approach. A key learning was that in the past attempts to improve quality often began with step four, 'measures'. This, however, was found to lead to directionless implementation of measures, because the fundamental steps 'defining improvement objectives' and 'determining main problem areas' were not ascertained in a first step. Managers therefore had to identify improvement potential on the basis of strategic business planning and with the help of benchmarking and self-evaluation. Important questions to be asked included: How high are the non-conformance costs? Where do they originate from? Which problems are worth the effort of improving? Where should leverage be applied? Members of the Business Excellence Program team, who also focused managers' attention on the process, supported the first three steps. This was considered a key success factor, because without management attention, successful application of the Business Excellence measures was questionable. Steps four and five involved the systematic development and application of measures at the process level, supported by top management. The method chosen was Six Sigma, an approach that involved various (mainly statistical) techniques and tools for optimizing process chains and which had also been used successfully by other companies. So-called 'Black Belts'[11] were also used in putting the quality initiative on a firm path within Energy Solutions. Step six was still ongoing at the time of the field study, but involved the constant monitoring of the initiative with the help of case studies, analysis, defining improvement goals, and knowledge sharing about the lessons learned in the initiative (*ElectroCorp Today*, vol 3, 2001; Head of Business Excellence Program, interview, November 2001).

In recognition of the importance of quality management in defending ElectroCorp's competitive position, 'Q-Days' were held regularly in order to raise awareness among employees and to share best practices in quality management. The case-study evidence showed that success depended on three basic factors (Head of Business Excellence Program, interview, November 2001): management attention, transparency and qualification and training programs.

Several interviewees emphasized that a high level of personal support by top management was considered particularly crucial to 'set an example', and laid the groundwork for quality improvements. Quantification along the entire sequence of business processes created the transparency required to achieve set targets and to monitor where deviations from these targets occurred. Finally, qualification and training programs as part of the Business Excellence Program empowered employees to carry out quality projects successfully (Head of Business Excellence Program, interview, November 2001; Head of Competitive Intelligence CS Networks Sales, interview, November 2001).

The Portfolio Optimization Program foresaw the turning of ElectroCorp into a true e-business company. As part of this exercise, the e-business transformation team ascertained what the key success factors of ElectroCorp in an e-business context were. One of the key learnings of the team was that the ElectroCorp brand name represented one of the least surmountable barriers to entry. Various media in the case study emphasized that this brand name stood for trust and individualized solutions for ElectroCorp's customers (direct observation, employee forum, October 2001; Chief Knowledge Officer, interview, November 2001). Interviewees said that while the concept of branding was hardly a new one, it took on added significance in the new online environment. The widespread accessibility and availability of the Internet, coupled with the comparatively low cost of entry for new competitors, effectively leveled the playing field, because competitors were just a 'mouse click away'

(Head of Corporate Development, interview, September 2001). The ElectroCorp brand name, trusted for more than 150 years, represented one of the most important assets of ElectroCorp in defending its position in an e-business context, and interviewees were convinced that 'price does not rule the Web, trust does' (Davenport and Probst, 2000: 233; Chief Knowledge Officer, interview, November 2001; direct observation, employee forum, October 2001).

CS2003 focused mainly on reducing costs in defending ElectroCorp's position in general and the position of the Communications Solutions division in particular. At the time of the field study, the full extent of cost-cutting measures under the auspices of CS2003 could not yet be fully appreciated, and were therefore not considered for inclusion in this analysis.

Step Three: Realizing Imaginative Strategies

This step in the strategy-making process is primarily about monitoring, control and learning. It consists of activities that seek to ensure that strategy and the competitive environment do not drift apart as the strategy progresses and the environment changes. When twinned with the first thrust in strategy making, describing imagination, realizing imaginative strategies includes such activities as: discriminating generic strategies; cultivating competitive angst; and creating a fit with the environment.

Discriminating generic strategies

The case-study evidence showed ample evidence of the usage of the Porterian 'generic strategies'. In fact, the strategy-making jargon at ElectroCorp was an almost verbatim echo of many of Porter's concepts. Thus, concepts of 'cost leadership', 'differentiation leadership' or 'focused strategies' pervaded all three projects investigated (the Business Excellence Program, the Portfolio Optimization Program and CS2003), and could be ascertained throughout all media consulted for the study (for example, Head of Corporate Development, interview, September 2001; direct observation, employee forum, November 2001; direct observation, employee forum, October 2001; direct observation May 2001; *ElectroCorp Today*, vol 3, 2001). Perhaps the most interesting aspect of this focus on discriminating generic strategies at ElectroCorp was their long-term orientation. Throughout the entire field study, there was strong evidence of continuity as one of the keys in ElectroCorp's strategy-making approach (for example, CEO, speech, January 2001; direct observation, employee forum, October 2001; Head of Corporate Development, interview, September 2001). In the words of the CEO:

> ElectroCorp is proud of its 150-year-old tradition. And our Business Excellence Program today bases its core elements on the values and strategies of our founder

... Part of this company philosophy is that we think and work with a view to the future. *We don't believe in the short-term 'get in, get out' strategy* many believe we should follow ... (CEO, speech, February 1997; emphasis added)

The Business Excellence Program, the Portfolio Optimization Program and CS2003 invariably emphasized the long-term nature of the generic strategies underlying the key projects investigated. Perhaps the best illustration of this approach to extend the current strategy without major shifts or quantum leaps, was epitomized by the very motto of CS2003: 'We stick to our targets – we do what we say' (CEO, speech, June 2001).

In the case of CS2003, the targets mentioned by the CEO referred to revenue growth estimates based on the calculations of December 2000, that is, in bullish market conditions. Despite the unexpected market downturn, particularly in the Communications Solutions divisions, ElectroCorp's approach for discriminating generic strategies was to sustain long-term growth and revenue targets for the individual divisions for fiscal 2003. To cite the CEO:

Where are we heading? Last December we negotiated medium-term target margin agreements with each group. They apply to the fiscal year 2003, which is literally the day after tomorrow. We derived these targets from comparisons with our competitors, from expectations of the capital market, and from analyses of our own potential. These margins – measured as a ratio of earnings before income tax to sales – range from 4–6 per cent for Industrial Services, to 11–13 per cent for Automation, as well as Healthcare. Taking our groups and operations as a whole, we have an earning before income and taxes trend in the range of +20 per cent a year ... (CEO, speech, 13 June 2001)

It was particularly intriguing to examine where the emphasis on the long term in generating generic strategies came from. In ascertaining the case-study evidence, it became clear that shareholder expectations were the driving force behind sustaining generic strategies, even in the face of deteriorating market performance (direct observation, employee forum, November 2001; Head of Corporate Development, interview, September 2001). It furthermore appeared that while the influence of capital markets on strategy-making behavior was considerable, ElectroCorp was also reluctant to succumb to them:

... let me make one thing clear here: I receive considerable tips, advice, recommendations and good council [from analysts] ... Some of it is obviously delivered in undertones that are intended to generate a certain pressure. I listen closely to these opinions ... But, in the end, things will remain as they are: our company will not be managed by analysts. We can do that ourselves. And the analysts have in the meantime largely accepted this fact. In fact, some even manage a strained smile when I say we are so successful because we did not follow much of the analysts' advice, but followed our own course ... (CEO, speech, June 2001)

Nevertheless, the effect of shareholder expectations seemed to be a driving force behind the discrimination of generic strategies in order to achieve targets once set: 'The growing influence of financial markets on corporate governance is another phenomenon. This may not be news in the Anglo-Saxon business world, but it is a huge challenge in other regions…' (CEO, speech, June 2000).

Cultivating competitive angst

Cultivating competitive angst was widely practiced at ElectroCorp. All three programs investigated (the Business Excellence Program, the Portfolio Optimization Program and CS2003) cultivated competitive angst (Head of Corporate Development, interview, September 2001; direct observation, employee forum, October 2001; CEO, speech, February 2001). Perhaps the most dramatic evocation of ElectroCorp's adoption of this imagination lever was found in a speech by the CEO: 'New competitors are popping up virtually overnight … [C]ompetition is taking on dimensions no one could have imagined a decade ago. It started out as a wind, became a storm, and is developing into a hurricane…' (CEO, speech, June 2000).

While competitive angst was cultivated in many areas, including cost positions, innovation capacity, turnover figures and revenue growth margins (direct observation, employee forum May 2001; Head of Competitive Intelligence, CS Network Sales, interview, November 2001), it was mostly used as a means to alert corporate managers to ElectroCorp's working capital situation vis-à-vis competitors. As was discussed earlier on, the Business Excellence Program featured a specific module titled 'asset management' which was geared towards reducing the amount of working capital in the different business units. While performance in asset management was measured against differentiated targets (asset intensive industries such as the Automotive and Rail business unit, which was building trains, would naturally require higher working capital than, for example, the consulting business unit), the overall asset management situation was considered unsatisfactory at the time of the field study:

> … the asset management situation hasn't fundamentally improved to date …, but in fact has worsened on a comparable basis [with our competitors] … we will have to approach the situation in a different way. And we will have to do so because the circumstances today make this more imperative than ever. Why aren't we making progress despite the good intentions and initiatives? … [L]ook at any of the competitors where such 'sins' are not tolerated … Why can't we make progress in asset management without these crisis situations? (CFO, speech, June 2001)

The tool traditionally used at ElectroCorp for cultivating competitive angst was benchmarking.

> ElectroCorp was never afraid to benchmark against the best ... This leads to a
> sustained competition for the best processes and business models. We have bench-
> marked 85 per cent of our costs on corporate level against best-in-class partners. We
> then developed appropriate measures to analyse problem areas and to come up with
> solutions within the Business Excellence Program ... (Member of the Corporate
> Board (Business Excellence Program), interview, January 2001)

In a benchmarking project in the Industrial Automation division, for example, a serious cost gap relative to the division's major competitor, Mitsubishi,
was revealed. Competitive angst was cultivated by extrapolating that this cost
gap could quadruple within the space of four years (Head of Business
Excellence Program, interview, November 2001). ElectroCorp's approach to
nurturing competitive angst lead to achieving 108 per cent of the target savings
within three years. In other words, the cost gap relative to Mitsubishi had been
closed (Former Member of the Corporate Executive Committee, interview,
ElectroCorp Today, October 1999).

Cultivating competitive angst was found to be particularly useful in divisions
that traditionally enjoyed a good position and were therefore less inclined to
respond to appeals for competitive angst. To illustrate: in the prosperous
Automation division, a substantial potential for cost savings was found in the
purchasing department. The most important obstacles to overcome included the
attitude shared by many employees that 'we are the global market leaders, so we
must be good enough' (direct observation, employee forum, October 2001).
Competitive angst was needed so that the new ideas and proposals for cost
cutting could be realized without prejudice and negative sentiments. The following quote from a Former Member of the Corporate Executive Committee illustrates the need and potential benefit of nurturing competitive angst even if, and
especially if, cultivating competitive angst seems unfounded:

> In many of our business fields we are already better than our best competitors, in
> other words, we are a benchmark for other companies. This applies to 60 per cent
> of our total business. But as a world-class company we should really be at about 80
> per cent. In order to determine our position in a given field, we have to conduct
> repeated benchmarking assessments that measure our performance against that of
> our main competitors ... (Former Member of the Corporate Executive Committee,
> interview, *ElectroCorp Today*, October 1999)

Creating a fit with the environment

The notion of creating a fit with the environment was a recurring theme
throughout various media in the case-study evidence (CEO, speech, February
2000; participant observation, workshop, June 2000; *ElectroCorp Today*, vol
4, 2001; Former Head of Communications Solutions Networks Sales (retired),
interview, December 2001; Corporate Technology Officer, interview,
December 2001). To illustrate with a quote from the CEO:

... deregulation, privatization and globalization trends are creating an *entirely new business environment* for our customers, and for us as well ... To survive in this emerging arena, you must act, not react. Our strategy centers on innovation and growth. These two pillars, combined with targeted improvements in our business, will help us achieve the productivity gains necessary for the new business environment ... (CEO, speech, February 1998, emphasis added)

At the time of the field study, the notion of creating a fit with the environment was timely. Following an outstanding performance in the fiscal year 2000, ElectroCorp started the year with great optimism. Several interviewees noted that the company was caught up in the general market euphoria (Former Head of Communications Solutions Networks Sales (retired), interview, December 2001; Head of Corporate Development, interview, September 2001). In particular, it seemed that in the age of the Internet, economic cycles were a relic of the past. Perhaps as a result of this belief, the company's growth curves of fiscal 2000 were extrapolated to the plans of the following year. Since then, however, ElectroCorp has had to substantially scale back its expectations and, at times, make serious cutbacks in the plans of the overall company and some of its business units, most notably the Communications Solutions business units (CEO, speech, June 2001). Under these circumstances, the Chairman of the Supervisory Board characterized ElectroCorp's clear commitment to creating a fit with the environment as follows: 'The quality of a company and its management can be seen in how early they spot negative – and positive – deviations from their plans and forecasts, and how rapidly they plan and implement adjustments to the new situation' (Chairman of the Supervisory Board, speech, June 2001).

In various media, the field study evidence consistently found emphasis that a very important measure to create a fit with the environment is:

... agility in planning and logistical systems. A problem practically all contenders in the telecommunications industry have been struggling with is the inflexibility of their planning and logistical systems ... Particularly difficult is emancipating oneself from the constraints of past planning figures. One of our competitors, for example, kept up turnover figures by simply delivering more products to the retailers, resulting in tremendous write-offs, because the market for these products had gone ... (Former Head of CS Networks Sales (retired), interview, 5 December 2001)

In various instances the case-study evidence furthermore emphasized a number of constants that stood behind ElectroCorp's commitment to create a fit with the environment (Chairman of the Supervisory Board, speech, June 2001; CEO speech, June 2001; Head of Corporate Development, interview, September 2001). These commitments were:

- ElectroCorp would continue to be a pure electrical engineering and electronics company, one with a portfolio that is broader than most of its competitors.

- ElectroCorp's technology base is as broad, and all business units should profit from this diversity. The key here lay in the area of information and communications technology, which had penetrated all sectors in which the company was active.
- All groups should furthermore profit from ElectroCorp's worldwide presence, and from the broadly distributed regional value creation and its comprehensive global sales network that enabled the company to keep close to its customers.
- Finally, all groups should profit from the strength of the ElectroCorp brand, which should open doors and ensure a feeling of confidence and trust among the company's customers.

At the time of the field study, the company was focusing on the task of adjusting its activities to a changed business climate, particularly in the Communications Solutions sector. To accomplish this, ElectroCorp focused its energy on minimizing deviations from its original targets and ensuring that it reached its medium-term targets in the fiscal year 2003 (CS2003). This was particularly pressing, since ElectroCorp had communicated these targets to and awakened expectations in the capital market and public (Chairman of the Supervisory Board, speech, June 2001). This suggested that the very nature of CS2003 was geared towards re-establishing a fit with the environment (*ElectroCorp Today*, vol 4, 2001).

CREATIVE IMAGINATION IN STRATEGY MAKING AT ELECTROCORP

The second major thrust in strategy making can be labelled 'creative imagination'. Derived from resource-based perspectives in the strategy content literature, creative imagination seeks to evoke new possibilities through combination, recombination and transformation of things and concepts.

Step One: Envisaging Imaginative Strategies

Under the umbrella of the second thrust, creative imagination, envisaging imaginative strategies has, in the literature, included: concentrating on core competencies, propagating strategic intent; and transcending competitors.

Concentrating on core competencies
The Business Excellence Program, as well as the Portfolio Optimization

Program, featured a special pointer dedicated to concentrating on core competencies. The CEO emphasized: 'By focusing and combining the unique and
unbeatable array of competencies within our company, we will keep the
competitive edge...' (CEO, speech, February 2001).

This emphasis on concentrating on core competencies was very evident
throughout the data sources consulted in the field study. Interestingly, the
interview data showed that core competencies were most often expressed not
in terms of abstract capacities, capabilities or competencies, but in terms of the
different ElectroCorp business units. When asked what the core competencies
of ElectroCorp were, interviewees at corporate level would consistently name
the corporate divisions (for example, Department Head, Strategic Marketing,
interview, December 2001; Vice President Corporate Technology Strategic
Marketing, interview, November 2001; Head of Corporate Development,
interview, September 2001).

A key task in concentrating on core competencies, which was emphasized
consistently in various media throughout the case-study evidence, was that of
harmonizing multiple technologies. The CEO commented on the harmoniz-
ation of technologies as follows:

> ... [o]ur synergies come from the cross-industry technologies used throughout our
> operations. Communications solutions technology specifically is increasingly pene-
> trating and networking all our groups. I see our expertise in communications tech-
> nology as an enormous competitive advantage, since no other company in the world
> enjoys an equally strong position ... (CEO, speech, February 2001)

As the quote suggests, ElectroCorp paid particular attention to the
networking of core competencies within the individual units, as well as
across units. The notion of networking core competencies represented a
recurring theme in the field study (for example, Head of Knowledge
Management CS Networks Sales, interview, February 2000 and November
2001; Former Head of CS Networks Sales (retired), interview, February
2000 and December 2001; participant observation, June 2000; direct observation, October 2001; Davenport and Probst, 2000), and is epitomized in a
quote from the CEO:

> ... [T]here's another ingredient ... that I'd like to call the *idea of networking*.
> Supported by the spread of digitalization in electronics, our components, products
> and plants are increasingly being networked into complete systems. This is happen-
> ing across all our business activities. Our broad spectrum of knowledge enables us
> to overlay these physical networks with networks of knowledge. We are putting this
> networked knowledge to use across all of our activities to benefit our customers ...
> We are the leading systems house for complex projects that require a combination
> of hardware, software and services ... (CEO, speech, February 1999; emphasis
> added)

The instrumental role of the multidivisional firm and the synergies between the divisions in the context of networking was highlighted in various media throughout the case-study evidence:

> We intend to use our *unique combination of competencies* to develop strengths and customer attractiveness ... You can call it synergies if you like, but whatever the case, customer benefit is the result. This explains why we have no intention of breaking up the consolidated competencies that make ElectroCorp strong and unique. Regardless of the motive behind them, all recommendations to split ElectroCorp into individual companies – some even speak of dismantling the company – are out of the question. In our special constellation, one plus one is more than two ... (CEO, speech 1997; emphasis added)

The conjecture that the portfolio of ElectroCorp's business units was key in identifying and nurturing core competencies was frequently heard in the case-study evidence. While ElectroCorp operated in a broad field of electronics and electrical engineering, its focus was on those fields where it had a genuine chance of gaining and keeping a leading position in the global market, and in which profit from the company's broad spectrum of competencies could be captured. The core competencies on which ElectroCorp wanted to concentrate were predominantly in the realm of the engineering of major software packages, the application of microelectronics, and expertise in information technology networking (for example, Knowledge Manager (b), CS Networks Sales, interview, January 2000; direct observation, employee forum, October 2001; participant observation, workshop, June 2000). In concentrating on core competencies, the aim was to develop as many end products as possible from an existing organizational knowledge base (Corporate Knowledge Management Business Excellence Program Manager, interview, November 2001). The head of the Business Excellence Program at ElectroCorp emphasized the role of recombining existing core competencies to create new products: 'Trend-setting is not about upgrading version 3.1 to version 3.2, but about discontinuous innovation ... In doing this, we are focusing on ElectroCorp portfolio of core competencies and try to discover new ways of combining these competencies to create new markets' (Head of Business Excellence Program, interview, November 2001).

The field study also showed that a fundamental challenge in concentrating on core competencies revolves around delineating 'core' from 'non-core' competencies (Corporate Knowledge Management Business Excellence Program Manager, interview, November 2001; Head of Corporate Development, interview, September 2002; direct observation, employee forum, March 2001). ElectroCorp was doing this by drawing 'knowledge maps' as part of the Business Excellence Program. These knowledge maps illustrated where in the company what expertise was located (Chief

Knowledge Officer, interview, November 2001). The challenge in deciding what 'core' competencies were, and where they resided, was illustrated by the difficulty in deciding what 'best' practices within the ElectroCorp corporation were. The head of best practice sharing in the Business Excellence Program described this process as follows:

> Identifying core competencies is … about checking where in the corporation the best solution for a problem resides. This solution does not always have to be a new solution, but the solution has to be new in the context in which it is applied … [T]wo years ago, the Business Excellence award was won by the local company in India, using a methodology that was developed in Germany 15 years ago. Reapplication of this solution to the local company in India, however, created enormous leverage. This means that in identifying core competencies, the target context is what matters … (Corporate Knowledge Management Business Excellence Program Manager, interview, November 2001)

To address the important task of identifying core competencies, ElectroCorp developed a specific approach: the Business Excellence module 'best practice sharing' which featured a so-called Best Practice Marketplace, in which the definition of what 'best' practices constitute was negotiated through supply and demand (direct observation, Business Excellence Awards, December 2000; Corporate Knowledge Management Business Excellence Program Manager, interview, November 2001). A Best Practice Marketplace provided documented knowledge and pinpointed topic-related bearers of know-how in the company. This Marketplace made it possible for anyone either supplying or looking for practices to find one another via project documentation (Corporate Knowledge Management Business Excellence Program Manager, interview, November 2001; Chief Knowledge Officer, interview, November 2001). The person offering a practice described: the problem, the problem-solving approach, the solution process, the critical success factors, the expense involved and the results. The addresses of contacts available to answer queries completed the input (Corporate Knowledge Management Business Excellence Program Manager, interview, November 2001).

Interviewees explained that asking the employees to share their 'best' practices was, however, often met with much resistance. The case-study evidence showed that many employees did not have the confidence to contribute their normal, everyday work processes and experiences as 'best practices'. It was therefore necessary for all participants in best practice sharing to understand that naming an experience a 'best practice' may be done by the original contributor, but is more likely to be done by a 're-user' of a variation, or similar application, of the original contribution (direct observation, employee forum, March 2001; Corporate Knowledge Management Business Excellence Program Manager, interview, November 2001). Through constantly negotiating and re-negotiating what constituted 'best' practices at ElectroCorp, the corporation's core competencies could be delineated (Corporate Knowledge Management Business Excellence Program Manager, interview, November 2001).

Propagating strategic intent

As the CEO's quote below foreshadows, propagating strategic intent featured strongly in the case-study evidence in all three projects investigated.

> Innovation ... ultimately means spotting new technology trends, new business concepts, new opportunities ahead of the competition. It literally means *seeing the future* – and shaping it. I like to think this strategy is similar to the one used by Wayne Gretzky, probably the greatest hockey player in history. When he was asked about his secret for leading the National Hockey League in goals year after year, he replied: 'I skate to where the puck is going to be, not where it has been'... (CEO, speech, June 2000; emphasis added)

In recognition of the need to actually visualize a strategic intent, or 'a look into the future' (Member of Corporate Executive Committee, June 2001), ElectroCorp launched a new publication called *Visions of Tomorrow* as part of the Business Excellence Program. In this publication, the corporate technology department, in collaboration with the individual business units, had developed a tool for propagating strategic intent throughout ElectroCorp. *Visions of Tomorrow* were studies presenting ElectroCorp's technological visions and strategic intent for five corporate key areas: Communications Solutions, Automation, Power, Automotive and Rail, and Healthcare (Head of Automotive and Rail Corporate Management, interview, December 2001.

A common denominator underlying all five corporate key areas was substantially increasing the service business on an unprecedented scale (that is, to over 50 per cent of the total revenue). To illustrate: at the time of the research, services accounted for over 15 billion Euros in sales, or 25 per cent of the company's total (CEO, speech, February 2001). The reason for this increased emphasis on services was that they required far less net capital employed than manufacturing-generated income. The Communications Solutions segment led the way in creating new market space, with services accounting for 30 per cent of its sales (Corporate Knowledge Management Business Excellence Program Manager, interview, November 2001; Head of Knowledge Management CS Networks Sales, interview, November 2001; direct observation, employee forum, October 2001). At the time of the field study, a so-called 'Service Board' was in the process of being set up at corporate board level in order to offer top management support to the increasing activity in the service sector (CEO, speech, June 2001; Head of Corporate Project World Class Services, interview, January 2002). A senior manager from the Automotive and Rail business summarized the situation as follows:

> [W]e had to increase the service business on an unprecedented scale. Turning service into more than 50 per cent of the overall value added of a given deal was certainly one of the most challenging goals ... Service is the key to success in Automotive and Rail. Service business can be understood as a long-term partnership with the customer, in which we offer him everything he may need to keep the system running ... In particular, it involves ensuring RAMS, that is, Reliability, Availability, Maintainability and Serviceability. For example, to serve the needs of the market well, you must make a credible commitment to your customer that you, not he, will ensure that the train you delivered will be up and running for the next 20 years. (Head of Service Management, Automotive & Rail, interview, December 2001)

The second key project investigated, the Portfolio Optimization Program, in itself can be seen as the paragon of propagating strategic intent. It was developed from the need to make credible, but ambitious, statements of direction to the ElectroCorp shareholders after a period of deteriorating financial performance. In 1999, the CEO announced at the Annual Shareholders' Meeting that ElectroCorp would soon be 'a different company' (CEO, speech, February 1999). During the year preceding this announcement, analysts were becoming increasingly skeptical of the company's value-generation potential. Some analysts were even demanding the break up of the conglomerate structure of ElectroCorp, believing that the value of the sum of its parts would be greater than the total value (CEO, February 1999). The Portfolio Optimization Program was launched as a set of concrete measures to re-establish the trust of the analysts. One of the ten points, in particular, reflected the strategic intent of the company: the listing on the New York Stock Exchange and the conversion of all accounting measures to the US GAAP system as a prerequisite for this listing.

The company presented selected key figures under the US GAAP accounting standard for the first time at the end of fiscal 2000. Starting with the fiscal year 2001, all financial reporting was to be in accordance with US GAAP. The conversion was not only a prerequisite for listing on the New York Stock Exchange, it also made financial reporting much more transparent and enabled a direct comparison with competitors. With its Wall Street listing, the company underscored the importance it attached to the US market and obtained an additional acquisition currency for possible purchases. To illustrate this importance: the US, where ElectroCorp had sales of $25 billion and over 90 000 employees (almost a quarter of its entire workforce), was the company's single-most important market. In fact, ElectroCorp was the largest foreign investor in the US in the field of electronics and electrical engineering (CEO, speech, November 2001).

Finally, as part of CS2003, the company propagated the strategic intent of moving all its business operations into leading positions. At the time of the field study, this intent focused mainly on the Communications Solutions business units. As the Vice President and Communications Solutions CEO succinctly described:

> Analysts are convinced, and perhaps rightly so ... that ElectroCorp's share price is a function of the Communications Solutions segment. The idea at Communications Solutions Networks is not about restructuring an ailing business unit, the idea is to put the entire ElectroCorp ship back on course – while mending a few rusty patches, of course ... (Vice President and Communications Solutions CEO interview, November 2001)

The strategic intent was to achieve either number 1 or 2 positions for the Communications Solutions businesses, since only businesses in top competitive positions posted long-term earnings that exceeded the cost of capital. As part of CS2003, the company had compiled statistics that showed that only businesses in top positions could achieve the aim of earnings that exceeded the cost of capital. Businesses in number 3 positions could often not earn their cost of capital over the long term. The strategic intent was therefore clear: the groups in the ElectroCorp portfolio had to do everything they could to put their businesses into leading positions and keep them there (CEO, speeches, February 2000, November 2001; direct observation, employee forum, October 2001; *ElectroCorp Today*, vol 4, 2001).

An interesting new insight that emerged in the case-study evidence related to the barriers to successfully propagating strategic intent. In an interview with the former head of Communications Services Networks Sales Germany, it became clear that the key stumbling block in propagating strategic intent was the sales force:

> If sales representatives have the opportunity to revert to selling the product they are used to, they will do so. This can be a problem, because you will find it difficult to push your new products. How does one remedy this situation? There is no 'silver bullet' answer to this problem. If you prevent your sales force from selling the old products, for example by adjusting motivation and reward systems, your core business goes down the drain, and with it an important source of cash for financing the fledgling business. However, if sales reps do have an option, they will continue selling the old product ... (Former Head of CS Networks Sales (retired), interview, December 2001)

Transcending competitors

Transcending competitors through innovation had a long tradition at ElectroCorp, as the following quote from ElectroCorp's founder shows:

A key reason for the blossoming of our factories lies in using our own innovations as their basis ... This approach has never failed to enable us to be quicker than our competitors. This advantage usually persisted until we managed to get even further ahead by continuous improvement of our innovation ... (Founder, 1966)

In the field study, particularly as part of the Business Excellence Program, transcending competitors was a key imagination lever for ElectroCorp. By contrast, the Portfolio Optimization Program and CS2003 exhibited transcending competitors to a lesser degree and sometimes even emphasized the need to 'catch up with competitors' (CEO, speech, November 2001), rather than to transcend them.

In the Business Excellence Program, however, the case-study evidence demonstrated a firm commitment by ElectroCorp to transcend competitors not only on the level of end products, but also on the level of core products, and core competencies (Former Head of CS Networks Sales (retired), interview, December 2001; Corporate Technology Officer, interview, December 2001; direct observation, employee forum, October 2001). This became evident from the differentiated way in which ElectroCorp managers understood the word 'competition'. A member of the board defined competition as follows:

Today, competition means innovation and productivity competition in many areas of business. We're ahead of technology and market share, for instance, but in many others, unfortunately, we're not yet up there with the best in efficiency, design to cost, and profitability ... (Member of the Corporate Executive Committee, interviewed in ElectroCorp Today, January 1999)

Transcending competitors often went hand in hand with drafting unique selling propositions in a radically new way. This observation could be triangulated, using a variety of case study media (for example, Former Head of CS Networks Sales (retired), interview, December 2001; Head of Business Excellence Program, Healthcare, interview, December 2001; direct observation, employee forum, October 2001). However, it also became obvious that the basis for transcending competitors need not necessarily be a radical innovation. The following quote by the Business Excellence Program manager at ElectroCorp Healthcare was exemplary for this insight:

Drafting unique selling propositions does not always have to entail radical innovations. In innovating our products, we did not go for a radical approach. Instead, we enhanced existing product features. As an example, a new technology made it possible for our magnetic resonance systems to operate three times quicker. For our customers, this was a radical improvement of their workflow process. It meant that they could treat many more patients in a much shorter time than ever before ... To find these areas where radical improvements of customer value are possible, we often have to innovate around the core functionality of the product ... (Head of Business Excellence Program, Healthcare, interview, December 2001)

In transcending competitors, a recurring theme in the case-study data was to ruthlessly adopt the perspective of the customer in order to discover whether a new product would actually be superior to the old, and whether it would consequently provide superior value (Former Head of CS Networks Sales (retired), interview, December 2001; participant observation, workshop, June 2000). An interesting example of adopting the customer's perspective in transcending competitors was emphasized later in the same interview with the Business Excellence Program manager at ElectroCorp Healthcare:

> ... we looked at existing products from the customer perspective. While this may sound trivial, it is not. Usually, in Healthcare, you look at it from the technological perspective ... What we did was ask our customers: 'what would you want from us if you knew what is technologically doable?' The result of this was sophisticated magnetic resonance systems that did not use the traditional tunnel-technology, but instead used an 'open' design. The result: patients did not feel as claustrophobic, and our direct customers, the medical doctors, were happy ... (Head of Business Excellence Program, Healthcare, interview, December 2001)

Different interviewees, however, also consistently emphasized a downside to listening to the customer. The common denominator in these interviews was that often the customers themselves do not know what they wanted, and hence listening to them in order to find out how to best transcend competitors can lead to the wrong conclusions (Former Head of CS Networks Sales (retired), interview, December 2001; Head of Business Excellence Program, Healthcare, interview, December 2001). In the words of a senior development manager at the mobile phones business unit:

> ... we must ask ourselves, why do we consistently walk in one direction once we have taken this direction? ... Part of the story is the customer. Like us, the customer is trapped in walking into the same direction he's always walked ... (Senior Development Manager, interview, November 2001)

Thus, the case-study evidence showed that listening to the customer in transcending competitors was a double-edged sword (Former Head of CS Networks Sales (retired), interview, December 2001). The former Head of Sales Germany of Communications Solutions Networks offered the solution to this problem:

> In building innovation capability, you may also talk with customers ... However, you need to talk to the right people. All too often when sales representatives talk to their customers, they take the lift downwards – to the cellar, where the technicians sit. Instead, they should take the lift upwards, to the top floor, where management sits ... Technicians are often deeply preoccupied with upgrading existing technology, rather than thinking around the existing technology. More often than not, you get the wrong idea of what the customer really wants or what is good for the

customer from only listening to technicians ... (Former Head of CS Networks Sales (retired), interview, December 2001)

Step Two: Conceiving Imaginative Strategies

Conceiving imaginative strategies in this part of the strategy-making matrix can be seen to include the following activities: redefining industry boundaries, leveraging internal resources and building the intelligent enterprise.

Redefining industry boundaries

The theoretical framework outlined three bases along which industries can be re-defined: capacity-driven industries, customer-driven industries and knowledge-driven industries. The industries ElectroCorp competed in can best be described as knowledge intensive. To quote the CEO: 'Between 60 and 80 per cent of the value-added we generate is linked directly to knowledge – and the proportion is growing' (CEO, speech January 2000).

In emphasizing the importance of knowledge as a key value-adder, ElectroCorp made a clear commitment to looking at the resource-side in redefining industry boundaries (Head of Knowledge Management CS Networks Sales, interview, November 2001). The central question in redefining industry boundaries at ElectroCorp was: are the current businesses an adequate reflection of the market needs, buyer preferences and technological requirements? (Vice President Corporate Technology Strategic Marketing, interview, November 2001; *ElectroCorp Today*, vol 1, 2001; Head of CS Networks, interviewed in *ElectroCorp Today*, November 2001). The case-study evidence demonstrated that often customers, and in particular corporate customers, would not pay heed to the definition of industry boundaries, but would instead demand highly integrated solutions that often cut across several of the industries served by ElectroCorp. In the theoretical framework outlined here, I called this 'blurring industry boundaries', and this tendency could also be observed in the case-study evidence:

> Blurring of industry boundaries is happening on a large scale in the Communications Solutions sector. It's called TIME. Time stands for Telecom, Internet, Media and Entertainment. In a couple of years from now biology will also form part of this ... In fact, the very notion of Communications Solutions as a business unit combining two formerly separate areas at ElectroCorp is an illustration of blurring industry boundaries ... (Vice President and Communications Solutions CEO, interview, November 2001)

Given the blurring of industry boundaries, ElectroCorp managers considered it expedient not to define industries too narrowly. To cite a colorful evocation of this point by the CEO of the Communications Solutions business unit:

Industry boundaries is an elusive concept. I quite like Jack Welch's approach of not drawing the boundaries too closely. First to keep employees from relaxing, because they think they can clearly define the environment they are operating in and thereby ignore other important environments. Second, if 'industry' is defined more loosely, my scope of perception is widened too, and I am more sensitive to developments in related industries that might have an impact on my own industry. If we only think in terms of telephony networks, and nothing but the network, we have a problem. No question: it's good to think about the developments of networks, how existing networks can be improved, and can be made more efficient and customer-friendly. But if we do this, we fail to realize forces that impact the network as such. That's the 'frog's perspective'. I see the net and nothing but the net. What I see is the number of data bits that gets transported, I wonder how more data can get transported and that kind of thing … I don't grab the steer by its horns, all I do is perhaps get hold of its tail … (Vice President and Communications Solutions CEO, interview, November 2001).

In redefining industry boundaries, the common denominator across the industries ElectroCorp competed in was the knowledge needed by the individual business units (Chief Knowledge Officer, interview, November 2001; external consultant, interview, May 2000). ElectroCorp, as part of the Business Excellence Program, started an initiative that attempted to redefine industry boundaries irrespective of the traditional industry definitions, and markets served. This initiative was called 'Knowledge Strategy Process'. It was an instrument for determining strategy and action plans that were based on an assessment of the knowledge needed to deliver customers an integrated solution, irrespective of the industries that were involved in putting this solution together (Chief Knowledge Officer, interview, November 2001; Vice President and Communications Solutions CEO, interview, November 2001; Head of Corporate Knowledge Strategy, interview, November 2001).

The Knowledge Strategy Process methodology redefined industry boundaries by using the concept of 'knowledge areas', rather than using the served industries. Knowledge areas were clusters of product and process skills that typically cut across business units and their industries. These knowledge areas were categorized in terms of their proficiency, codification and diffusion. Proficiency referred to the abilities, skills and the expertise needed to build a solution. Proficiency was considered to be always tied to a person. By contrast, the second category for knowledge areas, diffusion, reflected to what degree abilities and expertise were distributed across the organization and across the individual industries, and how the processes for such distribution and networking were functioning. The last category for knowledge areas was codification, which conveyed to what extent and in which media knowledge was documented or recorded. Knowledge areas could address markets, products, technologies, materials, components, as well as processes (Head of Corporate Knowledge Strategy, interview, November 2001). Redefining industry boundaries using the Knowledge Strategy Process methodology was done by answering four questions:

- The first question was: what is the most significant business perspective for the near future? This could be a product line, a process innovation, a business or an organizational transformation. It aimed at identifying the most relevant business perspectives for the near future. The time frame for this was contingent on the business unit, and the common cycles within this business unit. To illustrate: nuclear power plants (Construction Technologies business unit) would have a longer time horizon than mobile phones (Communications Solutions Mobile business unit).
- The second question was: which knowledge areas are significant for the business perspectives selected? In the Knowledge Strategy Process methodology, this question was answered in a brainstorming session with senior management, customers and line employees. The result was a list of 12 knowledge areas. For this process, a knowledge area constituted the various experiences, skills and abilities. It touched upon considerations that ranged from whether a business unit had the know-how for developing energy-saving engines right through to its expertise in general project management.
- The third question was: what is the status of our knowledge areas and where can the company improve? This activity focused on the fitness of the knowledge areas in terms of the three dimensions (proficiency, diffusion and codification). The strategy-making team estimated the actual and target status along three key questions: Do we have an expert working in this area, if not, where can the expert be found (proficiency)? How well is the relevant knowledge distributed in the company, and how are the processes used for this distribution functioning (proficiency)? How is the knowledge documented, in reports, structured descriptions or standardized forms, such as best practices (codification)?
- The fourth question was: what is our plan and how do we monitor progress? In the final step, it was decided how the individual knowledge areas identified in the previous steps could be structured to create synergies. During this process, managers from different units came together to brainstorm areas of overlap in the knowledge areas identified, and how this would impact their current industry definition.

Leveraging internal resources
All three projects investigated for this study (the Business Excellence Program, the Portfolio Optimization Program and CS2003) strongly emphasized the need

for leveraging internal resources. The key question in leveraging resources as outlined by the theoretical framework, 'How can we exploit our limited resources effectively and efficiently?', was corroborated in interviews, archival data and direct observations (Head of Business Excellence Program, interview, November 2001; Vice President Corporate Technology Strategic Marketing, interview, November 2001; direct observation, employee forum, September 2001; *ElectroCorp Today*, vol 2, 2001). The importance of leveraging in particular internal knowledge resources was strongly emphasized by the CEO in various speeches. To cite one example:

> [O]ur knowledge-based activities will continue growing in importance. Ultimately our success will depend on the knowledge and capabilities of our managers and employees and how well we make this know-how available throughout our global ElectroCorp network ... (CEO, speech, December 1997)

The rationale for leveraging internal resources was epitomized in the proverbial 'if ElectroCorp only knew what ElectroCorp knows'. The case-study evidence showed that a company employing more than 450 000 employees worldwide represented an enormous asset – the relationships that these people built with suppliers, customers, partners, governments and institutions every single day constituted an internal resource worth leveraging (Chief Knowledge Officer, interview, November 2001). However, the fact that these 450 000 people were dispersed over 190 countries also represented a challenge in leveraging this asset. It was clear that:

> [t]here aren't too many problems that one or the other of our eight business segments hasn't already solved. Whether it's installing a complete metropolitan subway system, constructing a pharmaceuticals plant on a turnkey basis or putting up an office tower with the latest building management and communications technology – you can bet that at least one of the more than 400 000 ElectroCorp experts in at least one of the 190 countries where we are active has tackled the job before ... (CEO, speech, January 2000)

Leveraging internal resources at ElectroCorp was done to take advantage of the 'law of increasing returns' (Head of Knowledge Management CS Networks Sales, interview, November 2001). For example, the number of business options, quality improvements, cost reductions and process optimizations could be increased, thanks to the repeated use of the knowledge of how to set up a complex telephone network, without requiring further major investment, and R&D costs (Corporate Knowledge Management Business Excellence Program Manager, interview, November 2001). ElectroCorp Communications Solutions Networks and the introduction of Knowledge Web, an Intranet-based knowledge-sharing platform provided a telling illustration for leveraging internal resources, particularly knowledge resources.

ElectroCorp Communications Solutions Networks faced a significant increase in the complexity of its business, due to the deregulation of the telecommunications equipment supplier market. This deregulation resulted in an increase in new entrants to the market. On average these companies were far more entrepreneurial than the incumbents, highly sensitive to price, and they insisted on rapid innovation. Their emphasis was on customized product and service packages, which were highly knowledge-intensive (Head of Knowledge Management CS Networks Sales, interviews, February 2000 and November 2001).

This meant that Communications Solutions Networks faced the challenge of having to reduce costs and innovate new products and services simultaneously, at a pace not experienced previously. But the changing telecommunications landscape also brought new opportunities: while the new business reality threatened the profit margins of the established business, it also opened up new business in the service- and knowledge-intensive business, which had much higher profit margins. The new entrants needed fresh business analysis and planning to accommodate the rapidly changing markets in which they operated, but many did not have the resources or experience to handle this. Most of them were also start-up ventures without sufficient capital to make cash equipment purchases, which led to their demanding new means of financing and innovative contracts. In the deregulated telecommunications market, a customer could therefore expect a supplier, like Communications Solutions Networks, to provide most of the services involved in running a telecommunications-service business, including financing, business planning, engineering and operation. The complex service and product packages that a telecommunications-services provider wishes to sell to his end user have become known as 'solutions' (Head of Knowledge Management CS Networks Sales, interview, November 2001; Knowledge Manager (b), interview, January 2000).

As a result, solution creation and solution selling became key competitive levers for Communications Solutions Networks. This meant that the individual sales representative at Communications Solutions Networks had to effectively sit with the customer and develop an integrated solution for the customer's business problem. The sales representative had to act more like a consultant than like a person simply selling a pre-packaged product or applications (Knowledge Manager (b), interview, January 2001). One former sales representative reasoned:

> We will have to unlearn thinking in packaged products and applications. The way we work together is the most important clue to success. Once we start negotiations about a new project with the customer, we quickly have to identify internal and external qualified people to build and operate these new businesses jointly with the customer. Because of the multifaceted knowledge needed, we have to learn how to

source our knowledge from convenient sources. We have to get used to integrating internal and external know-how ... (Knowledge Manager (b), interview, January 2000)

The case-study evidence consistently demonstrated that ElectroCorp could no longer simply rely on former product knowledge (Chief Knowledge Officer, interview, November 2001). Where in the past ElectroCorp's sales representatives in the Communications Solutions business unit had often anticipated customer needs even before they had been articulated, they now had to guess, sense and discuss the complex needs of the new entrants to the telecommunications market. Doing so meant that the salesperson had to gather information about the new clients and develop in-depth knowledge about the customer's way of doing business beforehand. Unlike their established customer who had placed orders in a relatively foreseeable way, these new customers had latent wishes that had to be leveraged. One interviewee illustrated this as follows:

What we need most is intimate customer knowledge, especially knowledge about the customer's economic branch. We have to make pro-active suggestions about where our customer's business may go and in which field he may be operating within the next few years. To date we have only boarded the sales process when it comes to ordering products and applications. The challenge is to start discussions much earlier: We have to play the role of a strategy-management consultant who is able to interpret trends and to jointly design new business opportunities with the customer ... (Head of Knowledge Management CS Networks Sales, interview, November 2001)

It was clear to ElectroCorp that the new consulting role would be far more time consuming and demanding than simply 'moving boxes', as the product selling business was often called in the company (participant observation, knowledge forum, October 2000). Successful solution selling required that the organizational set-up and competencies needed to be geared towards purpose-fully identifying and quickly sharing relevant information and knowledge across markets around the world, and continually refining Communications Solutions Networks's competencies to keep up with market developments. The goal was to detect local innovations and leverage them on a global scale (Knowledge Manager (b), interview, January 2001; direct observation, employee forum, October 2001). In the words of the CEO: 'Companies like ElectroCorp have to exploit their expertise more systematically and more intensively than ever before' (CEO, speech, January, 2000).

The case study showed that a prerequisite for leveraging internal knowledge resources was the ability to transfer the explicit elements of knowledge that can be easily transferred, or stored in databases, as well as the more tacit elements of knowledge that arise from discussions and business development with a customer. Each of these types of knowledge elements demands fundamentally different transfer and management mechanisms. Interviewees emphasized that tacit knowledge is bound to the individual mind, and cannot be transferred without actually transferring the person. Knowledge codified in databases, manuals and project debriefs, however, can be transferred with relative ease (Knowledge Manager (a), interview, February 2000; Knowledge Manager (b), interview, January 2000).

The aim of the Knowledge Web initiative for leveraging internal resources was therefore to focus on explicit as well as tacit knowledge. To accomplish this, Knowledge Web leveraged four kinds of knowledge.

1. Cognitive knowledge, or *know-what*, was defined as basic technical mastery and was achieved through extensive training and certification. For Knowledge Web this meant technical knowledge, for example in the form of pricing concepts, represented an essential, but insufficient, aspect to ensure commercial viability.
2. Skills, or *know-how,* referred to effective execution and application of abstract rules and regulations to the real-world context. Knowledge Web achieved this through the feedback given by sales professionals in debriefing projects.
3. Systems understanding, or *know-why*, referred to a deep understanding of cause-and-effect relationships underlying an experience. In a global sales and marketing context, this enabled professionals to anticipate subtle aspects in their interaction with a customer. This understanding was especially important in view of the increased complexity of the sales process. For example, an experienced key account manager would instinctively know which components of a solution can be developed further, be leveraged and re-deployed in other countries, or even be re-invented to suit different requirements. Systems understanding therefore represented a particularly important area of intervention.
4. Self-motivated creativity, or *care-why,* refers to active and caring involvement in a given cause. For Knowledge Web this meant systematically identifying and promoting highly motivated and creative groups of employees. Indeed, such groups often outperformed other groups with greater resources.

Building the intelligent enterprise
The theoretical framework constructed in Chapter 2 outlined that a firm's value chain is embedded in a system of interlinked value chains, sometimes called a 'value system'. This value system includes the value chains of suppliers of raw materials and components that are interconnected by 'knowledge links', suggesting that building the intelligent enterprise means focusing on

developing 'best in world capabilities' in selected activities (as described in the previous section), while outsourcing other, less critical, activities (as will be described in this section).

The vision that guided the Business Excellence Program can best be described as a strong focusing of the organization on what it does best, while at the same time obtaining other resources and skills from partners (Head of Corporate Strategy (Cooperation Strategies and M&A Integration), interview, January 2002). According to the head of the Communications Solutions division:

> We are concentrating on our core competencies, while constantly replenishing them. At the same time, we are collaborating with external partners in situations of mutual benefit. For example, we are currently entertaining the thought of development partnerships for games to be used in mobile phones. In doing this, we are following a simple rule of thumb, and that is favorization of in-house production over co-option of external partners. In following this approach ... we can learn from our partners and also become more agile in reacting to changes in the market environment. (Head of Communications Solutions, interview in *ElectroCorp Today*, April 2001)

Building the intelligent enterprise at ElectroCorp was considered a key role in business development. Over the course of the Portfolio Optimization Program, it became clear that in order to reach overall performance objectives, ElectroCorp still had to improve its market position in many businesses. The first priority was to carry out such improvements through 'organic measures' (that is, leveraging internal resources), as this was considered to involve fewer risks than collaboration with external partners. Corporate development had analysed that, based on the company's overall sales volume, in 30 per cent of ElectroCorp's business the necessary position improvements could not be reached by organic measures, which showed a strong need for collaborating with external partners. This applied to both dynamic growth markets, where the necessary speed could only be achieved by mergers or entering local markets through acquisition of market shares, rather than by trying to enter through long-range price wars (Head of Corporate Strategy (Cooperation Strategies and M&A Integration), interview in *ElectroCorp Today*, April, 2001; Chief Knowledge Officer, interview, November 2001). The CEO emphasized in this context:

> We won't dissipate our strength, but continue to build on it. This calls for ongoing pruning of our business portfolio to ensure competitiveness and growth. We will continue to grow from within, but also rely on acquisitions and divestments. We will give up activities that have better prospects with other partners or in other constellations ... We will continue to acquire other companies if they can strengthen the competitive position of our core business in markets and technologies ... (CEO, speech, October 1997)

Knowledge assets, and the cost and speed with which they could be developed, were considered a key criterion in deciding whether to follow the 'organic' or 'external' route of development. The Chief Knowledge Officer made this very clear in an interview:

> In managing knowledge, we need to make sure that we understand both what the knowledge is that we have and what critical knowledge assets we don't have ... Once we have a good picture of our knowledge portfolio, what's in, what's missing, we can then decide what to do about the knowledge that is missing. Usually, the basis for making this decision is speed. Given the relentlessly increasing speed at which technology cycles change, speed is key ... Therefore, it often makes sense to co-opt the knowledge and capabilities of partners ... (Chief Knowledge Officer, interview, November 2001)

Building the intelligent enterprise at ElectroCorp revolved around partial 'outsourcing' of logistical risks to suppliers. For example, in the Automation division, the plastic parts section had room for improvement at the time of the field study. In the past, many of the plastic parts (such as screws, nipples, etc.) had been broken in transit and were unusable when they arrived at the production plant. The solution that was eventually developed foresaw that those parts that had to be assembled during production would now be purchased 'ready-assembled' from a single supplier. This would yield a saving of 500 000 Euros per year. Using this method, 108 per cent of the target savings would be achieved within three years (Head of Business Excellence Program, interview, November 2001, *ElectroCorp Today*, vol 3, 2001).

It also became clear in the case-study evidence that in building highly integrated solutions – complex packages of products and services – ElectroCorp had to increasingly use external partners. This necessitated a re-thinking of what core competencies were (Chief Knowledge Officer, interview, November 2001; Head of Corporate Strategy (Cooperation Strategies and M&A Integration), interview, January 2002; Vice President and Communications Solutions CEO, interview, November 2001). The project manager of the Business Excellence Program at ElectroCorp Healthcare succinctly summarized this re-thinking of core competencies as follows:

> Our definition of core competencies shifted from an emphasis on product excellence to one on process excellence. If, five years ago, you had asked me what our core competencies were, I'd have said 'building the world's best medical electronics'. Today, we have moved beyond this narrow definition of core competencies ... We don't have to do everything ourselves. We form partnerships with other firms to deliver integrated solutions. This means that we now see ourselves as the world's best integrator of the world's best products – even if we don't build all of these products ourselves ... (Head of Business Excellence Program, Healthcare, interview, December 2001)

A final point emphasized in the case-study evidence was that in building the intelligent enterprise, it was not enough to look for attractive partners, but it was also necessary to position ElectroCorp itself as an attractive partner for other companies looking for strategic partners (Head of Business Excellence Program, interview, November 2001). Three resources that made ElectroCorp a particularly attractive partner were emphasized in the case study: a strong brand name, a thoroughly developed business content and last, but not least, a global human network.

- The brand name, ElectroCorp, its history and tradition, its power of innovation and technology was considered the most important resource in building the intelligent enterprise.
- Another resource was ElectroCorp's global business content – the trans-actions and contacts with ElectroCorp's partners, suppliers, and par-ticularly with customers. ElectroCorp was active in more than 190 countries, and was continually founding businesses abroad and had an increasing number of global headquarters outside Germany. These contacts and transactions represented millions of internal and external transactions that made ElectroCorp an attractive partner in building the intelligent enterprise.
- A third resource was ElectroCorp's global human network. The 450 000+ employees globally were described as a tremendous asset in terms of the relationships that these people built with suppliers, customers, partners, governments and institutions.

Step Three: Realizing Imaginative Strategies

The third step in the strategy-making matrix involves keeping in touch with the strategy as it begins to interact with the business environment in all its permutations. Twinned with the thrust of creative imagination, we start to see activities such as: introducing multidimensional performance goals; drafting unique selling propositions; and creating new market space.

Introducing multidimensional performance goals

In order to introduce multidimensional performance objectives, ElectroCorp developed a 'Business Driver Scorecard' as part of the Business Excellence Program. The Business Driver Scorecard was often compared to a pilot's instrument panel, which showed whether the business was on course by reflecting all key operating data, including tangible and intangible resources (direct observation, employee forum, November, 2001). To illustrate: pilots carefully monitor their cockpit instruments and can make appropriate correc-tions the moment they notice they are off course. It was argued that company managers have a similarly complex task in keeping their day-to-day business firmly oriented on an overall strategy (Head of Business Excellence Program, interview, November 2001). To help simplify this task, Business Driver Scorecards were introduced in all ElectroCorp divisions. These scorecards provided a continuous, up-to-date overview of current operations, allowing management to steer business developments and quickly spot when a business started 'veering off-track' so that corrective action could be taken (Head of Business Excellence Program, interview, November 2001).

Multidimensional performance objectives were introduced at ElectroCorp by tailoring the individual Business Driver Scorecards to match a specific business and contained targets for individual functions and processes with a view to increasing the value of the company by focusing on tangible, as well as intangible assets (participant observation, workshop, June 2000; Head of Business Excellence Program, interview, November 2001). The CEO made the strategic significance of introducing multidimensional performance objectives very clear: 'Just as important in ensuring solid performance is the development and vigorous implementation of so-called balanced scorecards. This tool is used to enable management to monitor and steer – on a monthly or quarterly basis – the key business parameters needed for success' (CEO, speech, February 2000).

The Business Driver Scorecards of the Business Excellence Program were intended as an aid to ensure that day-to-day business could be controlled and measured holistically. ElectroCorp appreciated that this could only be done if the business unit knew where it stood at any given point in time, and not just at the end of the fiscal year (Head of Business Excellence Program, interview, November 2001). The Business Driver Scorecard offered a comprehensive overview of correlated business data as well as how these data were derived. In particular, it contained financial as well as non-financial measures (such as delivery times and employee motivation). Business Driver Scorecards were derived for each business unit individually, based on the business unit's strategy, but within the broad corporate framework so as to ensure compatibility with other units (Head of Business Excellence Program, interview, November 2001). The Business Driver Scorecard introduced multidimensional performance goals by focusing on four key perspectives:

- employees/innovation (employee motivation, employee turnover, percentage of new to established products, and R&D cycle time – measured until launch of prototype)
- customers/market (sales share of new products, customer satisfaction, quality index and sales share of emerging regions)
- internal processes (delivery dependability, delivery capability, yield; and down time)

- finance (orders received, economic value-added achieved and cash flow).

Operationalization of the above key perspectives can be illustrated by reference to Communications Solutions Networks. Communications Solutions Networks was the largest ElectroCorp division, and focused on wireline telephony; it introduced scorecards in all of its subdivisions and sales units. Introducing multidimensional performance objectives at this division comprised three steps. Since the scorecards comprised business drivers and related measures derived directly from the strategy, the initial phase focused on strategy development. The aim here was for management to reach a consensus on strategic targets and on the specific business drivers, which must be influenced to reach these targets. In the second phase, business drivers were identified and the appropriate performance measures were defined. These so-called key performance indicators were worked out by four teams corresponding to the four scorecard perspectives: employee/innovation, customer/market, internal processes and finances. At the conclusion of the second phase, the business drivers and performance measures developed by the teams were approved at a management workshop comprising all members of management. In the third phase, performance measures were linked to target figures and the means for realizing the scorecards were decided upon. The project concluded with approval of the scorecard in an additional management workshop (Head of Business Excellence Program, interview, November 2001). An interesting observation was that in the development workshops, a very helpful factor was the transparent, comprehensible, and rigorous development method, which was based on the Business Excellence methodology. Interviewees noted that the development workshops were characterized by a dose of pragmatism: rather than searching for a 100 per cent solution, this methodology focused on rapid conceptualization of the scorecard. The motto was 'keep it simple – and have fun' (Head of Business Excellence Program, interview, November 2001).

The Energy Solutions unit at ElectroCorp underwent a similar experience. This unit began introducing balanced scorecards in September 1998. The scorecards were introduced in a top-down approach, that is, proceeding from the group level to the divisions, subdivisions and segments. Internal consultants were available to support the various scorecard teams during the project. As with the example of Communications Solutions Networks, introduction of multidimensional performance objectives in this unit emphasized the need for pragmatism. To illustrate, with the help of standard tools (MS Excel, MS PowerPoint), the scorecards made a quick and convincing debut. In the medium term, it was necessary to integrate the scorecards into the existing IT infrastructure to ensure their acceptance as a core management tool (Head of Business Excellence Program, interview, November 2001).

It should also be emphasized that, with regard to the financial perspective, ElectroCorp attempted to make performance of the individual units as transparent and comparable across the units as possible. Transparency to ElectroCorp meant making both results and lack of results clearly visible. Particularly through the corporate-wide introduction of economic value-added, ElectroCorp established a uniform standard against which it consistently gauged performance throughout the company. In addition to a uniform measurement system, ElectroCorp emphasized the need for agreement on goals (*ElectroCorp Today*, vol 2, 2000). Furthermore, the case-study evidence showed that agreement on goals needed to be quantified, and to be related to the broader business goals of the respective departments. In the words of the CEO:

> All of our businesses have a single performance yardstick: economic value-added. Together with each group, we set specific business targets for the year. In quarterly performance reviews attended by all group board members, we check to see if there are deviations from these targets, and if necessary, determine what corrective measures are necessary. In addition, these quarterly reviews provide a far better understanding of company-wide concerns and issues. They enable us to identify synergies and implement the most effective ways to exploit them. (CEO, speech, February 2000)

Drafting unique selling propositions

The case-study evidence demonstrated that the most important strategic goal of ElectroCorp was to generate value for its customers better than anybody else could:

> I emphasize customer utility for one simple reason: the only justification for the existence of a company and its employees is that our customers need us and that we can serve their needs better and more efficiently than the competition can. That's why it is important for us to find out how the kind of products and solutions we offer can improve the products and processes of our customers – and thereby help them to make more money. Our prime goal has to be to maximize customer utility. (Member of the Corporate Executive Committee, interview in *ElectroCorp Today*, January 1999)

The Business Excellence Program brought a very interesting point to light: drafting unique selling propositions must not be based on cost alone. For example, a common theme in the Communications Solutions division was that the focus on turnover, rather than earnings before income tax as a basis for allocating benefits to the sales representatives, led them to close complicated deals that competitors would not want to do because they were not profitable enough (Head of Competitive Intelligence, CS Networks Sales, interview, November 2001). That this had to change was made very clear by the CEO:

[There is one] factor that has angered me for some time: the quality of the orders we take in. Sometimes I get the impression that some of our sales people still take pride in showing off their skills by acquiring especially complex and difficult contracts – orders which our competitors wouldn't want, or, at least, not under such conditions – simply because they would regard the risk of losing money on the deal as being too high ... (CEO, speech, June 2001)

So the question for ElectroCorp was: how can we draft unique selling propositions while making sure that the deals we close are profitable? ElectroCorp Healthcare developed an enlightening approach for drafting unique selling propositions in a way that was profitable for ElectroCorp and the customer:

Integrating customers into the innovation process was key at ElectroCorp Healthcare ... We used a co-joint analysis approach to get a deeper understanding of the wants and needs of our customers. This was done by forcing our customers to make trade-off decisions between various options. We would tell them, 'listen, if you want this product feature, how much are you prepared to pay for it?' or 'if you are not prepared to pay extra for it, which other feature of the product would you rather not have?' In this way, we literally forced them to make decisions based on whether a particular feature is (a) a must, (b) nice to have, or (c) not necessary. This process helped us to considerably streamline our portfolio and to create greater value for the customer ... (Head of Business Excellence Program, Healthcare, interview, December 2001)

As the above quote illustrates, developing a deep understanding of what the customer really wants was key to drafting unique selling propositions. In particular, the case-study evidence showed that incremental improvements of a given product design can lead to 'over-engineering' of a product (Head of Competitive Intelligence, CS Networks Sales, interview, November 2001; Former Head of CS Networks Sales (retired), interview, December 2001). A senior development manager from the mobile phones division explained:

Consumers are simply tired of all those new technological gadgets ... Often, they simply don't want to be part of the next technology cycle. After all, we all use our mobile phones to phone somebody ... perhaps for one or two other functions as well, but that's it ... Where do we go with mobile phones? We certainly can't make them any smaller – we could, but nobody would be able to use them anymore ... (Key Account Manager, interview, November 2001)

It furthermore became evident that ElectroCorp was using an emotional appeal in creating value for the customer in their consumer goods divisions. However, in the industrial goods divisions, a more functional appeal prevailed.

A telling example of using an *emotional*, rather than functional, appeal to generate customer value was found in the mobile phone segment of the

ElectroCorp corporation. In this segment, a new communications strategy was started that aimed at giving the ElectroCorp brand a more emotional appeal. This was deemed necessary, because market analyses and surveys had shown that the ElectroCorp brand was traditionally associated with a conservative electrical engineering company. It was further found that although the company was often recognized as being quality-conscious, reliable and innovative, many customers tended to perceive ElectroCorp as unapproachable and generally not customer-oriented (*ElectroCorp Today*, vol 4, 2001). To remedy these inadequacies, a campaign was launched to make ElectroCorp's positive features more visible through associating the company with specific adjectives, such as innovative, flexible, far-sighted, inquisitive, human, competent and global. The key in this campaign was to associate ElectroCorp with a more emotional appeal. ElectroCorp believed that a more emotional appeal, introduced for example through certain attractive images (such as a man blowing bubbles) and the choice of certain words (such as the slogan 'spread the love') would help position the ElectroCorp brand favorably among its younger customers. This was a major shift from the traditionally functional appeal of the company that was famous for its sophistication in telecommunications and electronics (*ElectroCorp Today*, vol 4, 2001; Key Account Manager, interview, November 2001).

A telling example of a functional, rather than an emotional, appeal was found in the Automotive and Rail Division. Here, ElectroCorp experienced a general change in customer offerings. Instead of simply offering highly capable manufactured goods, ElectroCorp and other firms are purveying a variety of value-added services to customers. Products themselves become part of 'total solutions' that include services that meet a customer need (External consultant, interview, May 2001). A senior manager in the Automotive and Rail business unit commented as follows:

> Providing customer value in the Automotive and Rail business involves two aspects. First, customers want to transfer some of the risk to you, and you have to be prepared to take it on. This means you give the customer something he can calculate with ... he knows 'I can rely on ElectroCorp to keep the system running, and it will cost me this and that amount of money, and not more'. Second, we are talking about economies of scale and scope. Since we are pooling maintenance activities, we can do them cheaper than the customer. Quite simply this means it makes sense for the customer to outsource them to us. This also means the customer will need less human resources, which leads to further cost reductions. In the aftermath of the global privatization and deregulation of the national railway systems, many of our customers realized that they no longer need to do everything themselves in order to keep their systems running ... The market changed from one of highly vertically integrated, state-owned enterprises to one of small, privatized, nimble players, who wanted to share at least some of their risks with their suppliers ... (Head of Service Management, Automotive and Rail, interview, December 2001)

Finally, as part of the Portfolio Optimization Program, the Center for E-Excellence was founded in order to turn ElectroCorp into an 'E-Company'. An important focus of this center of competence was to customize the experiences of buyers. As one manager put it, the ability to customize the experience of a customer by using the Internet, has given a new dimension to the established idea that 'the customer is always right'. The Internet offered unprecedented scrutiny by the customer in the form of online auctions and virtual market-places, where customers could compare ElectroCorp products with those of competitors. The availability of alternative products and services through the Internet meant that the customer no longer tolerated poor service, uncompetitive pricing, or services that were difficult to use. It was argued that tapping into this scrutiny would enable ElectroCorp to monitor the degree of customer satisfaction constantly. More importantly, it would help the company understand to what degree its knowledge about the customer is an authentic reflection of what the customer desires. This would eventually help ElectroCorp in further gearing customer experience towards what the customer desired.

Creating new market space

ElectroCorp had a long track record of creating new market space. In 2001, the final year of the field study, the company invested 5.6 billion Euros in research and development, investigating new opportunities in the market. About 57 000 employees saw to it that leading-edge technology was built into ElectroCorp's products. In addition to this, ElectroCorp researchers produced 8200 inventions in the fiscal year 2000. This equaled an average of 33 per day, and represented an increase of 10 per cent compared to 1999, and produced an output of 5280 new patent applications internationally. The field study furthermore revealed that ElectroCorp was in a top position in terms of expenditures on research and development among the top ten electrical and electronics companies: competitors spent between 1.7 billion and 5.6 billion Euros on research and development (Corporate Technology Officer, interview, December 2001). The focus on creating new market space was underscored in statements such as 'innovations are our lifeblood', which was a recurrent theme in various media investigated in the field study (for example, direct observation, employee forum, October 2001; Head of Knowledge Management CS Networks Sales, interview, November 2001; participant observation, workshop, June 2000; Member of Corporate Executive Committee, interview in *ElectroCorp Today*, January 2000). Indeed, the idea of creating new market space could be traced back to the company's origins more than 150 years ago:

> Our company's 150-year history began with pioneering innovations in electrical engineering. Innovation is today – and always will be – our strongest competitive advantage. ElectroCorp must be synonymous with innovation. Our goal is to offer

customers the finest technologies and most attractive products as quickly as possible, and at the most competitive prices. (CEO, speech, December 1997)

Thus, creation of new market space had traditionally been a major concern
for ElectroCorp and continued to play a key role at the time of the field study.
The central importance of creating new market space within the three key
projects investigated (the Business Excellence Program, specifically) was
illustrated by the CEO:

> We are expanding into strategically critical, high-growth sectors. Our internal inno-
> vation management is oriented towards this goal, and is a central part of our
> Business Excellence Program. In addition, we are critically analyzing all of our
> businesses to see where we can use existing know-how to penetrate and cover new
> market segments … (CEO, speech, December 2000)

A similar, if less vocal, emphasis could be found in the Portfolio
Optimization Program (direct observation, conference, 2000). CS2003 had
less of an emphasis on creating new market space, possibly because the focus
of CS2003 was on cost-cutting in the first instance, and stimulating growth
through creating new market space did not feature as strongly at the time of
the field study (Head of Business Excellence Program, interview, November
2001). By contrast, the Business Excellence Program put a stronger emphasis
on the coincidence of cost-cutting and creating new market space:

> [The] Business Excellence Program … contains elements of process optimization,
> quality management, and asset management. The original top idea was born from
> Kaizen and Total Quality principles … that's cost-cutting, of course. However,
> Business Excellence also puts a strong emphasis on innovation and sales stimula-
> tion … Sales stimulation seeks to find new markets for existing products, whereas
> innovation seeks to tackle new markets with new products, or seeks to position new
> products in existing markets. Both approaches focus on growth by identifying
> 'white spots' in the market. (Head of Business Excellence Program, interview,
> November 2001)

As the above quote illustrates, the Business Excellence Program put a
deliberate emphasis on the complementary nature of cost-cutting and creating
new market space, as evidenced by the Business Excellence modules 'cost
effectiveness', 'asset management', on the one hand, and 'sales stimulation
and innovation' on the other hand (*ElectroCorp Today*, vol 3, 2001; Head of
Business Excellence Program, interview, November 2001). Various media in
the case-study evidence consistently showed that cost-cutting measures and
productivity gains provide only short-term relief and are in themselves insufficient (for example, CEO, speech, February 2001; Corporate Knowledge
Management Business Excellence Program Manager, interview, November

2001; direct observation, employee forum, October 2001). It was interesting
to note that a significant consensus prevailed among the empirical data
sources as to the doubtful benefits of re-structuring programs in other
companies. It was frequently heard that a preoccupation with re-structuring
would prove fruitless if companies focused merely on the cost factor, at the
expense of focusing on sales stimulation and innovation. In this context, the
CEO emphasized: 'Boosting sales means growth, which is crucial for safe-
guarding the future as the essential complement to cost cutting. If we simply
reduce costs without growing at the same time, we will shrink.' (CEO,
speech, July 2001)

In this context, it must be appreciated that even in a period of general
economic downturn, ElectroCorp put a deliberate emphasis on creating new
market space by introducing a new innovation initiative, called 'Visions of
Tomorrow'. This strategy for 'inventing the future' (Corporate Technology
Officer, interview, December 2001) was initiated by the board and executed by
the corporate research and development department. *Visions of Tomorrow*
were detailed studies presenting ElectroCorp's technological visions for five
key corporate areas: Communications Solutions, Automation, Power,
Automotive and Rail, and Healthcare. These studies were intended to obtain
information on emerging technologies, their market potential, and new business areas that could lead to new market space (Corporate Technology Officer,
interview, December 2001; Head of Business Excellence Program, interview,
November 2001; Vice President Corporate Technology Strategic Marketing,
interview, November 2001).

The Visions of Tomorrow initiative was the result of the corporate research
and development department working with the operating groups for several
years to develop a methodology for creating new market space. This methodology involved two opposing perspectives, each of which reinforced, and at
the same time questioned, the other: extrapolation (from the present to the
future) and retropolation (from the future to the present).

Extrapolation started with the current business definition at business level
and at corporate level and centered on projecting current trends into the
future. The trends investigated emanated from three key areas: products,
technologies and customer requirements (*Visions of Tomorrow*, October
2001; Corporate Technology Officer, interview, December 2001).
Extrapolation could best be described as road-mapping, projecting the technologies and products of today into the future. The aim here was to anticipate, as precisely as possible, the point in time at which certain products and
services would become possible, or when a market need for them would
have arisen. It was frequently emphasized that it is essential to extrapolate
using the customer's perspective:

[An] important aspect of creating new markets is to start with people, not with technology. Often you find engineers coming up with sophisticated approaches that do not address concrete customer needs ... In creating new markets, it is much more important to focus on human beings, their ways of doing things, their habits, desires, and problems ... (Vice President Corporate Technology Strategic Marketing, interview, November 2001)

The advantage of extrapolation – an objective starting position – was also considered its biggest weakness, since the method failed to predict discontinuities and great leaps forward in the development process. Figuratively speaking, while:

road-mapping will take you on a journey along a well-built road, you won't see much of what's happening beyond the roadside. And you can never be sure the road isn't about to end suddenly, in which case it would have been better to turn off miles before ... (Corporate Technology Officer, interview, November, 2001)

Retropolation attempted to compensate for the weakness in extrapolating, and was designed as the complement to extrapolation. Using the logic of scenario planning, retropolation involved placing oneself imaginatively some ten, 20 or even 30 years into the future. The timescale depended on the area of activity under investigation. For example, it could be easier to make predictions about the nature of power generation and distribution in 30 years than it would be to make equally reasonable statements concerning information and communications technology (*Visions of Tomorrow*, October 2001; Corporate Technology Officer, interview, December 2001). Once a relevant time frame had been selected for retropolating trends, a comprehensive scenario could be devised, incorporating relevant factors such as the future development of social and political structures, environmental considerations, globalization, technological trends and customer requirements. The trick in retropolating was to backtrack to the present from the 'known' facts of the future scenario. In this way, by combining extrapolation and retropolation, it was possible to identify the kinds of challenges and opportunities that had to be taken into account when creating new market space (Corporate Technology Officer, interview, December 2001; Vice President Corporate Technology Strategic Marketing, interview, November 2001). For example:

At Communication Solutions Networks, we look into other industries. We ask ourselves: what can we do in the media industry, in entertainment, and how do these opportunities interact with our own product and competence portfolio, as it appears today? These are really good approaches, because they help us to mirror what is going on in the market ... (Vice President and Communications Solutions CEO, interview, November 2001)

CHALLENGING IMAGINATION IN STRATEGY MAKING AT ELECTROCORP

The third and final 'thrust' in the strategy-making matrix, challenging imagination, can be formulated as the mind's negation of what it has described or created in the previous two thrusts. Challenging imagination contradicts, deconstructs, defames and destroys.

Step One: Envisaging Imaginative Strategies

Ensuring coherence
The literature-based theoretical framework laid out in Chapter 2 emphasized that tending to two areas of corporate involvement can ensure coherence: the internal and the external arenas. The case-study evidence demonstrated that, externally, ElectroCorp's most important commitment was to concentrate on a focused growth in the electrical and electronics industry. The case-study evidence further demonstrated that the most important commitment of all in ensuring coherence internally was knowledge management and collaboration between the different business units.

The evidence regarding how ElectroCorp ensured coherence in the external arena, that is, with the corporate environment, is discussed first. Various sources in the case study pointed to the importance of ensuring coherence with the corporate environment. In particular, it was emphasized that ElectroCorp would first not diversify into unrelated fields and would, second, not split up into 'various parts', that is, give up the corporate, conglomerate form (CEO, speech, February 1999; Member of Corporate Executive Committee, interview in *ElectroCorp Today*, June 2001). This emphasis was particularly evident in the Business Excellence Program and in the Portfolio Optimization Program. In the words of the CEO:

> We will continue to cover more than just one field in the huge electrical and electronics growth market … ElectroCorp has comprehensive expertise across a wide variety of business segments. With our global presence, the know-how of excellent employees throughout the world, and the outstanding reputation of ElectroCorp, we can focus and consolidate our strengths to the benefit of our customers. Within our business segments we intend to focus on those fields in which we, as a global player, have a realistic chance of gaining and keeping a leading market position … (CEO, speech, February 1998)

The message that ElectroCorp would remain an electrical engineering and electronics company was found in various media in the case-study evidence (for example, Head of Corporate Development, interview, September 2001; CEO, speech, February 1999; Member of Corporate Executive Committee, interview in *ElectroCorp Today*, June 2001). In these media, it was empha-sized that ElectroCorp would continue to focus its activities on a manageable number of business segments in which the company could maintain or achieve a strong competitive position (CEO, speech, February 1999). Factors often mentioned in interviews and archival documents that would aid in these efforts were the breadth of technological know-how, the company's knowledge of customer needs established over the 150 years of its existence, and its global presence (Head of Corporate Development, interview, September 2001; Head of Knowledge Management CS Networks Sales, interview, November 2001; CEO, speech, February 2001). On occasion of an annual shareholders' meet-ing, the CEO emphasized:

> One thing is for certain: ElectroCorp will remain in its core business of electrical engineering and electronics and will not diversify into non-related fields. Recently, we have been hearing suggestions ... that ElectroCorp should split up into various parts. The reasoning is that such a move would increase the value of the company. We are not convinced by the argument. It ignores the fact that we draw our strength from our internal synergies ... We consequently use all the synergies offered by our broad spectrum of competencies. This is especially true of ... microelectronics. Microelectronics is a cross-industry technology in which we enjoy a world-class position and which is indispensable for each of our operating units ... (CEO, speech, February 1998)

The idea of an 'ElectroCorp fit' of new business opportunities seems to underlie the CEO's reasoning above. This notion of 'ElectroCorp fit', or the expected synergy-potential of business opportunities, was emphasized in an interview with the head of Strategic Marketing in the Corporate Technology department; further insight into the CEO's focus on internal synergies can be gained from the following excerpt from an interview:

> We have a three-step approach to assessing the viability of tackling a new market opportunity. Creating new markets is first and foremost about establishing the potential market's attractiveness. The question here is: what are the likely competi-tors to emerge in the market? and not the question: what are the existing competi-tors in this market? Another question is: does this market align with ElectroCorp's business? Call it 'ascertaining the *ElectroCorp fit*', if you wish. This question is even more difficult ... criteria include: do we have an established set of customers whom we can leverage to the new market? what are likely entry barriers to this market if we do not have easy access, for example through established distribution channels that we could leverage for the new product or service? The third question is: what are the lead times to generating a positive cash-flow in this market ...? A difficult question this one, and one that cannot be given a general answer to ... In concrete terms, we are looking at earnings before income tax to sales of a minimum of 10 per cent for the new market opportunity to be viable. (CEO, interview, November 2001)

Whereas the focus of ElectroCorp in the external arena was on synergy potential of business opportunities and the ElectroCorp fit, the focus in the internal arena of ensuring coherence was on account management. The case-study evidence demonstrated that the most important aspect of ensuring coherence in a diversified company such as ElectroCorp was account management as a means to overcome the challenges of cross-group collaboration in the delivery of integrated solutions to large customers (*ElectroCorp Today*, vol 4, 2001; Member of Corporate Executive Committee, interview in *ElectroCorp Today*, June 2001; Head of Competitive Intelligence, CS Network Sales, interview, November 2001). Account management was a pointer that was explicitly mentioned in the Business Excellence Program, and a member of the corporate board was specifically assigned to further the company's account management approach. This person described the rationale of account management as follows:

> Customers want complete solutions from a single source. However, our internal setup is often rather confusing to them. After all, it is of no consequence to them whether three or ten of our divisions are involved in the creation of their solution … (Member of Corporate Executive Committee, interview in *ElectroCorp Today*, June 2001)

In order to ensure coherence internally, the ElectroCorp corporation established an integrated account management program under the auspices of the Business Excellence Program. This approach to account management ensured that customers had a 'single point of entry' to the highly diversified ElectroCorp corporation. For example, in the Automation division, sales staff from various groups collaborated to set up cross-divisional account teams. One such team existed for every one of the Automation group's strategically important customers. These teams worked to develop customer relationships according to specific targets. What gave this approach the competitive edge over conventional customer care was that it enabled ElectroCorp to present a cogent and coordinated image across all the relevant groups. In one instance, this factor led a customer in the pharmaceutical industry to award ElectroCorp a contract even though it had initially decided to opt for a competitor (Head of Business Excellence Program, interview, November 2001; *ElectroCorp Today*, vol 3, 2001). In this context, an external consultant observed in an interview:

> ElectroCorp is … a highly diverse organization that participates in a wide variety of businesses. The company has certainly been called a conglomerate in its history. For decades, scholars of business and organizations have deliberated over how such collections of relatively independent businesses can get synergies or increased value through collaboration. How can the whole be made greater than the sum of the parts? Firms hesitate to ask individual business units to help each other for fear that

they will sub-optimize their own performance. But knowledge management offers a potential solution to this dilemma. If knowledge can be shared easily across business units, then one ElectroCorp business unit can take advantage of the learning and expertise from another ... (External consultant, interview, May 2000)

The external consultant, as well as others interviewed for the case study, demonstrated that ElectroCorp's approach to knowledge management was also unusual for the diversity of initiatives and applications that are underway within the company (Chief Knowledge Officer, interview, November 2001; Corporate Knowledge Management Business Excellence Program Manager, interview, November 2001; participant observation, workshop, June 2000). The external consultant recalled:

> Most firms that I have observed focus almost all of their efforts on one major initiative – most commonly a knowledge repository. At ElectroCorp, however, the variety of initiatives and applications ... is much greater. There are also a wide variety of knowledge content domains being addressed within the firm, including best practices, customer knowledge, competitive intelligence, product knowledge, financial knowledge, and so forth. The breadth of approaches and tools being employed across ElectroCorp is a good fit to the diversity and complexity of the organization itself ... (External consultant, interview, May 2000)

Thus, the ElectroCorp approach to ensuring coherence internally centered on managing the flow of knowledge between the individual units within ElectroCorp. In the same interview, the external consultant went on to note that while ElectroCorp had been an organization known in the past for its strong hierarchy, its approach to knowledge management was not hierarchical at all. Instead, the approach was relatively grass roots and bottom up:

> After ... business units began to develop knowledge initiatives, they looked around and noticed that others were doing the same thing. After a period of informal communication, the employees and managers, who were managing knowledge around the firm, began to form a semi-official community of practice themselves. Ultimately they began to feel that they needed a corporate group to facilitate the firm's broad efforts, and they were successful in convincing senior executives to create the function. The Corporate Knowledge Management function is still a small organization. Most of the knowledge management efforts are taking place in the business units, but the corporate group plays a valuable coordinating role ... (External consultant, interview, May 2000)

An interesting observation was that ensuring coherence in the internal arena not only meant developing synergies between the individual business units through knowledge management, but also developing synergies between the individual knowledge management initiatives themselves:

[A] tension in ElectroCorp will be between knowledge initiatives that support the entire firm, versus those that advance a particular business unit or even a smaller group within it. Firm-wide initiatives help to exploit the scale of ElectroCorp ... More specialized, focused initiatives will be more easily measured, and may be better supported by managers who are responsible for a unit's financial performance ... this is a creative tension that will play out over time. Thus far I believe ElectroCorp managers have handled it well – far better than most of the large, multi-business firms I have encountered ... (External consultant, interview, May 2000)

Defying old paradigms

ElectroCorp had long understood the importance of defying old paradigms. The company exhibited a variety of approaches by which old paradigms were defied, old ways of 'doing things around here' were challenged and path-dependent behavioral patterns were questioned (Head of Corporate Development, interview, September 2001). In the Business Excellence Program, there was a clear emphasis on the importance of defying old paradigms. The head of Corporate Strategic Marketing emphasized the importance of challenging ElectroCorp's core competencies as an integral part of the Business Excellence Program: 'Innovation does not come from squeezing the last drop of juice from core competencies ... Indeed, we often need to pro-actively 'cannibalize' what we considered our core competencies in the past' (Vice President Corporate Technology Strategic Marketing, interview, November 2001).

In addition to the Business Excellence Program, the case-study evidence in the Portfolio Optimization Program and CS2003 also emphasized the need for defying old paradigms. This need was seen as a function of the past successes achieved by using a specific paradigm, such as the telex technology. Put differently, the more successful ElectroCorp became in exploiting a specific technology such as telexes, the more important the need was to defy this very paradigm at the time when it was most successful. Various media throughout the case-study evidence supported this paradox of challenging 'ways of doing things around here' before, rather than after, the value of established practices depreciated (Former Head of CS Networks Sales (retired), interview, December 2001; *ElectroCorp Today*, vol 3, 2001; direct observation, employee forum, November 2001). Indeed, it was discovered that past successes could lead to:

systematic biases against innovation ... Particularly if a new technology competes with an old one, reactions and biases against the new technology can kill its commercial potential immediately. The fax machine is a good example. Since the telex technology provided excellent profits that could be cannibalized by the fax technology, the inventor of the fax technology sold the fax to the Japanese. The rest is history ... (Former Head of CS Networks Sales (retired), interview, December 2001)

One interviewee revealed a very interesting underlying reason why ElectroCorp employees of German nationality particularly find defying old paradigms difficult:

> A deterring factor ... is the German tertiary education system ... After we leave school, and even in school, we are turned into specialists who no longer look left or right. Japan is another example of this approach ... This [approach] can be very effective when efficiency is the name of the game. The Japanese taught us a lesson in the 1980s from which we have yet to recover. The problem is that the super-efficient company is not necessarily the most innovative company. Squeezing another drop of juice from our core competencies doesn't do the trick in hyper-competitive environments in which our competitors are squeezing just as hard as we are. 'Me too' is a killer here ... (Vice President Corporate Technology Strategic Marketing, interview, November 2001)

Another problem that necessitated defying old paradigms was termed the 'functionality trap', the result of ever-increasing levels of functionality in a product or service as a result of incremental innovation:

> The problem with established products is that innovating them tends to be incremental. Today, our PWX 300 telephones have some 4000 functions ... One question is if the customer actually needs or utilizes all these functions. Another question is whether this kind of functionality is replicable in a different technology. With Voice over Internet Protocol technology,[12] it certainly isn't replicable yet ... It's very difficult to fall into this 'functionality trap' of ever increasing the performance of an existing product without asking if this is appropriate given customer needs and market and technology trends. (Former Head of CS Networks Sales (retired), interview, December 2001)

Given the deeply ingrained nature of 'ways of doing things around here', often radical approaches to defying old paradigms were necessary. CS2003, but also the Business Excellence Program, and the Portfolio Optimization Program, made use of defying old paradigms as a 'shock therapy'. This was particularly evident in the new approach to portfolio management, which no longer supported cross-subsidies between the individual business units. It was repeatedly emphasized, that 'no-one should feel safe in or comfortable in such divisions simply because the group as a whole is doing well. Let me emphasize once again, we will not support cross-subsidies' (CEO, speech, June 2001). At the 2001 annual business conference, the CEO went further:

> Word has gotten around that the term 'core business' has more or less been stricken from our vocabulary, because it can lead to divisions labeled core business, feeling safe and protected by their dictum: 'after all, we are one of the company's core businesses – nothing will happen to us, no matter what our results are like'. Absolutely wrong. No one enjoys such security at ElectroCorp. Those who fail to achieve their margin targets and sustain them are up for disposition. And we are not just playing with words here. We are serious ... (CEO, speech, June 2001)

While such 'shock therapies' approach to defying old paradigms were being encouraged, a more subtle approach was simultaneously being advocated in the case-study evidence. Interviewees sometimes favored a more softly-softly approach over the shock therapy, because sudden defiance of old paradigms, particularly where they referred to capabilities and skills that were considered core competencies, could lead to demotivation and frustration (Head of Business Excellence Program, interview, November 2001; direct observation, employee forum October 2001). The case-study evidence demonstrated that a balance was needed between challenging old ways of doing things in order for the company not to suffer from its depreciating intellectual capital, while doing this with a sense of appreciation and respect for the past achievements and successes of employees. A senior manager at corporate technology argued that defying old paradigms:

> ... is a highly sensitive process, and one that needs to be done extremely carefully. You can't simply tell your employees that their core competencies have turned into core incompetencies over night. After all, what you want is their buy-in, and shouting in their faces that they're incompetent does not help. Instead, in getting rid of counter-productive 'ways we do things around here', we need to show our colleagues quick wins, even if they are minutely small ... (Vice President Corporate Technology Strategic Marketing, interview, November 2001)

One way of defying old paradigms using a subtle, rather than shock, therapy was using a deliberate lack of prior industry knowledge. Lack of prior industry knowledge was seen as instrumental in order to 'not get locked into the industry paradigm' (direct observation, employee forum, November 2001; Former Head of CS Networks Sales (retired), interview, December 2001). In June 2002 the ElectroCorp Board replaced the CEO of its Communications Solutions Networks division with the executive who had up until then been working to turn around the Automotive and Rail unit. When challenged on the ground of his lack of prior industry knowledge in the telecommunications sector, the new CEO of Communications Solutions Networks replied: 'those who think that knowledge of the telecom industry is important here have not understood the situation at Communications Solutions Networks' (direct observation, employee forum, October 2001).

Fostering a culture of constructive dissent
Data collection on fostering a culture of constructive dissent was far more difficult than for any of the other imagination levers. Evidence was, perhaps unsurprisingly, virtually absent from the interview data. There was some, but unsystematic, evidence in the participant observation data (particularly participant observation, workshop, June 2000), and in direct observation data (for example direct observation, employee forum, October 2001). Overall,

however, no systematic evidence for fostering a culture of constructive dissent could be found in data sources other than those of historical or archival nature, and the account in this section concentrates mainly on transcripts of Annual Shareholders' Meetings and conferences.

An unusual illustration for fostering a culture of constructive dissent, which is worth citing, was found in the transcripts of the 1998 annual ElectroCorp International Conference. The fact that fostering a culture of constructive dissent made it possible for an organization to survive a good 150 years was made clear by an unusual guest speaker. A member of Germany's Andechs Monastery surprised ElectroCorp managers with a cryptic presentation on the rules of his order as a management tool that enabled the Benedictines to survive ten times as long as ElectroCorp. One of the main rules, according to the monk, is to 'stop grumbling'. This indicated that managers discussing things off the record was a waste of time, instead, the right way appeared to be to 'roll up your sleeves and tackle the problem' (*ElectroCorp Today*, vol 3, 1998).

In contrast to the Benedictine's insights, the CEO made it very clear in several Shareholder Meetings that ElectroCorp is in fact not a company inclined to nurture a culture of constructive dissent. He emphasized that at ElectroCorp, 'We must see common ground and not things that divide us. And there must also be a willingness to make compromises, and quick compromises at that' (CEO, speech, June 2001). Indeed, the case-study evidence pointed out that ElectroCorp's management culture involved the joint agreement of clear targets by employees and their superiors (direct observation, employee forum, November 2001; direct observation, employee forum, October 2001). The key was to enable employees across hierarchical levels to buy-in to strategy-making frameworks such as the Business Excellence Program, the Portfolio Optimization Program and CS2003. The result of this endeavor formed the basis for the so-called 'Employee Dialogue'. The Employee Dialogue comprised a series of discussions, on which employee promotion and demotion was based within ElectroCorp. The Business Excellence Program had specifically developed a method for arriving at an individual employee or manager's contribution to the achievement of the business targets. This method was the so-called 'Business Excellence Target Agreement Process'. It involved target agreements on three levels (CEO, speech, June 2001; direct observation, employee forum, November 2001):

- Vertical consistency of targets. Targets for individual employees were derived from the business targets. The sum of the individual targets was the overall target.
- Horizontal consistency of targets. Avoidance of competing or overlapping targets at the same hierarchical level.

- Rapid implementation of the target agreement process. Targets were agreed upon with all employees of a division, or sub-division, within approximately two months.

The key element of the Business Excellence Target Agreement Process was the target agreement cascade. This approach was characterized by a series of workshops, in which the business targets were broken down to arrive at targets for individual employees. The participation of three hierarchy levels (middle management, lower management and front-line employees) ensured the horizontal and vertical consistency of the targets. Personal development targets and (where not already agreed upon in the workshops) management and cooperation targets supplementary to the business targets, as well as written agreement of targets, were dealt with on an ongoing basis in the 'Employee Dialogue' discussions (Head of Business Excellence Program, interview, November 2001; Corporate Knowledge Management Business Excellence Program Manager, interview, November 2001).

Step Two: Conceiving Imaginative Strategies

Deconstructing value chains
ElectroCorp took special advantage of deconstructing value chains to establish new business opportunities through e-business applications. Despite the increasing disillusionment about e-business in other companies, ElectroCorp made a conscious effort to profit from the separation of the flow of physical goods from the flow of information goods. The following remark is worth relating in this regard:

> The 'E' has lost some of its appeal, because many of the companies that claimed to be 'e-companies' didn't have any substance ... The hype [surrounding e-business] is reminiscent of the fairy-tale 'The Emperor's new clothes'. It took people a while to realize that the emperor is actually naked ... (CEO, interview, June 2001)

In all three key projects investigated (Business Excellence Program, the Portfolio Optimization Program, and CS2003), the field study provided a case in point in illustrating the deconstruction of value chains. The deconstruction of the industry value chain, and the implications this had for ElectroCorp's value chain in the telecommunications unit, provides the most telling example. From the inception of the telephone service until the 1980s, telecommunication equipment customers around the world were mostly of one type: the monolithic, integrated telephone company. The entire set of activities involved in providing telephone service to the end user, that is, the entire value chain from the planning of the network to its operation to customer acquisition and care were concentrated in a single entity. With fully integrated customers, it was also natural for the supplier of the telecommunications equipment to be fully integrated. A single customer in a monopoly position would not naturally have found an advantage in integrating offerings from diverse suppliers, because even if there had been a cost advantage to be gained in such a practice, a monopoly was not naturally cost-sensitive (external consulting group publication, 1998; participant observation, workshop, June 2000; Head of Knowledge Management CS Networks Sales, interviews, February 2000 and November 2001).

Interviewees emphasized that this situation, however, had changed: in order to provide more competitive pricing and service to customers, governments had over the previous two decades been deregulating the telecommunications services market. In addition to the deregulation of markets, technological advances in electronics and computer science led to an explosion of new products and service offerings in the telecommunication services market (participant observation, workshop, June 2000; Former Head of Communications Solutions Networks Sales (b), interview, February 2000). This world-wide deregulation process of telecommunication had broad implications for the telecommunications value chain. The most important of these was that the formerly integrated, monolithic telephone companies of the past were becoming an anachronism. Where once it had been possible for a company to shift costs between services, for example by charging a high price for long distance calls that cost little to supply, and using the margins on this lucrative long-distance service to subsidize residential service, after deregulation competing long-distance service companies with no residential business to subsidize, could beat the incumbents on prices, and cost-shifting was no longer possible. Induced by the new competitive landscape in the telecommunications supplier business, many of the new entrants to the market were complex packages of services and products, rather than simply products (Former Head of Communications Solutions Networks Sales (b), interview, February 2000; Former Head of Communications Solutions Networks Sales (a), interview, February 2000; external consulting group publication, 1998). According to the CEO:

> Today's customers are a new breed. They very often demand integrated and innovative solutions from one source – everything from planning, financing, engineering, and components to construction, commissioning and operation. We have to provide this full spectrum, plus backing what we deliver with the best possible service … (CEO, speech, June 2000)

Thus, at the time when some elements of the telecommunications equipment value chain started to resemble commodities, which yielded significantly lower profit margins, the telecommunications solution selling business was becoming more important because of its higher value-added. This meant that the individual salesperson had to coordinate the many aspects of the telecommunications equipment offering, including financing, business analysis and network planning. Interviews emphasized that this could be time-consuming, difficult and complicated (Former Head of Communications Solutions Networks Sales (b), interview, February 2000; Former Head of Communications Solutions Networks Sales (a), interview, February 2000). This meant that the flows of physical products had to be separated from the flows of knowledge products in order to profit from deconstructing value chains (external consulting group publication, 1998; participant observation, workshop, June 2000).

Deconstruction of the value chain into its physical and electronic components was particularly evident in ElectroCorp's global business content, that is, the transactions and contacts with ElectroCorp's partners, suppliers and customers (Chief Knowledge Officer, interview, November 2001). These contacts and transactions represented trillions of internal and external transactions that were vital for successful e-business and new opportunities, and emphasized the need for competing on 'reach':

> In one of our Industry groups [in Communications Solutions Networks] ... customers can choose from among 50 000 products in a virtual mall. Overall, we expect to generate at least one-quarter of our business online in the near future. And our consumer business such as telephones or computers should very soon be well over 50 per cent ... (CEO, speech, June 2000)

The case-study evidence showed that in a broader sense the greater reach represented millions of contacts with suppliers and partners, and especially customers. Interviewees explained that during these contacts it was predominantly knowledge, that is, the non-physical component, that was being exchanged (Head of Knowledge Management CS Networks Sales, interview, November 2001; External Consultant, interview, May 2000). Leveraging these contacts by using the company's extensive experience of knowledge management therefore represented vast opportunities not only for cost savings, but also for further increasing revenue. According to the CEO, this meant:

> ... completely changing our internal processes. We are electronically networking everything from R&D, procurement and production to marketing, sales and services. Time and location are becoming irrelevant factors in the value chain. The driving factors here are speed, flexibility, responsiveness, reliability and quality ... (CEO, speech, June 2000)

The deconstruction of value chains also emphasized the importance of competing not only on 'reach' but also on 'rich' information, as illustrated by the following quote by the board member with special responsibility for e-business:

For the first time it is possible to deliver information that is both rich and comprehensive to a circle of addressees of unprecedented scope. For business conducted via the Internet, this means: transparency inexorably leads to unprecedented comparability among competitors and their offerings. Customer relations are likely to be less stable than in the future ... This is why we are developing radically new business models at ElectroCorp in order to make the entire corporation Internet-fit ... (Member of the Corporate Board (e-business), interview, December 2000)

The Portfolio Optimization Program specifically accentuated competition on both richness and reach. Indeed, one aspect was engineering the 'e-readiness' of the entire company. 'E-readiness' was an important part of the Portfolio Optimization Program, and 1 billion Euros were invested in this part of the Portfolio Optimization Program. Expected savings were between 1 and 2 per cent, equaling 1.5 billion Euros. ElectroCorp used an integrated, across-the-board approach in 'e-readiness', as described by the CEO: 'electronically networking the entire value chain and all of its processes – externally with our customers, suppliers, and partners, and internally with our employees' (CEO, speech, February 2001).

To master the challenges of deconstructing value chains, ElectroCorp established five elements as constituents of the 'e-readiness' initiative (Chief Knowledge Officer, interview, November 2001):

- First, e-knowledge management was set up to make the company's pool of knowledge available to all employees across all regions and businesses, in order to ensure that 'everyone at ElectroCorp knows what ElectroCorp knows' (CEO, speech, February 2001).
- The second element was e-procurement, which offered enormous potential for greater efficiency. ElectroCorp was aiming at handling 50 per cent of its 35 billion Euro annual purchasing volume via the Internet to gain additional savings.
- E-commerce was the third element of the 'e-readiness' plan. It envisaged handling 25 per cent of ElectroCorp's total business volume and 50 per cent of the company's consumer business online.
- The fourth element was the electronic networking of all of ElectroCorp's internal processes, or the so-called supply-chain management, which were being integrated and standardized to create a single, company-wide solution.
- Finally, 'e-readiness' envisaged marketing ElectroCorp expertise in e-business to external customers.

Results of deconstructing the value chain at ElectroCorp that were visible at the time the empirical study was conducted, included conducting 10 per cent of the overall buy-side volume (equaling 35 million Euros) online (CEO, interview, June 2001).

Co-opting customer competence
Co-opting customer competence, particularly by Internet-enabled means, was in an emerging state at ElectroCorp at the time of the field study. However, several initiatives were noticeable, particularly in the Business Excellence Program and Portfolio Optimization Program. The Portfolio Optimization Program, especially, emphasized ElectroCorp's transition to an 'e-company'. ElectroCorp's approaches to co-opted customer competence were centering around Internet-enabled means, such as direct dialoguing with the customer through online forums, customers directly posting urgent requests to ElectroCorp employees, online chat rooms for customers on the ElectroCorp home page, but also direct, face-to-face interaction with individual or corporate customers in the product development process (Member of the Corporate Board (e-business), interview, December 2000). ElectroCorp's commitment to co-opting customer competence was illustrated by the CEO:

> First and foremost is customer orientation. Any company worth its salt these days has written this one in stone ... It means closely involving customers in every phase of the development process ... This intense partnership with customers has another positive aspect. Companies with the most demanding, the most knowledgeable and the most creative customers will trounce the competition in the end ... (CEO, speech, June 2000)

As part of the Portfolio Optimization program, customers had been integrated into the development process and consulted on which product features they really required and what sort of prices they were willing to pay. The surprising insight emerging from this endeavor was that the benchmark values determined during the process were up to 50 per cent lower than standard market costs and prices. In one project at the Automation group, for example, specifically in the area of machine-tool control technology, a product had undergone constant upgrading, and increasing modification for specialist applications. The result was an over-priced and over-segmented product range. The approach taken to rectify the situation was to consult key customers, conduct analytical studies to define, jointly with the customer, the optimum features for successful machine-tool controls and the viable market price (Head of Business Excellence Program, interview, November 2001; CEO, speech, June 2001).

It was very interesting to see how ElectroCorp employees reacted to this unprecedented move to co-opt customer competence in order to obtain a clearer picture of the way in which ElectroCorp products were perceived. In a speech, the CEO remembered:

> The initial reaction to the identified requirements was 'impossible in Standort Deutschland'. Subsequently, a small, highly motivated team of developers was

removed from their normal working environments and hence from their skeptical colleagues. The team was successful and the new generation of ElectroCorp machine-tool controls was launched on the market, competitively priced and more efficient that the preceding generation ... (CEO, speech, June 2001)

In another example, ElectroCorp used co-opting customer competence as an integral part of the account management system. A case in point was ElectroCorp's interaction with a major corporate customer:

> [W]e sit down with our customer and determine what his future requirement will be, analysing business possibilities and developing an action plan. We meet with our ... counterparts twice a year to discuss the value creation chains – the central question being, of course, what ElectroCorp can do to optimize processes. This is because, obviously, we want to help [the customer] to do better business ... What our customers want today is a strategic partner for mutual benefit, and that is why our approach has been a win-win situation for everyone concerned ... (*ElectroCorp Today*, vol 4, 2001).

As the quote above illustrates, co-opting customer competence was extensively practiced through 'face-to-face' meetings with individual or corporate customers, in order to uncover areas where joint value creation was possible. E-business offered unprecedented opportunities for co-opting customer competence through engaging in direct and in-depth dialogue with the customer. For a company with a long history of providing customer satisfaction, a logical question was: how can new technologies, such as the Internet, be used to engage in active dialogue and knowledge sharing with new and established customers in order to provide better products and services to them?

In recognition of the central importance of e-business, ElectroCorp founded the Center for E-Excellence in May 2000. It provided the impetus for transforming existing business models, and creating new business through the Internet, and selling self-experience e-business solutions. The Center for E-Excellence provided corporate-level support for existing e-business services and guidelines, facilitated sharing of best e-practices, and the mobilization of innovative e-business ideas. In short, the Center for E-Excellence sought to enable the progression from traditional to electronic modes of operating within the company, in which co-opting customer competence was a key element (participant observation, workshop, June 2000; *ElectroCorp Today*, vol 1, 2001).

ElectroCorp's approach to co-opting customer competence was one of leveraging its expertise in knowledge management. Various media throughout the case-study evidence showed that traditional knowledge management centers on the intra-organizational context. In other words, it enables knowledge flows between employees. By contrast, co-opting customer competence broadens this perspective of knowledge management beyond the intra-organizational realm and also includes those outside the organization (Head of Knowledge Management CS Networks Sales, interview, November 2001; external consultant, interview, May 2000). As one knowledge manager commented:

> Traditional knowledge management systems tackle the problem of 'if only we knew what we know' – this has changed and turned into an 'if only we knew what our customers know'. (Head of Knowledge Management CS Networks Sales, interview, November 2001).

The key role of knowledge management in the process of co-opting the competence, the knowledge, and the skills of ElectroCorp's customers was illustrated by a quote from the head of the e-business transformation initiative at ElectroCorp:

> Growing alliances, networks and collaboration among organizations have in the past largely ignored the customer. The Internet has changed this. It has empowered customers to engage in dialogue and knowledge sharing with the company. The valuable experience gained through years of managing knowledge now helps us to design ElectroCorp's e-business model to engineer this knowledge sharing ... ElectroCorp has a firm understanding of and expertise in managing knowledge within corporate boundaries. The logical next step is to ... extend the management of knowledge to customers. This represents an exciting and challenging task, because the barriers to knowledge sharing and networking in the intra-organizational context are exacerbated once the organization broadens its horizon to include its customers. (E-commerce Manager, interview, 2000)

Several media in the case-study evidence demonstrated the potential contribution of co-opting customer competence to value creation. This was particularly evident in the Communications Solutions unit. Here, it had traditionally been the customer who formulated a demand that was then forwarded by the salesperson to the telecommunication supplier's ordering system. Then, in the solution-selling business, the salesperson himself often had to proactively present a business idea to customers, to help them develop innovative business strategies. This took the customer and the salesperson time, personal meetings, and negotiations before the objective of a project and some milestones could be defined. The challenge was that the customers often articulated their intentions and needs in broad terms only. Thus, the salesperson adopted the role of a business consultant, rather than a mere product seller. Effectively, what was traded between salesperson and customer was knowledge, and much of this knowledge could also be exchanged via the Internet. This would alleviate the time needed for personal interaction, which ultimately reduces costs for both ElectroCorp and its customers (participant observation, workshop June, 2000; Head of Competitive Intelligence, CS Network Sales, interview, November 2001).

Co-evolving with the knowledge landscape

The Business Excellence Program in itself represented a framework with the aim of enabling a company to co-evolve with the competitive landscape, rather than achieving a static 'fit' with a stable environment. Senior management realised that deregulation and globalization fundamentally changed the business landscape. Indeed, the case-study evidence showed that the Business Excellence Program was started as a response to the challenges posed. At the Shareholders' Meeting in February 2000, the CEO characterized ElectroCorp as:

> ... a living organism that must continually change and grow. In fact, change will always be one of the few constants in our company. We can sustain our success over the long term only – and that is the core point of all our portfolio measures – if we attain a leading competitive position in global markets for as many of our businesses as possible ... (CEO, speech, February 2000)

On the occasion of the celebration of ElectroCorp's 150th anniversary, the CEO noted: '[I]t is also clear that a company is not a permanent, immutable object, but a living, dynamic organism. How else can one reach the age of 150 and older?' (CEO, speech, February 1998).

Co-evolution with the knowledge landscape at ElectroCorp took the form of 'communities of practice'.[12] A the time of the field study, ElectroCorp was rated by an international commission as number three internationally and number one on a European level as far as co-evolution through communities of practice was concerned (External consultant report, 2002). Within ElectroCorp, communities of practice were perceived as an ideal way to overcome organizational and hierarchical boundaries, business processes and project-specific boundaries, as well as temporal, geographical, cultural and linguistic boundaries (Corporate Knowledge Management Business Excellence Program Manager, interview, November 2001). Communities of practice provided the company with benefits such as the creation and deepening of new knowledge, the ability to detect blind spots within the corporation, and the identification and usage of synergies. Moreover, they facilitated best practice sharing, swifter and more flexible reactions to changes in the corporate environment, the discovery of potential for improvement and innovations, as well as the standardization of terminologies and business processes.

The two observations above can be corroborated with an interview with ElectroCorp's Chief Knowledge Officer:

> Communities of practice exist in addition to the formal organizational structure. They cut across the structure, if you wish ... In many ways, communities of practice can be seen as the lubricant for the formal organizational structure ... communities of practice can be set up for a specific task at hand when the need arises, and

dissolve after the need is no longer there ... This is what makes communities of practice immensely powerful for staying flexible, while maintaining the formal organizational structure. (Chief Knowledge Officer, interview, November 2001)

Several initiatives, on both business unit and corporate level, were found that demonstrated ElectroCorp's approach to co-evolution with the knowledge landscape. The phenomenon of communities of practice started in 1998 with a request for central support by the previously informal 'Community of Practice Knowledge Management'. This, as the name implies, was a knowledge community concerned with exchanging knowledge management expertise. This community started life with 15 members. Over the years, ElectroCorp initiated various knowledge management activities and projects all over the world. People who had gained experience through these activities and met (more or less accidentally) began to exchange their experience and their knowledge. If a problem occurred, they would get in touch with one another. Informally, the members began telling one another stories about their successes or failures in the handling of knowledge until, finally, they formed the Community of Practice Knowledge Management (Head of Corporate Knowledge Strategy, interview, November 2001). After its inception in 1998, the community grew rapidly as a result of an ever-increasing interest in knowledge topics and the perception of the ElectroCorp staff and management of the enhanced importance of knowledge. Its size made its continued existence as a self-organized community of employees concerned with knowledge-related topics impossible. At the same time, the community wanted to involve more staff in actively contributing towards the transfer of knowledge across all hierarchical and group levels (Head of Corporate Knowledge Strategy, interview, November 2001; Chief Knowledge Officer, interview, November 2001).

During the study, speed was frequently emphasized as the most important aspect of co-evolving with the knowledge landscape. The Business Excellence Program was designed to take account of the pivotal significance of the time factor in a fiercely competitive environment. The comment that 'it is no longer about the big beating the small, but the fast beating the slow' was often heard (CEO, speech, February 2001; Head of Knowledge Management CS Networks Sales, interview, November 2001). Speed to market was seen as dependent on three interrelated factors. First, rather than an anonymous organization, a small, highly motivated, highly competent, consensus-oriented team was required. Second, a holistic approach was required, which embraced the entire development process, from assembly to distribution. This integrated concept had to serve as the guiding principle for all activities. Third, an innovation-friendly corporate climate, infused with a sense of urgency, was seen as key. This required research and development to be regarded not as a 'costly adjunct', but as a cornerstone for the success of the company (CEO, speech,

June 2001). The CEO of the Lighting Systems business unit, for example, made the importance of speed in co-evolving with the knowledge landscape very clear: 'the crucial thing is to recognize economic downturns at the earliest possible stage. This allows you to deal quickly with unexpected setbacks by implementing targeted production cutbacks, workforce adjustments and savings on overhead ...' (CEO Lighting Systems, interview in *ElectroCorp Today*, October 2001).

In order to maintain speed in reacting to sudden changes in the market, and in particular to recognize economic downturns at the earliest possible stage, the process of building communities of practice was divided into three phases (Chief Knowledge Officer, interview, November 2001; Corporate Knowledge Management Business Excellence Program Manager, interview, November 2001; Head of Corporate Knowledge Strategy, interview, November 2001) – the 'start-up phase', the 'run and improve phase' and the 'winding-down phase'.

The start-up phase was called 'pre-consideration'. A detailed checklist was provided which potential community initiators could consult to ascertain the extent to which initiating a community actually represented an appropriate approach to solving their current business problem. After this, the type of members that such a community would require was considered. Interviewees considered it important to survey members' common interests and motivate them. It was furthermore considered necessary to find a facilitator who planned and implemented the initiation. After this, a framework was set up that ensured the workability of the community. Finally the kick-off workshop was held. At this workshop members got to know one another, developed a joint understanding of the topics to be addressed, planned future activities, agreed on common objectives, and organized the structure of the community (Corporate Knowledge Management Business Excellence Program Manager, interview, November 2001).

When the community was established, it was considered critical that continuous improvement should take place (the 'run-and-improve phase'). Having successfully initiated a community, it was considered important to sustain the momentum in order to develop and sustain active knowledge sharing within the community. Importantly, the community had to become an important component in the everyday work of its members, in order to ultimately benefit the ElectroCorp corporation.

The case-study evidence showed that communities should only exist as long as the individual members could see benefits for themselves and their business. The community was therefore constantly adapting to the changes that took place in a knowledge-intensive environment. If the community was no longer deemed relevant, or if its set goals were no longer applicable, the community was discontinued. If it became necessary to close a community down, a final workshop reviewed its activities, processes and outputs. Important aspects of the community's knowledge were then either transferred to other communities or archived for later usage or use, if required, in related knowledge areas (Corporate Knowledge Management Business Excellence Program Manager, interview, November 2001; Head of Corporate Knowledge Strategy, interview, November 2001).

Step Three: Realizing Imaginative Strategies

Following simple rules
ElectroCorp used simple rules extensively throughout the three key projects investigated. To illustrate: the Portfolio Optimization Program can best be described as a list of ten simple rules that ElectroCorp ticked off one after the other (Corporate Development Analyst, interview, December 2001; direct observation, employee forum, April 2002). ElectroCorp's approach to simple rules in the Portfolio Optimization Program was much acclaimed by analysts, while the company's tenacity in following through the pointers stipulated in the Portfolio Optimization Program was admired throughout the business world (for example CEO, speech, December 2000). Perhaps the best-known simple rule forming part of the Portfolio Optimization Program within ElectroCorp, was a series of concise statements that applied to portfolio management.

> I am convinced that we can achieve enduring success only by winning and keeping top positions in our markets. This is why our Portfolio Optimization Program aims at placing virtually all businesses in leading global positions. If we do not achieve this goal with a business, we have four clear options: buy, cooperate, sell or close. This is the guiding principle behind the new orientation of our business portfolio ... (CEO, speech, December 1999)

The goal behind the simple rules mentioned in the quote above was: 'to bring the businesses into leading market positions. If a business is weak, there are five options for reaching this goal: fix, buy, cooperate, sell or close a business. I have always made it clear that the first option is the best: fix that which isn't working ...' (CEO, speech, June 2000).

At the time of the field study, ElectroCorp was active mainly in the 'buy' and 'cooperate' simple rules. In the buy category, ElectroCorp had completed two major acquisitions in the Energy Solutions Group, where two companies had been integrated. A third integration was under way, with a company in the automotive supplier business that produced speedometers for passenger cars (CEO, speech, February 2001; direct observation, employee forum, September 2001). The 'cooperate' simple rule applied to ElectroCorp's forming a 50/50 joint venture with a major computer company. This new company was intended to secure ElectroCorp's computer business over the long term (CEO, speech, December 1999). Another important example of the cooperate simple rule had been the partnering with another player, this time in mobile phone development (*ElectroCorp Today*, vol 1, 2000; Head of Corporate Development, interview, September 2001).

But simple rules could be found not only in the Portfolio Optimization Program. As part of the Business Excellence Program, ElectroCorp developed so-called 'power principles' with the help of an international survey involving 8000 employees.

> The principles [of the Business Excellence Program] point the way to the future for us. They help us orient our thoughts and actions. We need the principles ... they bring us a common identity across the company. This is very important for an international company such as ElectroCorp, which employs people from so many different nations and cultures ... (Head of Corporate Personnel, interview in *ElectroCorp Today*, October 1998)

It was interesting to see in what way the new corporate guiding principles were expected to interact with the corporate culture. When asked how he expected the new corporate guiding principles to shape ElectroCorp's culture, the corporate human resources chief and member of the board answered:

> It's the other way around. We didn't simply invent or prescribe the guiding principles. They grew out of the values expressed by our employees. In other words, out of our culture. We discovered what these values were by means of an international survey ... Our principles represent the values and wishes of employees throughout the company. (Head of Corporate Personnel, interview in *ElectroCorp Today*, October 1998)

In CS2003, there was also a clear focus on simple rules. However, here, they were more emergent and less formally stipulated when compared to the other two key projects investigated. For example, in changing the strategy at Communications Solutions Networks, a straightforward simple rule was 'revenue over volume' (Head of Communications Solutions Networks, interview in *ElectroCorp Today*, September 2001). This simple rule was not the result of a formal effort to instill simple rules in the company, but nevertheless recurred throughout various media in the case-study evidence (for example direct observation, employee forum, October 2001; CEO, speech, July 2001).

Focusing on heedful interaction
The literature-based theoretical framework set out in Chapter 2 emphasized two key aspects in focusing on heedful interaction: balancing internal replication of knowledge assets with their external replication. In other words, heedful interaction is about making knowledge fluid inside corporate boundaries,

while controlling external replication, that is, its flow outside corporate boundaries, for example in the long-term interaction with strategic partners.

While CS2003 placed less of an emphasis on heedful interaction, a key learning in the overall Business Excellence Program was that in order to make knowledge flow inside corporate boundaries, employees had to be purposefully motivated to not only use the knowledge of their colleagues elsewhere, but also to contribute their knowledge themselves. To this end, a sophisticated motivation and reward system, called 'Knowledge Web Shares', was introduced, which rewarded both the 'giver' as well as the 're-user' of knowledge. Similarly, external replication of knowledge assets was controlled in a project called the New Ventures Unit in Communications Solutions Networks. This project was conducted under the auspices of the Portfolio Optimization Program.

An interesting example of focusing on heedful interaction was found in the motivation and reward system called Knowledge Web Shares. This system appertained to the ElectroCorp-wide knowledge-sharing platform Knowledge Web, which was originally developed at Communications Solutions Networks and later implemented at corporate level. Several interviewees consistently emphasized that to make knowledge sharing happen, interactivity was required on an inter-departmental, inter-divisional and inter-functional level (Knowledge Manager (b), interview, January 2000; Former Head of Knowledge Management, CS Networks Sales, interview, February 2000; Chief Knowledge Officer, interview, November 2001). Interviewees emphasized that it was often difficult to accept and adopt another person's knowledge, especially if this person was from another division or department. One interviewee commented on this 'not invented here syndrome':

> Sometimes knowledge which has been brought in from external sources, such as other ElectroCorp departments or divisions, raises defence reactions. People often do not use it for the simple and stupid reason that they did not invent it. We have to develop people who can integrate suggestions from different origins and make a successful project from them. In short, make things happen, even if a project is composed of external inputs only ... (Former Head of CS Networks Sales, interview, February 2000)

In order to stimulate internal replication of knowledge assets, it was necessary to systematically identify and eliminate any organizational structures that could prevent knowledge from being shared, leveraged and enriched by different functions and departments. A critical success factor, therefore, was the establishment of a motivation and reward system that removed the fears and anxieties that could prevent the exchange of knowledge across divisions and departments (Chief Knowledge Officer, interview, November 2001). Knowledge, in particular tacit knowledge, was bound to a person. This meant that it could not be shared with others against such a person's will, and raised questions about motivating people to share their knowledge. Interviewees explained that getting a person to enhance other people's knowledge by voluntarily contributing his or her own did not happen easily. A further constraint was that knowledge sharing was considered a time-consuming and tedious exercise. This suggested that both the 'giver' as well as the 're-user' of knowledge had to be motivated (Former Head of CS Networks Sales, interview, February 2000; Chief Knowledge Officer, interview, November 2001; participant observation, workshop, June 2000).

The need to motivate and reward was therefore equally important for both the contributor or 'giver of knowledge' and the reuser or 'taker of knowledge'. The contributor, who received no direct reward for making experiences available, had to be specifically rewarded for the time invested in sharing his or her knowledge. The main reward for the reuser was the knowledge itself, which facilitated daily work (participant observation, knowledge forum, February 2001). For the reuser to benefit and thus gain the reward, Knowledge Web had to ensure that the available knowledge was truly useful. This was done through stringent quality control: the Knowledge Web Quality Assurance and Reward System was based on an airmiles scheme. Depending on the number of shares accumulated during a year, employees were awarded several incentives, such as conferences or journeys to attractive locations. The number of shares given to the contributor depended on the reuse feedback of the taker of knowledge, thus rewarding the usefulness of the transferred knowledge. The higher the usefulness of the knowledge, the higher the reward was. The feedback mechanism is also an important part of the quality assurance system. The quality of available knowledge could be quantified through reuse feedback from several knowledge reusers. Based on this feedback, knowledge of a low quality could be removed from Communications Solutions Knowledge Web, whereas high quality knowledge could be identified and developed further. Interviewees confirmed that this approach led to a constant improvement of the quality of the available knowledge (direct observation, employee forum, October 2001; Chief Knowledge Officer, interview November 2001).

In the Portfolio Optimization Program, an example of focusing on heedful interaction not only internally, as was the case in Knowledge Web Shares, but also externally (that is, with partners, suppliers and competitors) was also provided by the Communications Solutions Networks business unit. The importance of focusing on heedful interaction was illustrated as follows:

> One problem associated with collaborating with competitors can be illustrated in solution selling. In selling highly integrated telecom solutions, ElectroCorp could not do everything by itself, and had to co-opt the competence of other firms with which we also compete. An example is Data Management Systems, the supplier of data management solutions. ElectroCorp was forming a partnership with DMS in

combining ElectroCorp's expertise in telecom solutions with DMS's expertise in data management. Some say ElectroCorp eventually turned out to be the biggest re-seller of DMS products, and ironically helped building up an enormous customer base for its partner company... (Head of Competitive Intelligence, CS Network Sales, interview, November 2001)

The importance of focusing on heedful interaction when collaborating with competitors was underlined in an interview with the assistant to the CEO of the Communications Solutions business unit:

There is a certain degree of duality. The boundaries between competitors and suppliers blur in the solution-selling business. We cooperate with a number of play-ers, including DMS, for example, in building local area networks for our customers. So these competitors are also our suppliers ... (Assistant to the CEO of the Communications Solutions business, interview, November 2001)

In response to the challenges of heedful interaction, a 'New Ventures Unit' was formed in order to track innovations with the help of internal and external partners, and to select and implement ideas that could be converted into successful business ventures at Communications Solutions Networks. The leader of the project described the work of his team as 'scouting the world for people with ideas and a willingness to take risks inside and outside Communications Solutions Networks' (direct observation, employee forum, September 2001). Nurturing new ventures in this way also involved looking for promising firms in which to invest. Communications Solutions Networks provided capital, logistical support and consulting services to these new venture ideas with the aim of gaining additional access to innovative products and technologies in careful interaction with external partners, many of whom were competitors (assistant to the CEO of the Communications Solutions busi-ness, interview, November 2001). Three forms of focusing on heedful interac-tion in the 'New Ventures Unit' could be delineated (direct observation, employee forum, September 2001; Vice President and Communications Solutions CEO, interview, November 2001):

- If an ElectroCorp employee generated the initial business idea, a 'spin-off', that is, an independent company, which developed from Communications Solutions Networks and in which the group secured an equity stake, would be founded.
- If the initial business idea did not originate from within Communications Solutions Networks, a so-called 'start-up' was estab-lished. When this had been done, Communications Solutions Networks took a stake in this small, external company and assisted its founders with business development and marketing.

- A promising idea could also be passed on to a Communications Solutions Networks business unit, where, as an 'internal venture', it could then be converted into products and solutions and launched on the market.

Focusing on heedful interaction involved a three-step process: investigate, nurture and develop. A business idea was first discussed with the appropriate business unit. If the unit was not interested in developing the idea, then a proposal could be submitted to the New Ventures Unit. Here the idea underwent a thorough examination, involving questions such as: What is special about the business idea? How might it benefit the customer? How might Communications Solutions Networks benefit from it? What pre-emptive measures must be taken to ensure that the partnership surrounding the nurturing of the idea proceeds along tracks compatible with the original rationale of the partnership? What structural provisions must be in place to ensure that adequate protection of intellectual property rights takes place? (direct observation, employee forum, September 2001; Vice President and Communications Solutions CEO, interview, November 2001).

Building shared identity

In challenging imagination in strategy making, the established view of focusing on only the shareholders or stakeholders, the customers or owners of a business is one-sided. By contrast, shared identity, the final imagination lever in the strategy-making matrix, advocates an integrated approach: one that is geared to building shared identity among shareholders and stakeholders such as the wider social and political arena, employees and customers.

ElectroCorp pursued an integrated approach. Particularly noteworthy in this context is the Business Excellence Program, which by definition set out to increase corporate value in an integrated manner – not only for shareholders, but for customers, investors, business partners and employees. The CEO emphasized that it was necessary for ElectroCorp to 'attain world-class strength through learning and cooperation ... We are committed to learning from the best – from our most demanding customers, from leading companies in other industries, and from those in our company who demonstrate best practices' (CEO, speech, December 1997). Thus, increasing corporate value was frequently linked to shared identity and integration at ElectroCorp:

... in every part of our business, we want to make earnings exceed our capital expenditures. By the same token we want people outside the company to value us highly. Any increase in the value of the company will be directly reflected in our share price ... In addition to such short-term results, we also need sustained growth in the value of ElectroCorp. This can only be accomplished by improving our competitiveness. Only then will we be the first choice of customers, investors and employees, and only then can we guarantee long-term job security ... (Former Member of the Corporate Executive Committee, interview in *ElectroCorp Today*, October 1999).

In this context, the CEO also emphasized:

> ... excellent technology is not enough. Above all, our employees have to be open to one another, ready and willing to learn and share their knowledge. We have therefore taken a number of concrete steps to encourage cooperation. For example, we have, as part of our Business Excellence Program, reorganized the way we share information, experience and know-how. Through these measures, we are on the road to becoming a real learning company: an organization that absorbs ideas from the outside world by regularly benchmarking its activities against those of its best competitors and that shares best practice examples internally, holding up world-class achievements for everyone to emulate. And this is what knowledge management is all about: it is people business. That means the experience and abilities of our people are – and will continue to be – of ever-greater importance for our company's competitiveness and profitability. (CEO, speech, January 2000)

Furthermore, ElectroCorp had a 150-year history of building shared identity, starting with its founder, who encouraged shared leisure activities by building parks and organizing recreational events (Founder, 1966). At the time of the field study, a new corporate responsibility initiative was launched that extended the founder's original spirit beyond the bounds of the company (*ElectroCorp Today*, vol 2, 2001; Head of Corporate Personnel, interview in *ElectroCorp Today*, February 2001). The board member assigned to oversee issues of corporate responsibility explained its rationale as follows:

> Corporate responsibility is the social responsibility of a business corporation. It seeks to emulate the behavior of a 'good citizen' on corporate level, that is of a citizen who is actively involved in furthering the common good. To quote John F. Kennedy: 'Don't just ask for what the state can do for you, but also think about your own contribution to the common good.' Corporate responsibility is a basis for ElectroCorp's dealings with our partners ... it is a key ingredient of our mission statement and we are active in all countries of operation. (Head of Corporate Personnel, interview in *ElectroCorp Today*, November 2001)

The corporate responsibility initiative focused on seven areas of intervention (*ElectroCorp Today*, vol 2, 2001), from learning, research and training, the environment, public welfare to sports and leisure, and arts and culture. A formal publication, the *Corporate Responsibility Report*, was issued annually to complement the *Annual Report*, which focused primarily on financial data. The CEO described this integrated approach to corporate reporting as follows:

As a global network of innovation, ElectroCorp is a part of society, as a successful company ... We see ourselves as a corporate citizen, a member of society in all 190 countries where we do business – that is, in practically every part of the world ... In the Annual Report, the emphasis is on business success, company strategies, corporate messages, and company image ... The Corporate Responsibility Report provides details of all our social activities and the commitments we make to a more humane world. [Both] aspects form the basis for our thoughts and actions. They go together, they are interrelated and they are connected by the technical solutions and the knowledge of our 450 000 employees around the world. (CEO, *Corporate Responsibility Report* 2000)

Another example of building shared identity is the Portfolio Optimization Program and its emphasis on an internationally compatible approach to financial reporting, that is the program's concentration on one single performance measurement yardstick, against which performance was gauged consistently throughout the entire company. This performance yardstick was economic value-added – profits less capital costs. Introducing economic value-added as the standardized performance measurement yardstick helped ElectroCorp to foster transparency and consistency among its units and local companies. In order to remain competitive in the future, all groups within ElectroCorp worked to constantly increase their economic value-added (CEO, speech, November 2001; Head of Business Excellence Program, interview, November 2001). This was corroborated in another interview:

With the new performance measurement approach ... ElectroCorp had also established a clear focus on rewarding earnings, rather than rewarding turnover. At the customer interface, this meant that sales representatives would no longer be rewarded for increasing turnover, but would only be rewarded for making a sale that would contribute value. Indeed, sales representatives would now be penalized for not selling in-house components of a solution... (Head of Competitive Intelligence, CS Networks Sales, interview, November 2001)

NOTES

1. The name of the company studied and the names of all its divisions, employees, strategic programs, events and publications have been changed to preserve the company's anonymity. References are available for the purposes of academic study, provided a confidentiality agreement with ElectroCorp has been signed.
2. See Eisenhardt (1989) for the most important problems associated with retrospective data.
3. Some top managers who had previously left the company were included as well.
4. An interesting new technique for conducting the interviews emerged during the first few: it transpired that once the tape recorder was switched off, the interviewees tended to relax, and provided more interesting data than when they were being recorded. To take advantage of this tendency, the 'switch-off effect' gradually became a very powerful tool for eliciting high quality data. The researcher thus learned to use the switch-off button strategically during the interviews. To ensure confidentiality in this process, the interviewees reviewed all transcripts before they were utilized for the case study.

5. Both the interview tapes, as well as Microsoft Word revision mode versions of the summaries of the interviews before and after they were sent to the interviewees for appraisal, are available from the researcher for the purpose of scientific study, provided that a confidentiality agreement has been signed with ElectroCorp.

6. All names of business areas have been changed in order to protect the anonymity of the organization studied.

7. Economic value-added denotes profits minus capital costs (see, for example, Bontis, Dragonetti, Jacobsen and Roos, 1999).

8. Working capital is made up of receivables and inventories less payables and downpayments received. Working capital and fixed assets together constitute a company's business assets.

9. Non-conformance costs were defined as costs for finding and clearing non-conformance or weaknesses and their causes that result in products or services not meeting their requirements.

10. Black Belts were specialists in Six Sigma techniques who obtained intensive training, and were then used as project managers in rolling out Six Sigma.

11. Voice over Internet Protocol (VoIP) was then a new technology that transferred telephone conversations over the Internet, rather than over traditional wireline networks.

12. A community of practice is a group of people who are linked together by a common ability or a shared interest, and consequently possess common practical experience, specialist information and intuitive knowledge. Members typically share information, experience and insights and are supported by various tools.

5. Conclusions and implications

In this final chapter, I would like to wrap up some of the main insights from the fascinating story of strategy making and dissemination at ElectroCorp during the volatile years of the early twenty-first century. Hopefully, doing so will make it clear for current and future managers why and how imagination represents a key lever in strategy making in general and during a crisis in particular. At the start of the empirical study that I carried out at ElectroCorp in the early 2000s, two questions were fixed in my mind: first, what is the relative importance of the three imaginations in crafting strategy imaginatively? And second, what is the role and importance of sequencing the steps in crafting strategy imaginatively?

THE RELATIVE IMPORTANCE OF THE THREE IMAGINATIONS IN STRATEGY MAKING

The strategy-making framework presented here offers a blueprint for thinking about strategy during a crisis, and suggests answers to persistent questions and paradoxes that surround the topic. A key claim of the strategy-making matrix is that no single one of the three imaginations is universally sufficient in an imaginative approach to strategy making in the diversified firm.

There was strong evidence in the case study for all three imaginations. Although the three imaginations were present throughout the three key projects investigated, and in particular in the umbrella project, the Business Excellence Program, some imaginations were more dominant in specific steps of the strategy-making process than others. The Business Excellence Program, for example, started with a strong focus on internal firm resources and capabilities (creative imagination). Based on a thorough analysis of core competencies, decisions were taken to focus on certain competencies, while outsourcing others (Head of Business Excellence Program, interview, November 2001). Due to fundamental external discontinuities, particularly in ElectroCorp's core business in the telecommunications sector, ElectroCorp then moved into descriptive imagination, where the industry context was carefully analysed, and implications for the (re-)definition of core competencies were drawn. Eventually the company focused on purposefully defying 'ways of doing things around here' (challenging imagination).

Thus, all three imaginations clearly played an important role in the process of crafting strategy imaginatively. However, creative imagination seemed to be a prerequisite for the other two imaginations. Imaginative strategy making was first and foremost based on a deep understanding of firm-idiosyncratic resources and competencies. Furthermore, particularly in diversified firms such as ElectroCorp, the focus was on looking into ways to best exploit the synergies between the different competencies situated in the individual business units examined in the empirical study. ElectroCorp's CEO noted: 'By focusing and combining the unique and unbeatable array of competencies within our company, we will keep the competitive edge' (CEO, speech, February 2001). When asked what the core competencies of ElectroCorp were, interviewees at corporate level would consistently name ElectroCorp's business units (for example, Department Head Strategic Marketing, interview, December 2001; Vice President Corporate Technology Strategic Marketing, interview, November 2001; Head of Corporate Development, interview, September 2001).

However, creative imagination also had its limits. Although creative imagination was the fundamental basis upon which strategy at ElectroCorp was built, over-emphasis on core competencies could lead to a false sense of security and complacency among the individual business units that thought of themselves as 'ElectroCorp's core competencies', or belonging to the 'core business', and this called for challenging imagination. This is precisely what the CEO did when he questioned the fundamental focus on core competencies in the course of the third key project investigated, CS2003: 'the term "core business" has more or less been stricken from our vocabulary, because it can lead to divisions that are labeled core business, feeling safe and protected by their dictum: "after all, we are one of the company's core businesses – nothing will happen to us, no matter what our results are like" ' (CEO, speech, June 2001).

Finally, descriptive imagination added the important 'external' perspective on the industry environment and dynamics that put contingencies to the definition and development of core competencies. At the time of the field study, this focus on the external environment was very pronounced. Following an outstanding performance in the fiscal year 2000, ElectroCorp started the year with great optimism, because the company's growth curves of the fiscal year 2000 were extrapolated to the plans for 2003. After that, however, ElectroCorp was forced to substantially scale back its expectations and at times seriously cut back the plans of the overall company and some of its business units, most notably the Communications Solutions business units. The latter were characterized by a dramatic downturn in the mobile phone market, a technological shift in telephony technology toward Internet Protocol and optical networks, and weak investment activities by enterprise customers (CEO, speech, June 2001; direct observation, employee forum, October 2001).

Role and Importance of Sequencing Steps in the Strategy-Making Process

There was strong evidence in the case study confirming the three generic steps in the strategy making matrix, which I have called envisaging, conceiving and realizing. In fact, the very motto of the Business Excellence Program reflected ElectroCorp's focus on these steps: clear goals, concrete measures and rigorous consequences (see Figure 5.1).

The case-study evidence indicates that the process of crafting strategy imaginatively starts with determining the agenda with issues that are currently recognized as strategic at corporate or business unit level. At ElectroCorp, strategic issues were defined as events, developments or trends that are potentially important for the future development of the organization. The first generic step in strategy making in the empirical evidence was about determining objectives, that is, to determine a strategic direction for the firm and its divisions and business environments. Both the umbrella project as well as the two sub-projects reflected this. The Business Excellence Program started with the setting of two clear goals. The first goal was the introduction of a new performance yardstick (value-added) against which performance was gauged consistently throughout the entire company. The second measure centered on innovation and growth, and defined clear goals and pilot projects. Five key leverage points were identified: portfolio optimization, reduction of tied-up assets, earnings-oriented sales, cost reduction, and quality (CEO, speech, February 1999; Head of Business Excellence Program, interview, November 2001). This was consistent with the theoretical framework, which emphasized that the first generic step in strategy making is about determining objectives, that is, to determine a strategic direction for the firm and its divisions and business environments (Chakravarthy and Lorange, 1991: 4), and that envisaging strategy is about creating 'a plan – some sort of consciously intended course of action, a guideline (or set of guidelines) to deal with a situation. By this definition, strategies have two essential characteristics: they are made in advance of the actions to which they apply and they are developed consciously and purposefully' (Mintzberg, Quinn and Goshal, 1995: 13).

The case-study evidence further demonstrated the setting of concrete measures as an important second step (conceiving strategies). In other words, ElectroCorp understood that envisaging a strategy is not sufficient; a concept is needed that encompasses the resulting behavior. I called this step 'conceiving strategies'. While envisaging strategies focuses on the intellectual

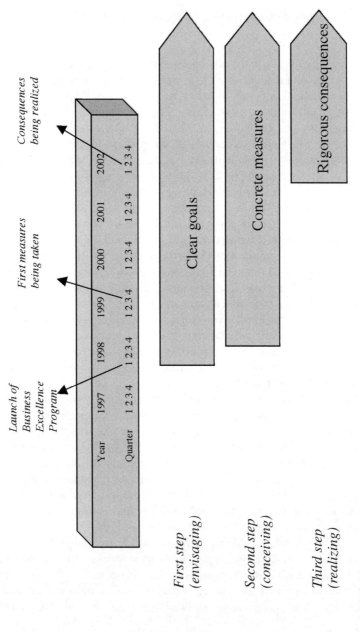

Source: Author.

Figure 5.1   ElectroCorp's strategy-making process

processes of ascertaining what a company might do, conceiving strategies focuses on deciding what a company can do, and bringing these considerations together in optimal equilibrium. ElectroCorp focused on issues of portfolio optimization, the application of the Business Excellence Program, the creation of new business opportunities, and personnel management (Head of Business Excellence Program, interview, November 2001; Member of the Corporate Board (Business Excellence Program), speech, June 2001; CEO, speech, June 2001). ElectroCorp's approach was consistent with the theoretical framework, which emphasized that conceiving strategies is a phase that encompasses activities such as assessing the organization's ability to implement strategy (Eisenstat and Beer, 1994; Beer and Nohria, 2001), evaluating strategic alternatives (Lyles, 1994), budgeting and establishing action programs (Lorange, 1980). Thus, in line with the theoretical part, while envisaging strategies focused on the intellectual processes of ascertaining what the company might do, conceiving strategies focused on deciding what a company can do, bringing these considerations together in optimal equilibrium (Mintzberg, Quinn and Goshal, 1995: 57).

The third step in the Business Excellence Program was 'definite consequences', which correspond to the third step – realizing strategies – in the theoretical framework. The Business Excellence Program prescribed holistic success measurement with balanced scorecards, incentive systems and personnel development. The theoretical framework showed that realizing strategies is closely related to organizational learning, and encompasses nurturing capability for continuous innovation, energizing the organization, sustaining formal commitment to the strategy made, and maintaining an entrepreneurial spirit. Realizing strategies can therefore be seen as the logical step following the conception of a given strategy. It constitutes a feedback loop and its primary purpose is monitoring, control and learning. For example, at Communications Solutions Networks, the largest business unit at ElectroCorp, a team developed scorecards for all of its subdivisions and sales units. Since the scorecards comprised business drivers and related measures derived directly from the strategy, the initial phase focused on strategy development (envisaging strategies). The aim here was for management to reach a consensus on strategic targets and on the specific business drivers that must be influenced to reach these targets. In the second phase, business drivers were identified and the appropriate performance measures were defined (conceiving strategies). These so-called key performance indicators were defined by four teams corresponding to the four scorecard perspectives: market/customer, internal processes, employee/knowledge, and finances. At the conclusion of the second phase, the business drivers and performance measures developed by the teams were approved in a management workshop comprised of all members of management. In the third phase (realizing strategies), performance measures were linked to target figures and the

means for realizing the scorecards were decided upon in order to enable organizational learning and through measuring of progress along the key perspectives of the scorecard (Head of Business Excellence Program, interview,
December 2001).

It should also be appreciated, however, that while the three steps of the
umbrella project investigated correspond very well with the theoretical framework, the sequence of the activities underlying these steps often took place in
parallel or even reverse order. For instance, the Business Excellence Project
started with the setting of clear goals such as the introduction of the new
performance yardstick, and the measures to achieve innovation and growth
(Member of the Corporate Board (Business Excellence Program), speech,
June 2001). At the same time, however, the balanced scorecard project
described above was started, and this project focused on realizing strategies.
Thus, the case-study evidence showed that the first and the last step, envisaging and realizing strategies, could also be seen as parallel activities. In other
words, there seems to be a feedback mechanism between the two. This feedback mechanism between envisaging and realizing strategies was confirmed in
various media in the case study (for example Head of Corporate Development,
interview, September 2001; direct observation, employee forum, October
2001; CEO, speech, June 2001). So it seems that particularly the first and the
last step of the strategy-making matrix constitute inextricably interwoven
strategic activities, which is probably the reason for their overlapping to some
extent in the present empirical study.

CONCLUSIONS

The overall conclusion is that imaginative strategy making involves the use of
three distinct imagination thrusts (descriptive imagination, creative imagination and challenging imagination), while taking into consideration the three
steps of the strategy-making process (envisaging, conceiving and realizing).
By combining the three imagination thrusts and the three steps in the strategy-
making process, the strategy-making matrix formalizes the individual propositions comprising the theoretical argument on two levels of granularity:[1]

- The juxtaposition of the three generic steps of the strategy-making
  process with the three basic thrusts of strategy making yields a three by
  three matrix (comprising a total of nine boxes). This matrix can be seen
  as a keen and concise conceptual scheme for thinking about imagination
  in strategy making.
- The strategy-making matrix identifies the activities, or, as I have termed
  them, the 'imagination levers' for each of the three thrusts in each step

of the strategy-making process. Using this approach, a total of 27 imagination levers (three imagination levers for each of the nine boxes) arise, and detail the theoretical argument of the strategy-making matrix. This conceptualization intends to offer a rich framework for crafting strategy imaginatively.

The overall contribution of this work can be assessed from a theoretical and from an empirical perspective. First, theoretically-speaking, the study contributes to the existing discussion on strategy making in that it integrates into a single framework a number of previously non-integrated theories from the strategy content and strategy process research realms. The theoretical contribution: following the recommendations by Bower (1970) and Burgelman (1983), the present study has found it useful to focus the analysis on particular strategic projects, rather than on the process of crafting strategy in general. The units of analysis therefore were three specific strategy-making projects that were ongoing at the time of the research. Analysis of these projects allowed the construction of a theoretically-based and empirically-grounded framework for crafting strategy imaginatively which described the sequence of the stages and their associated key activities in terms of the three different imaginations. The primary level of analysis in building the theoretical framework was the corporate level; the secondary level of analysis was the business unit level. In line with the single-embedded case study method (Yin, 1994), this permitted insights into how strategy was being made at ElectroCorp on the two levels of analysis in this study. On the corporate level, the present research constitutes an in-depth case study of how one diversified, major transnational firm in a specific industry uses the activities in each step in crafting strategy imaginatively. On the business unit level, it allowed for the identification of steps and their associated key activities in six carefully sampled industrial settings (Communications Solutions Networks, Communications Solutions Mobile, Automation, Automotive and Rail, Healthcare, and Energy Solutions).

From an empirical perspective, this study has made three important contributions. First, it has provided valuable empirical data about a strategy-making process in a major diversified firm, which involved descriptive, creative, and challenging imagination. It should be appreciated that very few academics have previously had the opportunity to do such in-depth study of these three imaginations as they evolve in the context of one organization. Indeed strategy-making research has often been criticized for its lack of empirical grounding (for example, Eisenhardt and Martin, 2000; Eisenhardt and Galunic, 2001; Williamson, 1999; Priem and Butler, 2001a). Scholars have explained this inadequacy as being due to the difficulty researchers have in obtaining access to organizations: studying strategy-making procedures implies significant researcher commitment and organizational access (van den Ven, 1992: 181, Mintzberg, 1979: 583). Only one previous study was found which included some elements of all three imaginations (Roos and Victor, 1999). However, in contrast to the present work, that study was not based on empirical research.

Second, this work adds valuable empirical data in the realm of disciplined imagination (Szulanski and Doz, 1995; Szulanski and Amin, 2001). Disciplined imagination refers to the process of introducing diversity in the strategy-making process, which is achieved by examining reality from a variety of perspectives, and by consistently applying a specific set of multiple frames of reference (Szulanski and Amin, 2001: 548). Judging from the most prominent thinkers in strategy making, this emphasis seems well warranted. Szulanski and Doz have made it very clear that, 'Perhaps one of the main hurdles for the progress of strategic management ... has been and still is the absence of tools to map what people have in their mind' (Szulanski and Doz, 1995: 17). The strategy-making matrix is in the spirit of disciplined imagination, but also contributes to and extends the findings of Szulanski and Doz. By emphasizing the consistent application of the three imaginations using a three-step approach, the strategy-making matrix attempts to provide a rigorous framework, one that consistently structures and systematizes what managers have in mind. This disciplined imagination in the strategy-making matrix manifests itself in the degree of consistency by which the three imaginations and the three steps are applied, which contributes to Szulanski and Doz's findings. This dissertation also contributes to Szulanski and Doz in that it provides detailed empirical evidence for the conjectures made. By contrast, Szulanski's work with both Doz and Amin was either of conceptual nature (Szulanski and Doz, 1995), or used anecdotal evidence only (Szulanski and Amin, 2001).

Third, by framing strategy making as an imaginative, dynamic process, the present study added valuable empirical data in the realm of dynamic capabilities. Eisenhardt and Martin have emphasized that imagination plays a key role in developing and nurturing dynamic capabilities (Eisenhardt and Martin, 2000: 1114). Very little is known about the management of dynamic capabilities (Eisenhardt and Martin, 2000) and their interaction with strategy making (Zollo and Winter, 2000). In particular, little is known about how dynamic capabilities interact with the three imaginations. Only two influential studies in the realm of dynamic capabilities were found (Eisenhardt and Martin, 2000; Teece, Pisano and Shuen, 1997). However, these papers, while important milestones in their field, were once again conceptual in nature. Only one study was found that looked into the topic of dynamic capabilities empirically (Zott, 2000). However, in contrast to the present study, the empirical data for the paper by Zott was based on a computer simulation, and not on an existing firm.

LIMITATIONS OF THE STUDY

The main conclusions and contributions of this study as outlined above should be seen in the light of several limitations, in particular those relating to generalizability and theoretical focus.

While grounded theorizing from single-embedded case studies has historically played an important role in the field of strategic management in general (for example, Mintzberg and McHugh, 1985; Bower, 1970), and in the field of strategy-making frameworks in particular (for example, Burgelman, 1983, 1994), such research suffers from the problem of questionable generalizability. Clearly, findings and propositions drawn from a single case study, like the present one, no matter how carefully sampled and researched, deserve to be regarded with a healthy caution (Burgelman, 1994: 53). In the present study, this problem is perhaps less acute because of the purposefully wide variety of industries covered, as discussed in Chapter 3. The wide variety of industries covered is in stark contrast to the custom in other case-study research. The much-acclaimed frameworks by Burgelman, for example, focus exclusively on the high-technology sector (for example, Burgelman, 1983, 1994). Similarly, Eisenhardt acknowledges that her research centers exclusively on the high-technology industry, which could severely compromise generalizability of her findings (for example, Eisenhardt and Brown, 1998). Moreover, this dissertation has attempted to compensate for the limited generalizability by explicitly positioning the theoretical framework within two well-established streams of thought (strategy process and strategy content research). However, it must still be acknowledged that the strategy-making matrix, as it is presented here, can lay claim only to being a tentative framework for crafting strategy imaginatively, and is in need of further research and validation in a wider variety of contextual settings.

The focus of this study was on strategy making, without paying explicit attention to the implementation of the strategy made, i.e. without focusing on strategic change (discussed in Chapter 1). However, several researchers have emphasized the interdependence of strategy making and strategy implementation or strategic change (for example, Roos and Victor, 1999; Eisenhardt and Martin, 2000). At the heart of these studies is the argument that while it may be analytically convenient to separate the two concepts, their distinction would seem difficult to reconcile with the reality of strategy-making processes (see, for example, Rumelt, Schendel and Teece, 1994: 20; Schendel, 1992: 2). This complex connection between strategy making and strategy implementation or strategic change has been illustrated in the 'Matrioshka approach', which suggests that both concepts can be seen as a set of Matrioshka dolls which fit within one another, to illustrate their interdependence (Hilb, 2001: 46). Nevertheless, despite or because of this interdependence, the concrete distinction between strategy making and strategy implementation has been a defining characteristic of strategy research since its inception in the 1960s and has also been adopted for the purposes of this study. Practically speaking, of course, the making of a strategy and its implementation are interdependent processes, and should be seen as two sides of the same coin. In line with Andrews et al. (1965: 17), crafting strategy, or the process by which a strategy is determined, was seen as independent from the process of actually implementing this strategy for analytical convenience. Clearly, further work would need to investigate both sides of the coin simultaneously.

THEORETICAL IMPLICATIONS AND FURTHER RESEARCH AVENUES

The integrated framework developed in this study is very helpful for deducing implications for existing major frameworks as well as for the advancement of theory through further research. The research reported here has supported a key statement in Priem and Butler's seminal article, which proclaimed that 'a *complete* model of competitive advantage would require the full integration of models of the competitive environment with the models of firm resources ... [Their] artificial separation may be restricting our ability to fully conceptualize strategy making' (Priem and Butler, 2001a: 64; emphasis added). The findings reported here have also extended Priem and Butler's notion of a 'complete' model, in that in addition to the frameworks associated with competitive environment (descriptive imagination) and firm resources (creative imagination), a third perspective needs to be included, namely, challenging imagination.

The three basic thrusts and the three generic steps were juxtaposed to form an integrated framework. I hope this framework will be seen as a valuable addition to the field of strategy making. A key reason behind the limited progress in the strategy-making realm has been the absence of a careful modeling based on standard concepts (Bower, cited in Lovas and Goshal, 2000: 892). In the absence of a rigorous yet robust underlying framework, research in strategy making has been neither focused, nor integrative.

By explicitly framing strategy making as an imaginative process, the strategy-making matrix builds on a long tradition within strategy-making research. Mintzberg's (1978) discussion of emergent strategy, Bower's (1970) framework of the resource allocation process, and Lovas and Goshal's more recent (2000) contribution of strategy as guided evolution, for instance, can be seen as imaginative in their underlying logic. In line with these major works, the strategy-making matrix claims that with the successive arising of new situations, re-examination of strategies is necessary to ensure the maintenance of effective alignment of strategy-making efforts with actualities. Thus, the strategy-making matrix shares the spirit of these frameworks by sharing the understanding of strategy making as an imaginative process: what is appropriate in crafting strategy depends on the situation and cannot be determined in a dogmatic or peremptory fashion.

Earlier contributions were, however, largely non-integrative and focused on either strategy process research literatures or insights from the strategy content realm. Although considerable research has been focused on strategy content in terms of specific industry structures (Porter, 1980, 1985, 1991, 1998, 2001), or resource structures (Barney, 1991; Prahalad and Hamel, 1990; Peteraf, 1993; Wernerfelt, 1984, 1995), less attention has been devoted to how these structures arise in the first place. In a similar fashion, while much strategy process research has examined contextual factors, decision-making processes, intuitive and analytic aspects (for example, Mintzberg, 1976; Mintzberg and Waters, 1985), less study has been done on specific managerial practices determining the origins of and the connection to these industry and resource positions. In other words, the conceptual development at the interface between strategy process and strategy content research has been in a preliminary state (for example, Schendel, 1992; Rumelt, Schendel and Teece, 1991, 1994; Chakravarthy and Doz, 1992). This suggests that a major contribution of the strategy-making matrix resides in its attempt to develop the interface between strategy content and strategy process research by juxtaposing the three generic steps (based on strategy process) with the three kinds of imagination (based on strategy content).

Further research could build on the insights derived from the strategy-making matrix and needs to investigate at least three issues:

- Further research needs to determine whether the conceptualization of strategy making as an imaginative process involving the complex interplay of the three imaginations and the three steps is idiosyncratic to ElectroCorp, or whether the findings can be replicated in other firms and/or non-profit and public sector organizations.
- Another interesting strand of inquiry could be to explicitly frame the three imaginations in terms of the contribution the firm can make to its stakeholders in particular. Stakeholder theory has burgeoned in recent years (see, for example, Patsch, 2001; Friedman and Miles, 2001). It seems timely to investigate if, and to what extent, the strategy-making matrix can be used to craft strategy imaginatively, i.e. so that the often disparate and diametrically opposed claims of different stakeholder groups are accommodated.
- Additionally, scholars could investigate whether and how one or more of the three imaginations is brought into sharper focus than the others

when the strategy-making matrix is used in different industries. An interesting conjecture to be tested here would be whether firms in more dynamic industries (for example, the software industry) would place a stronger emphasis on challenging imagination. A similar investigation might explore whether firms in highly asset-intensive, static industries (for example, the steel industry) would find it more difficult to challenge their established business model (and dispose of their extensive physical infrastructure), which would place a stronger emphasis on accurately capturing the dynamics within relatively static industry boundaries using descriptive imagination.

- Such research can usefully combine units of analysis on various levels of aggregation. This study looked at three key projects, all of which were successful at the time of the field study. This could introduce a 'survivor bias'. It seems therefore expedient to also include unsuccessful projects in a given organizational context, in order to allow for comparisons between successful and unsuccessful approaches.

In summary, I hope that the present book will incentivize others to engage in the arduous task of doing in-depth research in organizations to find out more about the key role of imagination in strategy making in general and during a crisis in particular. I also hope that organizations will not only tolerate but actively encourage the presence of external researchers, especially when times are difficult.

NOTES

1. 'The strategy-making matrix' conceptualization of the overall theoretical argument on two levels of granularity supports findings of a seminal article by Eisenhardt (1989: 547), who argued that a hallmark of good theory is parsimony and richness simultaneously.

References

Abell, D. (1980), *Defining the Business*, Englewood Cliffs, NJ: Prentice Hall.

Allison, M.A. and S. Kelly (1999), *The Complexity Advantage: How the Science of Complexity Can Help Your Business Achieve Peak Performance*, New York, NY: McGraw-Hill.

Amit, R. and P. Shoemaker (1993), 'Strategic assets and organizational rent', *Strategic Management Journal*, **14**(1), 33–46.

Ansoff, H.I. (1980), *The New Corporate Strategy*, New York, NY: McGraw-Hill.

Ansoff, H.I. (1965), *Corporate Strategy: An Analytical Approach to Business Policy for Growth and Expansion*, New York, NY: McGraw-Hill.

Andrews, K.R. (1971), *The Concept of Corporate Strategy*, Homewood, IL: Dow-Jones-Irwin.

Andrews, K.R., C.R. Learned and W. Guth (1965), *Business Policy: Text and Cases*, Homewood, IL: Richard D. Irwin.

Arthur, W.B. (1996), 'Increasing returns and the new world of business', *Harvard Business Review* (July–August), 100–109.

Bain, J.S. (1956), *Barriers to New Competition*, Cambridge, MA: Harvard University Press.

Bardaracco, J. (1991), *The Knowledge Link: How Firms Compete Through Strategic Alliances*, Boston, MA: Harvard Business School Press.

Barney, J.B. (2001), 'Is the resource-based view a useful perspective for strategic management? Yes', *Academy of Management Review*, **26**(1), 41–56.

Barney, J.B. (1991), 'Firm resources and sustained competitive advantage', *Journal of Management*, **17**(1), 99–120.

Bar-Yam, Y. (1997), *Dynamics of Complex Systems*, Cambridge, MA: Addison-Wesley.

Beer, M. and N. Nohria (2000), *Cracking the Code of Change*, Cambridge, MA: Harvard Business School Press.

Beinhocker, E.D. (1997), 'Strategy at the edge of chaos', *McKinsey Quarterly*, **1**, 24–39.

Belohlav, J. (1996), 'The evolving competitive paradigm', *Business Horizons*, March–April, 11–19.

Bontis, N., N.C. Dragonetti, K. Jacobsen and G. Roos (1999), 'The knowledge toolbox: a review of the tools available to measure and manage intangible resources', *European Management Journal*, **17**(4), 391–401.

Bower, J.L. (1970), *Managing the Resource Allocation Process*, Boston, MA: Harvard University Graduate School of Business Administration.

Brown, J., and P. Duguid (1998), 'Organizing knowledge', *California Management Review*, **3**(40), 90–111.

Burgelman, R.A. (2002), *Strategy as Destiny*, Cambridge, MA: Harvard Business School Press.

Burgelman, R.A. (1994), 'Fading memories: a process theory of strategic business exit in dynamic environments', *Administrative Science Quarterly*, **39**, 24–56.

Burgelman, R.A. (1983), 'A process model of internal corporate venturing in the diversified firm', *Administrative Science Quarterly*, **28**, 223–44.

Campbell, A. (2001), 'Letter to the editor: strategy as simple rules', *Harvard Business Review*, May, p.149.

Campbell, D.T. (1985), 'Degrees of freedom and case study', *Political Studies*, **8**, 178–93.

Campbell-Hunt, C. (2000), 'What have we learned about generic competitive strategy? A meta-analysis', *Strategic Management Journal*, **21**, 127–54.

Chakravarthy, B. (1997), 'A new strategy framework for coping with turbulence', *Sloan Management Review* (Winter), 69–82.

Chakravarthy, B. and Y. Doz (1992), 'Strategy process research: focusing on corporate self-renewal', *Strategic Management Journal*, **13** (Summer special issue), 5–14.

Chakravarthy, B. and P. Lorange (1991), *Managing the Strategy Process*, Englewood Cliffs, NJ: Prentice-Hall.

Chandler, A. (1962), *Strategy and Structure: Chapters in the History of the Industrial Enterprise*, Cambridge, MA: MIT Press.

Cilliers, P. (1998), *Complexity and Postmodernism*. London: Sage.

Clausewitz, K. (1998), *On War*, London: Penguin.

Coase, R.H. (1937), 'The nature of the firm', *Economica*, **4**, 386–405.

Cohen, W.M. and D.A. Levinthal (1990), 'Absorptive capacity: a new perspective on learning and innovation', *Administrative Science Quarterly*, **35**, 128–52.

Collis, D. and P. Ghemawat (1994), 'Industry analysis: understanding industry structure and dynamics', in L. Fahey and R.M. Randall (eds), *The Portable MBA in Strategy*, New York, NY: John Wiley and Sons, pp. 171–94.

Datta, D.K. and N. Rajagopalan (1998), 'Industry structure and CEO characteristics: an empirical study of succession events', *Strategic Management Journal*, **19**, 833–52.

Davenport, T.H. (1993), *Process Innovation: Reengineering Work Through Information Technology*, Boston, MA: Harvard Business School Press.

Davenport, T.H. and J.C. Beck (2001), *The Attention Economy*, Cambridge, MA: Harvard Business School Press.

Davenport, T.H. and G.J.B. Probst (2000), *Knowledge Management Case Book*, New York, NY: John Wiley and Sons.

Davenport, T.H. and L. Prusak (1998), *Working Knowledge*, Boston, MA: Harvard Business School Press.

Day, G.S. (1994), 'Evaluating strategic alternatives', in L. Fahey and R.M. Randall (eds), *The Portable MBA in Strategy*, New York, NY: John Wiley and Sons, pp. 297–317.

Denzin, N.K. and Y.S. Lincoln (1994), *Handbook of Qualitative Research*, London: Sage.

Derrida, J. (1988), *Limited Inc.*, Evanston, IL: Northwestern University Press.

Derrida, J. (1981), *Plato's Pharmacy*, Evanston, IL.: Athlon Press.

Despres, C. and D. Chauvel (1999), 'How to map knowledge management', *Financial Times*, March, pp. 4–6.

Dierckx, I. and K. Cool (1989), 'Asset stock accumulation and sustainability of competitive advantage: reply', *Management Science*, **35**(12), 1514.

Edvinsson, L. (1997), 'Developing intellectual capital at Skandia', *Long Range Planning*, **30**, 366–73.

Edvinsson, L. and M.S. Malone (1997), *Intellectual Capital: Realising Your Company's True Value by Finding its Hidden Brainpower*, New York, NY: Harper Business.

Eisenhardt, K.M. (1999), 'Strategy as strategic decision-making', *Sloan Management Review*, **40**(2), 65–72.

Eisenhardt, K.M. (1989), 'Building theories from case study research', *Academy of Management Review*, **14**(4), 532–50.

Eisenhardt, K.M. and S.L. Brown (1999), 'Patching: restitching business port-folios in dynamic markets', *Harvard Business Review*, May–June, 72–82.

Eisenhardt, K.M. and S.L. Brown (1998), *Competing on the Edge: Strategy as Structured Chaos*, Cambridge, MA: Harvard Business School Press.

Eisenhardt, K.M. and C.D. Galunic (2001), 'Architectural innovation and modular corporate forms', *Academy of Management Journal*, **4**(6).

Eisenhardt, K.M. and J.A. Martin (2000), 'Dynamic capabilities: what are they?', *Strategic Management Journal*, **21** (Winter special issue), 1105–21.

Eisenhardt, K.M. and D.N. Sull (2001), 'Strategy as simple rules', *Harvard Business Review*, January, 106–16.

Eisenhardt, K.M., J.L. Kahwajy and L.J. Bourgeois III (1997), 'How manage-ment teams can have a good fight', *Harvard Business Review*, July–August, 77–85.

Eisenstat, R.A. and M. Beer (1994), 'Strategic change: realigning the organ-ization to implement strategy', in L. Fahey and R.M. Randall (eds), *The Portable MBA in Strategy*, New York, NY: John Wiley and Sons, pp. 321–57.

Eppler, M. (2000), 'The concept of information quality: an interdisciplinary evaluation of information quality tools', University of St. Gallen working paper.

Eppler, M. and W. Kuepers (2001), 'The concept of irony and its application to management', University of St. Gallen, HSG working paper.

Evans, P.B. and T.S. Wurster (2000), *Blown to Bits*, Boston, MA: Harvard Business School Press.

Evans, P.B. and T.S. Wurster (1999), 'Getting real about virtual commerce', *Harvard Business Review*, November–December, 84–98.

Evans, P.B. and T.S. Wurster (1997), 'Strategy and the new economics of information', *Harvard Business Review*, September–October, 71–82.

Fahey, L. and H.K. Christensen (1986), 'Evaluating the research on strategy content', *Journal of Management*, 12(2), 167–83.

Farjoun, M. (2008), 'Strategy making, novelty, and analogical reasoning: commentary to Gavetti, Levinthal, and Rivkin (2005)', *Strategic Management Journal*, 29, 1001–16.

Floyd, S.W. and S. Wooldridge (1996), *The Strategic Middle Manager*. San Francisco, CA.: Jossey-Bass.

Foddy, W. (1993), *Constructing Questions for Interviews and Questionnaires*, Cambridge, MA: Cambridge University Press.

Fredrickson, J.W. (1984), 'The comprehensiveness of strategic decision processes: extension, observations, future directions', *Academy of Management Journal*, 27(3), 445–66.

Fredrickson, J.W. and T.R. Mitchell (1984), 'Strategic decision processes: comprehensiveness and performance in an industry with an unstable environment', *Academy of Management Journal*, 27(3), 399–423.

Friedman, A.L. and S. Miles (2001), 'Developing stakeholder theory', *Journal of Management Studies*, 39(1), 1–21.

Garvin, D.A. (1998), *Managing Quality: The Strategic and Competitive Edge*, New York: Free Press.

Gavetti, G., D. Levinthal and J. Rivkin (2005), 'Strategy making in novel and complex worlds: the power of analogy', *Strategic Management Journal*, 26: 691–712.

Ghemawat, P. (1991), *Commitment: The Dynamic of Strategy*, New York: Free Press.

Gibbert, M., M. Hoegl and L. Valikangas (2007), 'In praise of resource constraints", *MIT Sloan Management Review*, 48(3), 15–17.

Gibbert, M., P. Kugler and S. Voelpel (2000), 'Getting real about knowledge sharing: the Premium Bonus-on-Top system', in T.H. Davenport and G. Probst (eds), *Knowledge Management Case Book*, New York, NY: John Wiley and Sons, pp. 200–217.

Gibbert, M., M. Leibold and S. Voelpel (2001), 'Rejuvenating corporate intellectual capital by co-opting customer competence', *Journal of Intellectual Capital*, 2(2), 345–59.

Gibbert, M., W. Ruigrok and B. Wicki (2008), 'What passes as a rigorous case study?', *Strategic Management Journal*, **29**, 1465–74.

Ginsberg, A. and N. Venkatraman (1985), 'Contingency perspectives of organizational strategy: a critical review of empirical research', *Academy of Management Review*, **10**, 421–34.

Gluck, F., S. Kaufman and A. Walleck (1982), 'The four phases of strategic management', *Journal of Business Strategy*, **2**, 9–21.

Grant, R. (1997), 'The knowledge-based view of the firm: implications for management practice', *Long Range Planning*, **30**(3), 450–55.

Grant, R. (1996), 'Toward a knowledge based theory of the firm', *Strategic Management Journal*, **17**, 109–23.

Grindley P.C. and D.J. Teece (1997), 'Managing intellectual capital: licensing and cross-licensing in semiconductors and electronics', *California Management Review*, **39**(2), 8–39.

Hagardon, A.B. (1998), 'Firms as knowledge brokers: lessons in pursuing continuous innovation', *California Management Review*, **40**(3), 209–28.

Hamel, G. (2000), *Leading the Revolution*, Cambridge, MA: Harvard Business School Press.

Hamel, G. (1999), 'Bringing Silicon Valley inside', *Harvard Business Review*, September, 70–85.

Hamel, G. (1998), 'Strategy innovation and the quest for value', *Sloan Management Review*, **39**(2), 7–14.

Hamel, G. (1996), 'Strategy as revolution', *Harvard Business Review*, July–August, 69–82.

Hamel, G. (1991), 'Competition for competence and inter-partner learning within international strategic alliances', *Strategic Management Journal*, **12**, 83–103.

Hamel, G. and C.K. Prahalad (1996), 'Competing in the new economy: Managing out of bounds', *Strategic Management Journal*, **17**, 237–42.

Hamel, G. and C.K. Prahalad (1994a), *Competing for the Future*, Cambridge, MA: Harvard Business School Press.

Hamel, G. and C.K. Prahalad (1994b), 'Seeing the future first', *Fortune*, September, pp. 65–8.

Hamel, G. and C.K. Prahalad (1993), 'Strategy as stretch and leverage', *Harvard Business Review*, March–April, 75–84.

Hamel, G. and C.K. Prahalad (1991), 'Corporate imagination and expeditionary marketing', *Harvard Business Review*, July–August, 81–93.

Hamel, G. and C.K. Prahalad (1989), 'Strategic intent', *Harvard Business Review*, July–August, 63–76.

Hamel, G. and J.L. Sampler (1998), 'The e-corporation', *Fortune*, December, p. 7.

Hamel, G., Y. Doz and C.K. Prahalad (1989), 'Collaborate with your competitors and win', *Harvard Business Review*, January, 133–39.

Hammer, M. and J. Champy (1993), *Reengineering the Corporation: A Manifesto for Business Revolution*, London: Nicholas Brealey.

Harrington, J.H. (1991), *Business Process Improvement*, New York, NY: MacGraw-Hill.

Hart, S. (1992), 'An integrative framework for strategy-making processes', *Academy of Management Review*, **17**(2), 327–51.

Hart, S. (1991), 'Intentionality and autonomy in strategy-making process: modes, archetypes, and firm performance', *Advances in Strategic Management*, **7**, 97–127.

Hart, S. and C. Branbury (1994), 'How strategy-making processes can make a difference', *Strategic Management Journal*, **15**(3), 251–69.

Hayes, R.H. and S.C. Wheelwright(1979), 'Link manufacturing process and product life cycles', *Harvard Business Review* (January–February), 133–40.

Hebeler, J. and D. Van Doren (1997), 'Unfettered leverage: the ascendance of knowledge-rich products and processes', *Business Horizons* (July–August), 2–10.

Hedlund, G. (1994), 'A model of knowledge management and the N-Form corporation', *Strategic Management Journal*, **15**, 73–90.

Helfat, C.E. (2000), 'Guest editor's introduction to the special issue: the evolution of firm capabilities', *Strategic Management Journal*, **21** (Winter special issue), 955–9.

Henderson, B.D. (1979), *Henderson on Corporate Strategy*, Cambridge, MA: Abt Books.

Hilb, M. (2001), *Integriertes Personalmanagement* (9th edn), Neuwied, Germany: Luchterhand.

Hilb, M. (2000), *Transnationales Management der Human-Ressourcen: Das 4P Modell des Glocalpreneuring*, Neuwied, Germany: Luchterhand.

Hilb, M. (1998), *Integrierte Erfolgsbewertung von Unternehmen*, Neuwied, Germany: Luchterhand.

Hilb, M. (1997), *Integrierte Erfolgsbewertung von Unternehmen*, Berlin: Luchterhand.

Hilb, M. (1995), *Core Business Process Re-engineering: A Human Resources Perspective*, St. Gallen, Switzerland: University of St. Gallen.

Hoegl, M., M. Gibbert and D. Mazursky (2008), 'Financial constraints in innovation projects: when is less more?', *Research Policy*, **37**, 1382–91.

Huff, A. and R. Reger (1987), 'A review of strategy process research', *Journal of Management*, **13**(4), 211–36.

Itami, H. (1987), *Mobilizing Invisible Assets*, Cambridge, MA: Harvard University Press.

Jensen, M.C. (1988), *The Takeover Controversy: Analysis and Evidence*, Oxford: Oxford University Press.

Johnson, G. (1994), 'Strategic change: managing cultural processes', in L. Fahey and R.M. Randall (eds), *The Portable MBA in Strategy*, New York, NY: John Wiley, pp. 411–38.

Johnson, G. (1988), 'Rethinking incrementalism', *Strategic Management Journal*, **9**, 75–91.

Kaplan, R.S. and D.P. Norton (1996a), *The Balanced Scorecard*. Boston, MA: Harvard Business School Press.

Kaplan, R.S. and D.P. Norton (1996b), 'Using the balanced scorecard as a strategic management system', *Harvard Business Review* (January/February), 75–85.

Kauffman, S.A. (1995), *At Home in the Universe: The Search for Laws of Self Organization and Complexity*, New York, NY: Oxford University Press.

Kauffman, S.A. (1993), *The Origins of Order: Self Organization and Selection in Evolution*, New York, NY: Oxford University Press.

Kearney, R. (1988), *The Wake of Imagination: Toward a Postmodern Culture*, Minneapolis, MI: University of Minnesota Press.

Kim, W.C. and R. Mauborgne (2000), 'Knowing a winning business idea when you see one', *Harvard Business Review* (September–October), 129–37.

Kim, W.C. and R. Mauborgne (1999a), 'Strategy, value innovation and the knowledge economy', *Sloan Management Review* (Spring), 41–54.

Kim, W.C. and R. Mauborgne (1999b), 'Creating new market space', *Harvard Business Review* (January–February), 83–93.

Kim, W.C. and R. Mauborgne (1997a), 'Value innovation: The strategic logic of high growth', *Harvard Business Review* (January–February), 103–12.

Kim, W.C. and R. Mauborgne (1997b), 'Fair process: managing in the knowledge economy', *Harvard Business Review* (July–August), 65–76.

Kogut, B. and U. Zander (1996), 'What firms do? co-ordination, identity, and learning', *Organization Science*, **7**(5), 502–19.

Lane, D. and R. Maxfield (1996), 'Strategy under complexity: Fostering generative relationships', *Long Range Planning*, **29**(2), 215–31.

Leavitt, H.J. and J. Lipman-Blumen (1995), 'Hot groups', *Harvard Business Review* (July–August), 109–16.

Lei, D. and J. Slocum (1992), 'Global strategy, competence building and strategic alliances', *California Management Review*, **35**(1), 81–97.

Leibold, M. (2001), 'An increasingly complex world', in M. Leibold (ed.), *Business Strategy Systems*, Stellenbosch, South Africa: Content Solutions, pp. 3–14.

Leibold, M. and N.J. Slabbert (1994), 'Key political economy pointers for designing and managing strategic alliances in regional business environments', Best Paper Award presented at the third International World Business Congress, Penang, Malaysia.

Leibold, M., M. Gibbert and B. Kaes (2001), 'The knowledge management dilemma in international strategic alliances', *Bestuursdinamika*, **10**(2),

Leibold, M., B. Kaes and M. Gibbert (1999), 'An anatomy of intellectual capital: a synthesis of conceptual approaches and a research agenda for the future', *Bestuursdinamika*, **8**(2), 1–32.

Leonard-Barton, D. (1995), *Wellsprings of Knowledge*, Boston, MA: Harvard Business School Press.

Leonard-Barton, D. (1992), 'Core capabilities and core rigidities: a paradox in managing new product development', *Strategic Management Journal*, **13**, 111–25.

Lissack, M. and J. Roos (1999), *The Next Common Sense: Mastering Corporate Complexity Through Coherence*, London: Nicholas Brealey Publishing.

Lorange, P. (1980), *Corporate Planning: An Executive Viewpoint*, Englewood Cliffs, NJ: Prentice Hall.

Lovas, B. and S. Goshal (2000), 'Strategy as guided evolution', *Strategic Management Journal*, **21** (Winter special issue), 875–96.

Lumpkin, G.T. and G.G. Dess (1995), 'Simplicity as a strategy-making process: the effects of stage of organizational development and environmental performance', *Academy of Management Journal*, **38**(5), 1386–1408.

Lyles, M. (1994), 'Identifying and developing strategic alternatives', and in L. Fahey and R.M. Randall (eds), *The Portable MBA in Strategy*, New York, NY: John Wiley and Sons, pp. 273–96.

Lyotard, J.-F. (1984), *The Postmodern Condition: A Report on Knowledge*, Minneapolis, MI: University of Minnesota Press.

Mason, E.S. (1939), 'Price and production policies of large scale enterprises', *American Economic Review*, **29**(1), 61–74.

Miles, M.B. and A.M. Hubermann (1994), *Qualitative Data Analysis: an Expanded Sourcebook*, Thousand Oaks, CA: Sage.

Mintzberg, H. (1994), 'The fall and rise of strategic planning', *Harvard Business Review* (January–February), 107–14.

Mintzberg, H. (1979), 'An emerging strategy of direct research', *Administrative Science Quarterly*, **24**(4), 508–89.

Mintzberg, H. (1978), 'Patterns in strategy formulation', *Management Science*, **24**(9), 934–48.

Mintzberg, H. (1976), 'Planning on the left side and managing on the right', *Harvard Business Review* (July–August), 49–58.

Mintzberg, H. (1973a), *The Nature of Managerial Work*, New York, NY: Harpers and Row.

Mintzberg, H. and J. Lampel (1999), 'Reflecting on the strategy process', *Sloan Management Review*, **40**(3), 21–30.

Mintzberg, H. and A. McHugh (1985), 'Strategy formation in an adhocracy', *Administrative Science Quarterly*, **30**(1), 160–97.

Mintzberg, H. and J.B. Quinn (1991), *The Strategy Process*, Englewood Cliffs, NJ: Prentice-Hall.

Mintzberg, H. and J.A. Waters (1985), 'Of strategies, deliberate and emergent', *Strategic Management Journal*, **6**(2), 257–72.

Mintzberg, H., J.B. Quinn and S. Goshal (1995), *The Strategy Process*, Englewood Cliffs, NJ.: Prentice-Hall.

Mintzberg, H., D. Raisinghani and A. Theoret (1976), 'The structure of unstructured decision processes', *Administrative Science Quarterly*, **21**, 246–75.

Moldoveanu, M. (2009), 'Thinking strategically about strategic thinking: the computational structure and dynamics of managerial perception and problem solving', *Strategic Management Journal*, **30**, 737–63.

Montgomery, C. (1988), 'Guest editor's introduction to the special issue on research on the content of strategy', *Strategic Management Journal*, **9** (Summer special issue), 3–8.

Moore, J.F. (1993), 'Predators and prey', *Harvard Business Review* (May–June), 75–84.

Müller-Stewens, G. and C. Lechner (2001), *Strategisches Management: Wie strategische Initiativen wirksam werden*, Stuttgart, Germany: Schaeffer-Poeschl Verlag.

Nadler, D. and M. Tushman (1980), 'A diagnostic model for organizational behavior', in J.R. Hackman, E.E. Lawler and L. Porter (eds), *Perspectives on Behavior in Organizations*, New York, NY: McGraw-Hill, pp. 83–100.

Nalebuff, B. and A. Brandenburger (1996), *Co-opetition*, New York, NY: Doubleday.

Nanda, A. (1996), 'A critique of the resource-based view', in B. Moingeon and A. Edmondson (eds), *Organizational Learning and Competitive Advantage*, London: Sage, pp. 96–120.

Nasser, M.E. and F.J. Vivier (1995), *Mindset for the New Generation Organization: How Learning SA Companies Create Counter-trend Performance Despite Turbulence*, Cape Town, South Africa: Juta.

Nelson, R. (1991), 'Why do firms differ, and how does it matter?' *Strategic Management Journal* (Winter special issue), 61–74.

Nelson, R. and S. Winter (1982), *An Evolutionary Theory of Economic Change*, Cambridge, MA: Belknap Press.

New York Times (1998), 'Viewpoint: a corporate future built with new blocks', 29 March.

Nonaka, I. (1994), 'Dynamic theory of organizational knowledge creation', *Organization Science*, **5**(1), 223–38.

Nonaka, I. and H. Takeuchi (1995), *The Knowledge Creating Company*, New York: Oxford University Press.

Nonaka, I., P. Reinmoeller and D. Seinoo (1998), 'The ART of knowledge: systems to capitalize on market knowledge', *European Management Journal*, **16**(6), 673–84.

O'Dell, C. and C.J. Grayson (1998), 'If only we knew what we know: identification and transfer of internal best practices', *California Management Review*, **40**(3), 154–74.

Oliver, D. and J. Roos (2000), *Striking a Balance: Complexity and Knowledge Landscapes*, London: McGraw-Hill.

Orgland, M. (1995), 'Strategic change: initiating, managing and sustaining fundamental change in complex organizations', PhD thesis, University of St. Gallen, Switzerland.

Patsch, O. (2001), 'Anspruchsgruppenmanagement: Perspektiven, Reflexionen und Orientierungen', unpublished PhD thesis, University of St. Gallen, Switzerland.

Pennings, J.M. (1985), 'Introduction: on the nature and theory of strategic decisions', in J.M. Pennings (ed.), *Organizational Strategy and Change: New Views on Formulating and Implementing Strategic Decisions*, San Francisco, CA: Jossey-Bass, pp. 1–34.

Pehrsson, A. (2006), 'Business relatedness and performance: a study of managerial perceptions', *Strategic Management Journal*, **27**, 265–82.

Penrose, E. (1959), *Theory of the Growth of the Firm*, New York, NY: John Wiley and Sons.

Peteraf, M.A. (1993), 'The cornerstones of competitive advantage: a resource-based view', *Strategic Management Journal*, **14**(3), 179–91.

Peters, T.J. (1998), *The Circle of Innovation: You Can't Shrink Your Way to Greatness*, London: Macmillan.

Peters, T.J. (1992), *Liberation Management: Necessary Disorganization for the Nanosecond Nineties*, London: Macmillan.

Pettigrew, A.M. (1992), 'The character and significance of strategy process research', *Strategic Management Journal*, **13** (Summer special issue), 5–16.

Pettigrew, A.M. (1990), 'Longitudinal field research on change: Theory and practice', *Organization Science*, **1**(3), 267–92.

Polanyi, M. (1966), *The Tacit Dimension*, London: Routledge and Keegan Paul.

Polanyi, M. (1958), *Personal Knowledge*, Chicago, IL.: University of Chicago Press.

Porter, M. (2001), 'Strategy and the Internet', *Harvard Business Review* (March), 63–78.

Porter, M. (1998), *On Competition*. New York, NY: Free Press.

Porter, M. (1996), 'What is strategy?', *Harvard Business Review* (November–December), 61–78.

Porter, M. (1994), 'Global strategy: winning in the world-wide marketplace', in L. Fahey and R.M. Randall (eds), *The Portable MBA in Strategy*, New York, NY: John Wiley, pp. 108–41.

Porter, M. (1991), 'Towards a dynamic theory of strategy', *Strategic Management Journal*, **12**(4), 95–112.

Porter, M. (1990), *The Competitive Advantage of Nations*, New York, NY: The Free Press.

Porter, M. (1985), *Competitive Advantage*, New York, NY: Free Press.

Porter, M. (1980), *Competitive Strategy*. New York, NY: Free Press.

Powell, W.W. (1998), 'Learning from collaboration: knowledge and networks in the biotechnology and pharmaceutical industries', *California Management Review*, **40**(3), 228–40.

Prahalad, C.K. and G. Hamel (1990), 'The core competence of the corporation', *Harvard Business Review* (May–June), 79–91.

Prahalad, C.K. and V. Ramaswamy (2000), 'Co-opting customer competence', *Harvard Business Review* (January), 79–87.

Prahalad, C.K., L. Fahey and R.M. Randall (2001), 'Mapping the business landscape', in L. Fahey and R.M. Randall (eds), *The Portable MBA in Strategy*, New York, NY: John Wiley, pp. 171–88.

Priem, R.L. and J.E. Butler (2001a), 'Is the resource-based view a useful perspective for strategic management research?', *Academy of Management Review*, **26**(1), 22–40.

Priem, R.L. and J.E. Butler (2001b), 'Is the resource-based view a useful perspective for strategic management research? Yes', *Academy of Management Review*, **26**(1), 41–57.

Probst; G. (2000), 'Putting knowledge to work: Case writing as an organizational learning and knowledge management tool for the new economy', in G. Probst, and T.H. Davenport (eds), *Knowledge Management Case Book*, New York, NY: John Wiley and Sons, pp. 248–61.

Quinn, J.P. (1980), *Intelligent Enterprise: A Knowledge- and Service-based Paradigm for Industry*, New York, NY: The Free Press.

Quinn, J.P. (1994), 'Building the intelligent enterprise: leveraging resources, services, and technology', in L. Fahey and R.M. Randall (eds), *The Portable MBA in Strategy*, New York, NY: John Wiley, pp. 224–48.

Robinson, K.C. and P.P. McDougall (1998), 'The impact of alternative conceptualizations of industry structural elements on measures of performance for entrepreneurial manufacturing ventures', *Strategic Management Journal*, **19**, 1079–100.

Roos, J. and B. Victor (1999), 'Towards a new model of strategy-making as serious play', *European Management Journal*, **17**(4), 348–55.

Roos, J. and B. Victor (1998), 'In search of original strategies: How about some serious play?', *IMD Perspectives for Managers*, **56**(15), 1–4.

Roos, J., G. Roos, L. Edvinsson and N. Dragonetti (1998), *Intellectual Capital: Navigating in the New Business Landscape*, New York, NY: New York University Press.

Rubin, H.J. and I. Rubin (1995), *Qualitative Interviewing*, Thousand Oaks, CA: Sage.

Rumelt, R. (1991), 'How much does industry matter?', *Strategic Management Journal*, **12**, 167–85.

Rumelt, R. (1987), 'Towards a strategic theory of the firm', in D. Teece (ed.), *The Competitive Challenge*, Cambridge, MA: Ballinger, pp. 556–70.

Rumelt, R. (1984), 'Theory, strategy, and entrepreneurship', in D. Teece (ed.), *The Competitive Advantage: Strategies for Industrial Innovation and Renewal*, New York, NY: Harper and Row, pp. 137–58.

Rumelt, R., D. Schendel and D. Teece (1994), *Fundamental Issues in Strategy: A Research Agenda*, Boston, MA: Harvard Business School Press.

Rumelt, R., D. Schendel and D. Teece (1991), 'Strategic management and economics', *Strategic Management Journal*, **12** (Winter special issue), 5–29.

Ryle, G. (1949), *The Concept of Mind*, Chicago, IL.: Chicago University Press.

Saint-Onge, H. (1996), 'Tacit knowledge the key to the strategic alignment of intellectual capital', *Strategy and Leadership* (March–April), 10–14.

Sampler, J.L. (2001), 'Digital strategy', in L. Fahey and R.M. Randall (eds), *The Portable MBA in Strategy*, New York, NY: John Wiley, pp. 131–44.

Sampler, J.L. (1998), 'Redefining industry structure for the information age', *Strategic Management Journal*, **19**, 343–55.

Schendel, D.E. (1992), 'Introduction to the Winter 1992 special issue: fundamental themes in strategy process research', *Strategic Management Journal*, **13** (Winter special issue), 1–3.

Schendel, D.E. (1991), 'Editor's comments on the Winter special issue', *Strategic Management Journal*, **12** (Winter special issue), 1–3.

Schendel, D.E. (1988), 'Introduction to the special issue', *Strategic Management Journal*, **9** (Summer special issue), 1–2.

Schendel, D.E. and C.W. Hofer (1979), *Strategic Management: A New View of Business Policy and Planning*, Boston, MA: Little, Brown and Company.

Schoeffler, S. (1977), *Nine Basic Findings on Business Strategy*, The PIMSLETTER no. 1, Cambridge, MA: Strategic Planning Institute.

Schonberger, R. (1996), 'Strategic collaboration: breaching the castle walls', *Business Horizons* (March–April), 20–28.

Senge, P.M. (1990), *The Fifth Discipline: The Art and Practice of the Learning Organization*, New York: Doubleday/Century Business.

Shapiro, C. and H.R. Varian (1999), *Information Rules*, Boston, MA: Harvard Business School Press.

Simon, H. (1993), 'Strategy and organizational evolution', *Strategic Management Journal*, **14**(1), 131–42.

Spender, J. (1996a), 'Making knowledge the basis of a dynamic theory of the firm', *Strategic Management Journal*, **17**, 45–62.

Spender, J. (1996b), 'Competitive advantage from tacit knowledge?', in B. Moingeon, and A. Edmondson (eds), *Organizational Learning and Competitive Advantage*, London: Sage, pp. 56–73.

Stake, R.E. (1995), *The Art of Case Study Research*, London: Sage.

Stalk, G., P. Evans and L. Schulman (1992), 'Competing on capabilities: the new rules of corporate strategy', *Harvard Business Review* (March–April), 57–69.

Stern, C.W. and G. Stalk (1998), *Perspectives on Strategy From the Boston Consulting Group*, New York, NY: John Wiley and Sons.

Stewart, T. A. (1998), *Intellectual Capital: The New Wealth of Organizations*, London: Nicholas Brealey Publishing.

Sull, D. (1999), 'Case study: EasyJet's $500 million gamble', *European Management Journal*, **17**(1), 20–38.

Sullivan, P.H. (1998), *Profiting from Intellectual Capital: Extracting Value from Innovation*, New York, NY: Wiley and Sons.

Sun Tzu II (1997), *The Lost Art of War*, translated by T. Cleary, San Francisco, CA.: Harper Collins.

Sveiby, K.E. (1997), *The New Organizational Wealth*, San Francisco, CA: Berrett-Koehler Publishers.

Szulanski, G. and K. Amin (2001), 'Learning to make strategy: balancing discipline and imagination', *Long Range Planning*, **34**, 537–56.

Szulanski, G. and Y. Doz (1995), 'Strategy formulation as disciplined imagination', INSEAD working paper 95/96/SM.

Teece, D. (1998), 'Capturing value from knowledge assets: the new economy, markets for know-how and intangible assets', *California Management Review*, **40**(3), 55–79.

Teece, D., G. Pisano and A. Shuen (1997), 'Dynamic capabilities and strategic management', *Strategic Management Journal*, **18**, 509–33.

Teece, D., R.P. Rumelt, G. Dosi and S. Winter (1994), 'Understanding corporate coherence: theory and evidence', *Journal of Economic Behavior and Organization*, **23**(1), 1–30.

Thakur, M. (1998), 'Involving middle managers in strategy-making', *Long Range Planning*, **31**(5), 732–41.

Toffler, A. (1990), *Powershift*, New York, NY: Bantam Books.

Toffler, A. (1980), *The Third Wave*, New York, NY: Morrow.

van den Ven, A.H. (1992), 'Suggestions for studying strategy process: a research note', *Strategic Management Journal*, **13** (Summer special issue), 169–88.

van den Ven, A.H. and G.P. Huber (1990), 'Longitudinal field research methods for studying processes of organizational change', *Organization Science*, **1**(3), 743–61.

Venkatraman, N. (1989), 'The concept of fit in strategy research: Toward a verbal and statistical correspondence', *Academy of Management Review*, **14**, 423–44.

von Krogh, G. and J. Roos (1996), 'The epistemological challenge: Managing knowledge and intellectual capital', *European Management Journal*, **14**(4), 333–7.

von Krogh, G. and J. Roos (1995), *Organizational Epistemology*, London: Macmillan.

von Krogh, G. and S. Vicari (1993), 'An autopoiesis approach to experimental strategic learning', in P. Lorange, B. Chakarvarthy, J. Roos and A. de Ven (eds), *Implementing Strategic Processes: Change, Learning, and Co-operation*, Oxford: Blackwell, pp. 394–410.

von Krogh, G., K. Ichijo and I. Nonaka (2000), *Enabling Knowledge Creation*, Oxford: New Oxford University Press.

von Krogh, G., J. Roos and T. Hoerem (1997), 'Avoiding the phantom-limb effect', in G. von Krogh and J. Roos (eds), *Managing Knowledge: Perspectives on Cooperation and Competition*, London: Sage, pp. 137–54.

von Krogh, G., J. Roos and K. Slocum (1994), 'An essay on corporate epistemology', *Strategic Management Journal*, **15**, 53–71.

Wall Street Journal (2001), 'Starbucks: more stores are planned as net income climbs 34%', 27 July, p. B8.

Wall Street Journal Europe (1997), 'How to leapfrog the competition', 6 March, p. 13.

Weick, K. (1989), 'Theory construction as disciplined imagination', *Academy of Management Review*, **14**(4), 516–31,

Weick, K. and K.H. Roberts (1993), 'Collective mind in organizations: heedful interrelating on flight decks', *Administrative Science Quarterly*, **38**, 357–81.

Wernerfelt, B. (1995), 'The resource-based view of the firm: ten years after', *Strategic Management Journal*, **16**(4), 171–4.

Wernerfelt, B., (1984), 'A resource-based view of the firm', *Strategic Management Journal*, **5,** 171–80.

Williams, J. (1992), 'How sustainable is your competitive advantage?', *California Management Review*, **34**(2), 29–51.

Williamson, O.E. (1999), 'Strategy research: governance and competence perspectives', *Strategic Management Journal*, **20**(12), 1087–108.

Williamson, O.E. (1985), *The Economic Institutions of Capitalism*, New York, NY: Free Press.

Williamson, O.E. (1975), *Markets and Hierarchies: Analysis and Antitrust Implications*, New York, NY: Free Press.

Winter, S. (1987), 'Knowledge and competence as strategic assets', in D. Teece (ed.), *The Competitive Challenge*, Cambridge, MA: Ballinger, pp. 159–84.

Wooldridge, B. and S.W. Floyd (2001), *Strategy from the Middle*, Cambridge, MA: Harvard Business School Press.

Wooldridge, B. and S.W. Floyd (1990), 'The strategy process, middle management involvement and organizational performance', *Strategic Management Journal*, **11**, 231–41.

Yin, R.K. (1994), *Case Study Research: Design and Methods*, London: Sage.

Yoffie and Cusumano (1999), 'Judo strategy', *Harvard Business Review* (January–February), 70–82.

Zajac, E.J., M.S. Kraatz and R.K.F. Bresser (2000), 'Modeling the dynamics of strategic fit: a normative approach to strategic change', *Strategic Management Journal*, **21**, 429–53.

Zollo, M. and S. Winter (2000), 'From organizational routines to dynamic capabilities', School of the University of Philadelphia, Wharton working paper, Philadelphia, PA.

Zott, C. (2001), 'Value creation in e-business', INSEAD working paper, Fontainebleau, France.

Zott, C. (2000), 'Dynamic capabilities and the emergence of intra-industry differential firm performance: insights from a simulation study', INSEAD working paper, Fontainebleau, France.

Zuboff, S. (1988), *In the Age of the Smart Machine: The Future of Work and Power*, New York: Basic Books.

PRIMARY SOURCES[1]

Roos, J. (June 2000), personal communication, Imagination Lab meeting, Lausanne, Switzerland.

NOTE

1. References relating to interviews, speeches, direct and participant observation, and company-specific publications have been anonymized in the text. These references are available for academic purposes provided a confidentiality agreement has been signed with the corporation in question.

Index